THE INSIDER'S GUIDE TO

MALAYSIA & SINGAPORE

THE INSIDER'S GUIDES

AUSTRALIA • BALI • CALIFORNIA • CANADA • CHINA • EASTERN CANADA • FLORIDA • HAWAII •
HONG KONG • INDIA • INDONESIA • JAPAN • KENYA • KOREA • NEPAL •
NEW ENGLAND • NEW ZEALAND • MALAYSIA AND SINGAPORE • MEXICO •
RUSSIA • SPAIN • THAILAND • TURKEY • WESTERN CANADA

The Insider's Guide to Malaysia and Singapore
First Published 1993
Moorland Publishing Co Ltd
Moor Farm Road, Airfield Estate, Ashbourne, DE61HD, England
by arrangement with Novo Editions, S.A.
53 rue Beaudouin, 27700 Les Andelys, France
Telefax: (33) 32 54 54 50

© 1993 Novo Editions, S.A.

ISBN: 0 86190 258 0

Created, edited and produced by Novo Editions, S.A.
Editor in Chief: Allan Amsel
Original design concept: Hon Bing-wah
Picture editor and designer: Chan Sio Man
Text and artwork composed and information updated
using Ventura Publisher software

Printed by Samhwa Printing Company Limited, Seoul, Korea

THE INSIDER'S GUIDE TO

MALAYSIA
& SINGAPORE

By Sean Sheehan

Photographed by Alain Evrard

MPC

Contents

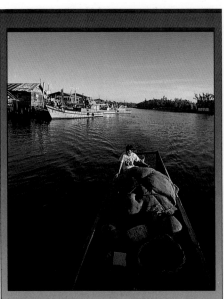

SABAH & SARAWAK

N

124 miles
200 km

BALABAC STRAITS

SULU SEA

SOUTH CHINA SEA

Tunku Abdul
Rahman Park

Kinabalu
National Park

Turtle
Island Park

PULAU GAYA

PULAU
SELINGAAN

Sandakan

Kota Kinabalu

Sepilok
Orangutan
Sanctuary

Beaufort

SABAH

Sigattal

Semporna

Miri

Marudi

Niah National Park

Long Miri

Bareo

SULAWESI SEA

Bintulu

SARAWAK

Long Geng

Sibu

Kanowit

Kapit

Bako
National
Park

Bako

Song

Rejang River

KALIMANTAN

Kuching

Skrang R.

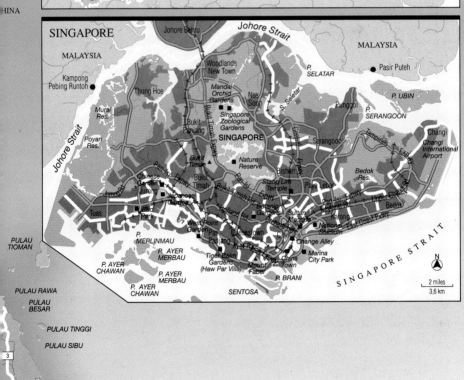

SINGAPORE

Johore Bahru

Johore Strait

MALAYSIA

MALAYSIA

Pasir Puteh

Kampong
Pebing Runtoh

Thong Hoe

Woodlands
New Town

Woodlands
New Town

P.
SELATAR

P. UBIN

Mandai
Orchid
Gardens

Nae
Sooh

S. Seletar

Punggol

P.
SERANGOON

Murai
Res.

Bukit
Panjang

Singapore
Zoological
Gardens

SINGAPORE

Serangoon

Changi

Changi
International
Airport

Poyan
Res.

Bukit
Timah

Nature
Reserve

Bishan

Bedok
Res.

Chinese
Garden

Bukit
Timah

Botanic
Gardens

Stang Lim
Temple

Payo Lebor

Jurong

Japanese
Garden

Holland Rd.

Sultan
Mosque

Katong

Bedok

Tuas

Bird
Park

West Point
Garden

Queenstown

City

National
Stadium

East Coast Pkwy

P.
MERLINMAU

P. AYER
MERBAU

Pasir
Panjang

Change Alley

Marina
City Park

PULAU
TIOMAN

P. AYER
CHAWAN

P. AYER
MERBAU

Tiger Balm
Gardens
(Haw Par Villa)

Mount
Faber

China
Town

SINGAPORE STRAIT

P. AYER
CHAWAN

SENTOSA

P. BRANI

N

2 miles
3,6 km

PULAU RAWA

PULAU
BESAR

PULAU TINGGI

PULAU SIBU

3

Kota Tinggi

92

SOUTH CHINA

SEA

ohore
ahru

Desaru

89

PORE

PULAU
BATAM

PULAU
BINTAN

HINA

Welcome
to
Malaysia
and
Singapore

STRUNG OUT over hundreds of miles of land and ocean, Malaysia and Singapore are strangely unique countries in which no two visits need ever be the same. They are lands of stunning cultural and geographical differences with food to suit every palate, accommodation ranging from the sublime to the bizarre, and activities for all ages, from white water rafting to ballroom dancing, and from jungle trekking to cut throat bargaining in the myriad of shopping complexes. The many histories of these once disparate communities could have come straight from a historical romance as settlers battled it out for domination over indigenous populations time and time again.

This book represents the best of six years' traveling and working in the two countries and offers up their most rewarding and delightful aspects for the short stay visitor or for those with time to visit the more remote, but no less fascinating, places and communities. It sets out to offer a perspective on the sometimes wild and violent history of the region, the cultural diversity of its peoples, makes suggestions for accommodation for all budgets and tastes, and offers inroads to the stunning variety of cuisines on offer. Most importantly of all, it offers a considered opinion on the attractiveness of the many resorts, parks, cities, historical sites and means of travel available. Places to visit, where to eat and stay, and how to reach the various towns, resorts and attractions are set out for West Malaysia, Sarawak and Sabah on the island of Borneo, and Singapore.

If you are wondering what a holiday in Malaysia and Singapore has to offer you, let us go on a brief journey around these lands. Beginning, as many people do, in the tiny island state of Singapore, the first time visitor will be stunned by its apparent westernization. On the drive from the airport along modern highways you will pass the architecturally diverse hotel complexes, the late twentieth century's answer to the beautiful cathedrals of earlier times. From your luxury hotel or from one of the many budget type Chinese style homestays you can venture out braving the tropical heat to countless shopping centers offering all the ethnic goodies of Asia. Or if history is more to your liking, Singapore's beautifully restored riverfront, many older buildings and relic of a past empire will tell their own tale. In the safe streets old Chinatown at night you can sample the nightly array of food to suit all budgets. Suitably fed, watered, and rested in Singapore, you can move on to the delights of the much larger and more nature oriented West Malaysia.

Just across the causeway to Johore Bahru, the traveler will notice a sudden change in pace and atmosphere. JB, as the locals affec-

tionately call it, is a raunchy, colorful but laid back city which comes into its own at night when Singaporians scurry across the causeway to sample the delights of its nightlife, shopping and restaurants. A shopper's paradise in its own right, Johore Bahru simply buzzes at night with all the excitement and chaos of a bigger Asian city. Further up the west coast, Malacca offers a pretty seaboard with evidence of its maritime history, quaint antique shops and the air of a quiet but ancient town. Further north

ABOVE: The calm beauty of a young Malay girl. OPPOSITE: The sleek lines of Kuala Lumpur's tower blocks define the curving grace of the Jame Mosque.

again, Penang and Langkawi are Malaysia's version of Mediterranean resorts but with none of the pollution and lots of vast empty beaches on which to get away from it all. From here a trip into Thailand is one of the options as the many hippy travelers of the sixties and seventies discovered or, if you can't bear to leave Malaysia, a journey west will bring you to the Malayan heartland.

But it is in Malaysia's east coast where the traveler will really discover the true glories of Malaysia. Its pristine beaches stretch endlessly into the distance and tiny unspoiled islands offer unparalleled snorkeling, fishing, windsurfing, sailing opportunities. At night one can sample homely Malay dishes from hawker centers or opt for the most elegant cuisines of Europe in the big resorts. In Kota Bharu the visitor will notice the distinctive dress, manners and lifestyle and the practice of ancient crafts such as batik work, silver and brass beating, kite-making, dance and music. Also to be found here is some very original and authentic cuisine.

For some the most enticing reason to visit Malaysia is to see vast and as yet almost undeveloped rain forest. Taman Negara, Malaysia's National Park, contains this and a range of wildlife from monitor lizards, which will try to take your lunch, to elephants and even the occasional tiger. It offers luxury accommodation or just a tent hidden away in the jungle and you can watch from a perch in the tree tops for the jungle's inhabitants or take exhilarating river trips down rapids to picnic spots deep in the heart of the forest.

Peninsular Malaysia isn't the only place to offer tropical beauty. Sabah and Sarawak also have their special places where a little effort will allow the visitor to see unique insectivorous plants, mangrove swamps, orang utan communities and the increasingly rare turtles which have laid their eggs for centuries on the islands off Sandakan. In Borneo you climb to the summit of Mount Kinabalu, and have an opportunity to observe the customs and lifestyle of the once head hunting Iban and the shy pale skinned forest dwelling Penan tribe.

After all this, Kuala Lumpur may seem to be an anticlimax but it too has its qualities. At first seeming chaotic and noisy, it has its

unique pace and atmosphere as well as its history reflected in the colonial architecture and excellent museums.

There are so many festivals that you will be bound to come across some celebration of a kind. The people of these countries have a special way of welcoming visitors and children are especially welcome in Singapore and Malaysia. In Malaysia children are held in particular esteem. Don't be surprised if local people ask if they can photograph your children, especially if they are blonde or scantily clad by Malay standards. The safety of Singapore's streets apparent to anyone streetwise in New York or London.

For some, the sheer variety of food and culinary diversity provides a reason in itself to visit the region and the styles can seem

Welcome to Malaysia and Singapore

bewildering at first. Cantonese, Teochew (Chiuchow), Malay, Nonya, North Indian, South Indian, Indonesian, Thai and Japanese all assault the senses. If you are a food buff, the cities of Singapore and Kuala Lumpur will be difficult to escape from. Restaurants abound and good food can cost anything from two or three to hundreds of dollars.

Malaysia and Singapore also serve as a good base to visit other countries in the region, and from Singapore's Changi Airport, one of the world's most comfortable, direct flights are available to Europe and the United States as well as to regional destinations. Boats travel from Singapore to many Indonesian islands while trains go north into Thailand. From Penang or Kota Bharu a trip to Thailand can be easily arranged

while Sabah lies close to the outlying islands of the Philippines.

Whether you choose a beach resort, a city hotel, a longhouse in the jungle; whether your ideal day trip is a trek in the rainforest or another around the consumer delights of Orchard Road in Singapore; whether you enjoy mountaineering, sunbathing, eating or partying or just a bit of everything, the the following sections will provide the information and advice to help make your visit to Singapore and Malaysia both memorable and enjoyable.

The Sarawak River near Kuching, Borneo.

The Countries and their People

HISTORICAL BACKGROUND

BEFORE THE EUROPEANS

Malay peninsula's geographical proximity to the sea route between India and China contributed tremendously to the development of its distinct cultures and traditions. The area's history evolved as the calm west coast of what is now Malalysia became a critical stop over for vessels from India which dared not venture beyond during the monsoon period when the sea off the east coast was dangerous to navigate. The valuable natural resources also shaped the country's future, as they still do today. Not only was tin and gold available, but also camphor, exotic feathers from the forests, and the cowrie shell from the coast (invaluable as a currency before the circulation of coins).

The Malays, who came down to the beaches and traded with the foreign merchants, were not the first inhabitants of the country. That distinction belongs to the Negritos from Melanesia and Polynesia. The Negritos took to the interior when the Malays arrived. The indigenous, non-Malay element in Malaysia's culture is even more apparent in East Malaysia — a part of the large island once called Borneo, now shared by Indonesia, Brunei and Malaysia. The Malaysian states of Sarawak and Sabah are peopled by a variety of tribes who have little ethnic connection to the Malays or the Negritos; such is the cultural kaleidoscope of Malaysia.

Migrants from southern China arrived sometime between 2500 and 1500 BC, and subsequent waves of migration produced the modern Malay race that is now spread across Indonesia, the Philippines and Malaysia itself. During the early Christian era the influence of India was felt and a lasting impression was made by the Indianized maritime empire from Sumatra and centered near Palembang. This Islamic empire lasted for centuries and held sway over the whole Malay peninsula. Colonists from Palembang in the thirteenth century founded a settlement on a tiny island which they bestowed with the honorific Sanskrit title of *Singapura*.

The Palembang empire, destroyed toward the end of the fourteenth century by a mightier Javanese kingdom, was a refugee from Palembang's nobility who fled to a small fishing village on the west coast of the Malay peninsula. The village became known as Melaka and within a hundred years it had developed into a cosmopolitan trading port. It was the town of Melaka that became the focus for the international trade between India and China and the legendary spice trade which connected the East with Europe. It was also through Melaka that

Islam became firmly entrenched; the Sufi mysticism blending comfortably with the spiritualism of the *kampong* (village) Malay peasants.

While the northern part of the peninsula remained undisturbed under the sovereignty of Siam (Thailand), the spice trade put the Malay peninsula on the map and quickly attracted the attention of European powers.

SPICE TRADERS AND COLONIZERS

The Portuguese were the first to relish the idea of seizing Melaka because they badly wanted to wrest control of the spice trade from the Muslim Arabs. Following on from their discovery of an all-sea passage to the East by Vasco da Gama in 1498, they saw a chance to by-pass the formerly inescapable land journey through Arab lands. A secure base in Southeast Asia was essential and by

OPPOSITE: Ethnic dress of Sabah, East Malaysia. ABOVE: The Sarawak River, life blood of the thriving city of Kuching.

the year 1511, Western influence had infiltrated Southeast Asia. A contemporary Portuguese account of Melaka — "Goods from all over the East are found here; goods from all over the West are sold here. It is at the end of the monsoon, where you find what you want, and sometimes more than what you are looking for" — reflects the strange mixture of commercial greed and genuine adventurism that drove those men to a then unknown land.

The city of Melaka fell to the Dutch in 1641, who extended their influence to the tin-producing states of Perak and Kedah, also on the western side. The east coast of Malaya and what is now Sarawak and Sabah remained untouched.

THE ANGLO-DUTCH TREATY

The Anglo-Dutch Treaty in 1619 divided the Spice Islands between the British and the Dutch. The British wanted their own base for the China run, where they sold opium and cotton, and at first the northeast of Borneo attracted their attention. Pirates here proved to be a big problem and so they looked elsewhere. A small island off the west coast of Malaya, Penang, attracted their attention. In 1786 Francis Light, a trader, took formal possession of Penang but despite its attractive position close to the tin-mining areas, Penang was too far north to serve as a trading center.

Enter Stamford Raffles, a free-wheeling English trader who became convinced that rivalry with the Dutch necessitated a new entrepôt that, unlike Penang, would be on the major trade routes. He settled for the small, almost uninhabited, island of Singapore and made it a free port. As Dutch economic power waned England's rose and Singapore has never looked back.

SARAWAK AND SABAH

An Englishman, James Brooke, arrived in Borneo in 1839 and helped the local ruler of Brunei to quash a rebellion, receiving, in return, a large measure of land which became his personal kingdom of Sarawak and he then established a dynasty that lasted until World War II. In his kingdom, ethnicity dictated occupation. The Malays were to help administer the country, the Chinese were to be brought in for trade and labour, and the native Ibans to act as military backup.

England's interest in northern Borneo what is now the state of Sabah, was partly a strategic one: keeping the Spanish influence out of the nearby Philippines.

The sole dynamic to England's interest in the peninsula of Malaya, Sarawak and Sabah was trade and commerce. Europe wanted antimony from Sarawak, tin (and later rubber) from the peninsula and gutta percha. This gum of the gutta percha tree provided a resin that was remarkably pliable and capable of protecting undersea telegraph cables. In an ominous nod to the future fare of the rain forests, the greedy entrepreneurs cut down the gutta percha trees in the thousands until none was left. The Chinese were also expressing an economic interest: camphor, the gum from the rattan palm, and birds' nests for eating were some of the delights that tempted them from across the sea.

THE GROWTH OF SINGAPORE AND MALAYSIA

The tiny island of Singapore served as the natural center for all this trade, and the duty-free port grew and prospered out of all proportion to its size. It received an enormous boost when new steamships made it through the even newer Suez canal, cutting 90 days off the London-Singapore trip, making Singapore the final coaling station for the last hop to the Far East. Singapore became what Melaka had been in the fifteenth century. Immigration was unrestricted and taxes exempt (except for the lucrative vices of opium, alcohol and gambling).

Tin and rubber production were alien activities to the indigenous Malay farmers or the forest-dwelling natives of Borneo. Tin mining was especially dangerous and only the needy and desperate would work for low wages in such risky work. So the British turned elsewhere and set about encouraging thousands of Chinese and Indians to come to the Straits Settlements, as the colonies

OPPOSITE: No longer Prime Minister but still a force for stability in Singapore — Lee Kuan Yew.

of Penang, Melaka and Singapore were known since their combination in 1826.

This policy, more than anything else perhaps, has shaped the critical nature of these modern nations. Although many emigrants probably intended to return to India and China, most never did. They stayed, married, had children — and the foundations for a future multiracial and multicultural Malaysia and Singapore were created. Many of the characteristics of modern Malaya and Singapore can be traced back to this policy of the British. The east coast of Malaya, where

to the humiliating surrender of the English in Singapore only three months later. The British were lined up in public on the *padang* in Singapore on the morning of February 17, 1942, kept waiting in the heat for hours, then ignominiously marched off to jail at Changi Prison, and the myth of white superiority went with them.

Thousands of Chinese were murdered while the Malays were encouraged to collaborate with the Japanese, who cynically fostered and fed ethnic Malay-Chinese rivalry. Many Chinese fled into the jungles and turned to

little tin and rubber existed, is still a predominantly Malay part of the country and here the Muslim influence is strongest. The west coast, by comparison, has a distinctly Chinese feel to it. Singapore, though containing all three cultures, seems a Chinese city through and through.

For the first three decades of the twentieth century the unchallenged British rule kept such a racial mix under control. World War II changed all that.

WORLD WAR II AND ITS AFTERMATH

The Japanese landed at Kota Bharu, in the northeast of the country, in December 1941 and began their blistering campaign that led

Maoist communism, an ideology that sustained their opposition to the British long after the Japanese had been defeated in 1945. A guerrilla war lasted through the early 1950s and never came to a proper end until 1989 when the legendary communist leader, Chin Peng, finally emerged from the jungle.

MODERN MALAYSIA AND SINGAPORE

Independence came to the Federation of Malaysia in 1957 after protracted discussions

ABOVE: The Boh Tea plantation in Malaysia where the tea is still hand picked, dried, graded and packaged. OPPOSITE: Commerce is the *raison d'etre* of Singapore and is carried out with fervor and determination.

about what to do with a land which the Malays felt was theirs, though economic power rested securely with the Chinese. That Malays did not have a clear numerical supremacy became a moot point when Sarawak and Sabah, with their large non-Chinese populations, expressed their willingness to join the new republic of Malaysia in 1963. The Chinese power bloc in Singapore continued to cause problems, however. Lee Kuan Yew, the leader of the Chinese, was seen to harbor political ambitions for leadership of the whole republic

and in 1965 Singapore was ejected from the coalition. Tension erupted in 1969 when racial riots broke out in Kuala Lumpur as a reaction by the Malays to a perceived Chinese threat caused by the a Chinese victory in a by-election.

Today Malaysia and Singapore are at peace, and despite occasional bickering, it seems unlikely that the unrest will return. Economic prosperity in both countries has proved to be the key to civic order and racial harmony. In Sabah, ironically, the prosperous natural resources, wood (what's left of it) and oil, have caused some recent dissent. Some politicians in Sabah are suggesting political separation on the grounds that too much of Sabah's wealth is siphoned off to peninsula Malaysia.

The Government and the Economy
Both countries follow a parliamentary democratic system modeled on that of the British, though both countries have managed to adopt this in a rather authoritarian manner. In Malaysia, power is firmly in the hands of

UMNO (New United Malays National Organization), whose intention it is to try to reverse the present economic advantages of the Chinese. A Muslim fundamentalist thrust comes from PAS (Parti Islam), which has some sway in the east of peninsula Malaysia but is unlikely to ever wield national power. The Prime Minister, Mahathir at the time of writing, balances the various ethnic and political forces with some success, though in 1987 a repressive Internal Security Act was used to imprison a variety of opponents including active environmentalists who were drawing attention to the destruction of the rain forests in Sarawak and Sabah. The Press is still effectively muzzled.

The economy of Malaysia is amazingly strong in terms of natural resources. Timber, palm oil and rubber have been large earners, though now oil is becoming the nation's most lucrative asset. In Southeast Asia, Malaysia's economy is only outshone by that of its southern neighbor, the island of Singapore.

The island of Singapore might be small, but economically it is booming. To appreciate the stature of this achievement one should keep in mind that Singapore has no natural resources, unless you count its surrounding waters which it has managed to turn into the world's busiest port that serves massive petroleum refineries. The promotion of English as the medium of educational instruction (Malaysia abandoned English in favor of the Malay language, a move which made more political than economic sense) has helped to create a business environment that continues to grow and prosper.

Unfortunately this economic success has been accompanied by a sorry state of political life. The ruler since independence in 1965 until 1990, Lee Kuan Yew, ruthlessly crushed any signs of dissent. It was only in 1989 that a political prisoner was released after 23 years in jail. A very strange and sad event was the arrest in 1987 of a score of church and social workers and members of the opposition. Trial was by television and their crime was an alleged Marxist plot to overthrow the government. The new Prime Minister, Goh Chok Tong, has a more tolerant image, but Lee's influence may well prove to have been permanent.

GEOGRAPHY

The geography of these two countries is quite alarming when you consider that the nation of Malaysia itself is divided by over 650 km (400 miles) of water. East Malaysia is comprised of Sabah and Sarawak on the island of Borneo, the world's third largest, and is a region where diminishing tracts of rainforest remain unlogged and where orangutan wander the forests. Mount Kinabalu, 4,094 m (13,432 ft) dominates

hills are fairly uninspiring. Bukit Timah Hill is a small and struggling nature reserve with wild macaques and any number of creepy crawlies while Faber Hill blended into the urban landscape long ago.

CLIMATE

The climate can come as a surprise. Everyone speaks of a wet season from November to the end of February but the term is misleading if you imagine lovely cool showers.

the Kinabalu National Park and is a beacon to air travelers crossing the country. Peninsular Malaysia too has large tracts of relatively unexplored mountainous forest although none of its peaks reach the majesty of Kinabalu. A flight over Malaysia reveals the enormous inroads being made into the forests, the tin workings looking like a huge moonscape and vast areas of oil palm plantation are intersected by brown access roads and the occasional small town.

Singapore's chief geographical feature is its enormous natural harbour, now considerably extended by several land reclamation projects. It is almost uniformly flat and was once marshy, although you would be hard put to find any marsh nowadays. Its two

The heavy rains can certainly spoil beach holidays on the east coast of Malaysia; indeed, many of the big resorts here close down completely and other places have reduced rates. Taman Negara, the large national park in peninsula Malaysia, also closes down for two months and it will be equally wet in Sarawak and Sabah, but you could easily spend one of these months in Singapore or Kuala Lumpur and be more aware of the heat than the rain. This is mainly because of the constantly high

ABOVE: Cloud formations can be appreciated from an amazing proximity and intensity on Mt. Kinabalu. OPPOSITE: Massed ranks of police parade at the Merdeka Day celebration in Kuala Lumpur.

humidity rate that rarely falls below 90 percent. Night-time temperatures seldom drop below 20°C and during the day it will usually be around 30°C. The west coast of Malaysia receives more rain from September through to the end of the year but not enough to put anyone off enjoying themselves.

A CULTURAL MIX

Anyone could be forgiven for thinking that Malaysia is populated by Malays and hence a Muslim country. But Malays only constitute around 50 percent of the nation's total population. The Chinese make up a good third, Indians a tenth, and if you are speaking just about Sarawak and Sabah, then it is difficult to think of these states as at all Malay in character, history or precious little else.

Singapore, like Malaysia, is truly multicultural: over 60 percent Chinese, 30 percent Malay, less than 10 percent Indian plus Eurasians and expatriates. The cultural diversity of both Malaysia and Singapore quite astonishing and is reflected in the many festivals that are celebrated in the traditions of the many ethnic groupings (see TRAVELERS' TIPS, page 192). The Chinese easily form the largest ethnic group in Singapore, and in Malaysia as a whole they constitute some 35 percent of the population. Most of them are descendants of poverty-stricken peasants who fled from southern China. But they came from different regions and brought their own dialects and customs. Mandarin is just one such dialect that both China and Singapore promote as a standard means of communication, but dialects remain strong. Hokkien forms the largest dialect group in Singapore, and common as well are Cantonese and Hainanese. These groups also exist in Malaysia, but the government insists that Malay is the national language and the speaking of any Chinese dialect is discouraged. In Sarawak and Sabah the Malays and Chinese make up about half of the population, with the upriver Ibans constituting 30 percent, and the remaining 20 percent made up of Bidayuh, Melanau, Kayan, Kenyah, Kelabit, Murut and Penan.

FOOD

The foods of both Malaysia and Singapore offer an amazing range of tastes, though Malaysia, while it offers excellent local food, cannot match the enormous variety of cuisines crying out for attention in Singapore.

Any trip to Malaysia and Singapore should be, in part, a gormandizing experience. The local cuisines (of which there are many) are heavily influenced by the origins of the many immigrants. From China, the rick-

shaw drivers, coolies and laborers came from three distinct areas, each with their own dialect, tradition and cooking style. You may feel you know all about Cantonese cooking from the restaurants of Europe, but they have little in common with what you will find here. Cantonese food is characterized by quickly stir-fried food, steeped in rich sauces. *Dim sum* is Cantonese in origin and consists of a selection of little steamed and fried pies and dumplings with both sweet and savory fillings. Sichuan food is very spicy and produces fast stir-fried food but without the distinctive sauces of

ABOVE: Fortune telling on the streets of Melaka. OPPOSITE: Inside the Sultan Mosque in Singapore.

Cantonese food. It also plays on the differences in textures between foods, putting in one dish such things as hard nuts with softer items like chicken. Typically wonderful dishes are dried chili chicken or prawns, where large amounts of inedible dried chilies are stir fried with the meat to give it a dry, chili taste. The majority of Singaporean Chinese are Hokkien speakers from Fujian, a very poor province whose cooking is definitely homely and more often represented in the hawker stalls than in classier restaurants. Most common are dishes such as *popiah* (like the spring rolls of Western Chinese restaurants) or stews of fish head or pork belly. The Teochew (Chiuchow) also brought a fairly simple style of cooking to Singapore with them, and recently restaurants serving Teochew food have become very popular. It is characterized by dishes which depend on the flavor of the food itself, rather than on rich spices. Food is steamed rather than stir fried. If you don't like lots of chili this might be the place to start. The pride of Chinese cooking is its imperial cuisine from Beijing, though it is not very common in Malaysia or Singapore since there are few native Mandarin speakers. It is wheat based, using pancakes, spring rolls, noodles and steamed buns instead of rice. Meat is most often barbecued, roasted or boiled, and delicate flavorings like shallots, chives and garlic are used. Its most popular dish is Peking duck, where the roasted skin of the duck is rolled up in pancakes and spread with sweet bean paste.

In addition to the Chinese cooking styles, there is also the Singaporean cooking which has drawn on all these styles and added its own particular ingredients, often seafood, chili and soy sauce. Most famous is chili crab or black pepper crab where the meat is served in the shell and coated with very hot sauce. Hot French rolls are served to soak up the spicy sauce. Another favorite is drunken prawns. The poor little fellows thresh themselves to inebriation and death in brandy. The head and prawn equivalent of lungs soak up the brandy and become the delicacy of the dish.

Indian cuisine is also well-represented here: south Indian breads like *dosa* or *paratha* or *bhatura* served with spicy sauces, banana leaf dishes with four or five curries served in a bed of rice on a banana leaf, rich north Indian curries based on nuts and cream, Indian Muslim food such as *roti prata*, or *murtabak*, pancakes either served plain with *dal* or wrapped around meat or vegetables, chicken *biryani*, which is cooked for hours in a huge vat of rice flavored with vegetables and spices, or *roti john*, french bread dipped in egg and meats and chili and fried. Tandoors are imported from India to produce meats typiical of tandoori cooking, seared on the sides of a clay oven and, of course, the excellent breads only possible with a tandoor, *naan*.

Malay food is heavily influenced by its Indonesian neighbor and often consists of curries using garlic, lemon grass and coconut. It is another homely style of cooking, and it is fully represented in the hawker stalls in Malaysia and Singapore.

Nonya food is, if you can imagine it, a cross between Chinese and Malay food developed by the Straits Chinese community in the early part of this century. Typical of this odd blend is *laksa*, a combination of Chinese noodles and Malay coconut curry.

Other than the cuisines of the three chief immigrant communities already mentioned here, most other Asian and European cuisines are represented in Malaysia and Singapore, but the dominant one is my favorite, Thai, which I think is one of the most exciting and tasty cooking styles in the world. Many restaurants serve excellent Thai dishes in both Singapore and Kuala Lumpur. Thai food is hot, spicy, sweet, textured, sour and mild, using stir-frying grilling and steaming. Stocks are based on coriander, chili, coconut, garlic, lemon grass, fish sauce and chicken stock. Most well known are *tom yam* soup, pineapple rice, and green chicken curry.

Whether you come to Malaysia and Singapore for the food, scenery wildlife, sea sports or a laze on a deserted beach, what you are sure to experience is an amazing mix of cultures, foods and sights that will delight and refresh even the most world-weary and jaded palate.

OPPOSITE TOP: The glories of a Malay buffet, Kuala Lumpur. OPPOSITE BOTTOM: Peranakan Place, Singapore, where open air dining, music, drink and tradition go hand in hand.

Kuala Lumpur– Malaysia's Capital

BACKGROUND

In 1857, a group of prospectors led by Raja Adullah, a Bugis chieftain, discovered rich open seams of tin, and a short time later a small trading post was established at the confluence of two rivers where the shallow waters upstream made navigation difficult. Beyond this point the water became too shallow for navigation, so it was there that early Chinese immigrants set off to seek their fortunes. This gave rise to the name

Kuala Lumpur (Muddy River Mouth). Fortunes were made and squandered as miners and merchants struggled for survival; at one stage a gang boss was even offering cash rewards for the delivery of his enemies' heads. Malay princes squabbled over rights to the tin, and soon the British saw the value of establishing order in the interests of peaceful trade. By the turn of the century, the shanty town was a capital, with a railway line and tin millionaires aping the colonialists by building European-style mansions.

By the early twentieth century, the rubber plantations added new sources of wealth, and Indians came in the thousands to tap the trees. Dunlop established a big office here, and the British owners set up their clubs and drank their gin until the Japanese cycled in and established a new order in 1942. Three years later they were gone, but Britain's colonial stranglehold was loosened, and in 1957 the city was freed by the declaration of independence.

GENERAL INFORMATION

The headquarters of the Tourist Development Corporation are at the top of the Putra World Trade Centre, ((03) 293-5188, but general information and maps are available at any of the Tourist Information Centres. There are two at the airport, one immediately outside the railway station, and one across the road from the station, ((03) 274-6063, and one on Jalan Parliamen, ((03) 293-6664. Out on Jalan Ampang the Malaysian Tourist Information Complex, ((03) 242-3929, can be found, and a whole holiday could be planned from here. This is the place to go if you want information on Malaysia as a whole. In addition there is an information service at ((03) 292-2722. The Tourist Police Unit can be contacted at ((03) 241-5522.

The *Visitor's Guide to Kuala Lumpur* is a useful free brochure that is updated every month.

Other telephone numbers that might prove useful:

Subang International Airport ((03) 746133.
Kuala Lumpur Railway Station (Reservations: North) ((03) 274-7434. (Reservations: South) ((03) 274-7443.
Complaints/Hotline ((03) 293-4531.
Malaysian Airlines ((03) 261-0555. The headquarters of MAS is in the MAS Building, Jalan Sultan Ismail, just opposite the Hilton Hotel. The 24-hour reservation number is ((03) 774-7000.
24-Hour Call Cabs ((03) 293-6211, 733-0507, 715352, 221-1011. 24-Hour Call Cabs ((03) 293-6211, 733-0507, 715352, 221-1011

GETTING AROUND

Taxis are highly recommended because they are cheap; any trip around town should cost around $M3. The majority are metered

The glittering skyline of Kuala Lumpur at night.

and if one is "broken" you can be sure the suggested rate is too much. Always check that the meter is turned on, and if it isn't, try for another cab. If this isn't feasible, engage in a bit of friendly bargaining. Around town there are many designated taxi stops and, although you can hail one anywhere, the stops are best during peak times. Waiting times can sometimes be infuriatingly long but no one seems unduly bothered. For longer distances there are special cab ranks and these cabs have no meters. Ask at your hotel how much these cabs should cost.

Stops for minibuses are often close to the taxi stops and they're handy for straight runs. Be forewarned, however, that they only

accept change. If you are not sure where the minibus is going, or even where you're going, ask someone for help. The *Visitor's Guide to Kuala Lumpur*, available from the tourist offices, has a useful map showing the various bus stations for out of town travel.

Car rental is readily available from Avis, ℂ (03) 242-3500, Hertz, ℂ (03) 243-3014, or Thrifty, ℂ (03) 230-2591. Check the Yellow Pages for more.

WHAT TO SEE

The town sights are conveniently packed into a small area, and if you are short of time I would suggest the following itinerary that takes in most of them on foot, starting at the railway station and ending in Chinatown. Allow yourself at least three hours and work backwards if this is more convenient.

Whether you arrive by train or not, the **Railway Station** should not be missed. No one term can represent an eclectic architectural style that successfully combines the Islamic, Mogul, Moorish, Gothic and Greek, and the surprising result is a visual treat. An excellent viewpoint can be had from the first floor of the similarly styled Railway Administration building directly across the road. Incidentally, the architect of both these buildings was a man of little experience. Before designing these places he had done nothing more than work on alterations to site plans!

Next door to the Railway Administration is the **National Art Gallery** and three blocks west of that, the **National Museum** (both open at 10 am). This museum and the one in Kuching are easily the best in this part of the world. Kuala Lumpur's museum is imaginatively conceived and its special exhibitions can be extraordinary. Next to the art gallery is a tourist information center. The art gallery is

perhaps still more famous for what it once was — the number one colonial hotel, the Majestic, used during World War II by the Japanese as their headquarters. One point of interest is that the interior of the former hotel has not been gutted; the domed exhibition area was the hotel's dining hall and ballroom and canvases now adorn the walls of what were once bedrooms.

Dawn at Kuala Lumpur's eclecticly styled railway station.

About six blocks north of the railway station is the 32-sided **Dayabumi**, a striking Islamic-influenced edifice that easily stands out from the majority of Kuala Lumpur's mundane skyscrapers. This building affords striking views of the town, though access is sometimes denied.

Continuing north brings you to an open green on the left, with Tudor style houses behind it, and on your right there are huge palace-like stone buildings. This was once the very nucleus of colonial Malaya, and the history of this patch of green marks many of

the significant stages in the evolution of modern Malaya. The green *padang* was once the playground for colonial sportsmen, and the mock-Tudor buildings housed their **Selangor Club**. This was where the expatriate tin and rubber merchants came to relax with a drink and watch cricket or play bridge. The club was first constructed in 1884 on top of what had been swamp land. The green was drained for a police training ground before being turned into a sporting green. It is here that football (soccer), now a popular sport among young Malaysians, was first introduced to the country. When the Japanese arrived in 1942 they reconverted the ground to agriculture, and banana plants and tapioca grew there for a brief while. The English converted it back to a sporting ground and play was resumed until 1957. On August 31 of that year the Malayan flag was raised for the first time to replace the Union Jack, and the national flag continues to hang from the 100 m (328 ft) flagpole that now decks **Merdeka** (Independence) **Square**.

The first stone building opposite the green is so similar in style to the one next to it that they are often confused or taken to be one. Both were designed by A.C. Norman in 1896. The first stone building, once the General Post Office, is the **Infokraf**, a craft center that displays and sells traditional items. The second building, the one that spouts the lacquered copper domes, now houses the Supreme Court and is known as the **Sultan Abdul Samad Building**.

Turn into Leboh Pasor Besar, the road that runs between these two stone buildings, and you'll soon come to a small girdered bridge. Look to your left and you have a view of **Masjid Jame** on Jalan Tun Perak. This is an elegant mosque, open to the public and significant for its location as much as its aesthetic appeal because it was on this very spot, at the muddy confluence of the two rivers, that the trading post for the pioneering tin miners was established.

Another short walk south will bring you to the **Central Market**. The Central Market was once just what the name indicates, but now it has been imaginatively transformed into a shopping mall with an emphasis on arts and crafts. The original slabs, used by the butchers and fishmongers to cut and display their produce, now host a variety of inexpensive consumer artifacts, and this is one of the best places for browsing for souvenirs and presents. The artistic atmosphere continues to be be enhanced by an active policy of encouraging street artists and entertainers to perform on the pedestrian streets outside, and a stroll around here in the early evening can be very entertaining.

Chinatown is a small area around Jalan Petaling just south of the Central Market. At night an open-air market springs up with stalls crowded with clothes, belts, cassettes and watches, and occasionally something novel makes an appearance — jewelry or fossils from Nepal for instance. During the day it is still a hive of activity, and there are a number of places here to rest and have a drink or meal. A block away on Jalan Bandar

OPPOSITE TOP and BOTTOM: The elegantly serene national mosque in Kuala Lumpur marks the spot where the first settlers landed.
ABOVE: A busy street in Kuala Lumpur's Chinatown.

Kuala Lumpur– Malaysia's Capital

rests the **Sri Maha Mariamman Temple**, one of the most spectacular Hindu temples in Malaysia because of its richly layered gopuram (gateway). Leave your footwear outside and feel free to wander in.

An alternative afternoon's sightseeing can be had at the **Lake Gardens**, particularly suited to those who need some peace and quiet or have children. Along Jalan Parliamen is the Lake itself, originally created in 1888, and for those who feel energetic enough, paddle boats wait patiently at the bank. Also in the Gardens is the national monument,

created by Felix de Weldon, creator of the famous Iwo Jima statue in Washington. The National Museum is close by, as are the orchid garden and deer park, where you can see the native Malaysian mouse deer, the smallest hoofed animal in the world. In the gardens is also a bird park, built into a natural valley. The entire area of over three hectares (eight acres) is covered in netting stretched from one side of the valley to the other and birds fly around freely. The site has made maximum use of the natural surroundings,

ABOVE: Merdeka Square, Kuala Lumpur, by night, showing the Federal Secretariat building and clock tower. OPPOSITE: Batu Caves, outside Kuala Lumpur, are a Hindu shrine and a tourist attraction.

including the stream at the bottom which provides habitat for waterfowl. A few birds are caged, however. The hornbills glare balefully out from their prisons wondering what they did to deserve incarceration while the other birds enjoy the pleasure of relative freedom. The bird park is still a little bare, so visiting at midday can be taxing as it is unbearably hot, and the few shady places that do exist will be well-populated by other sweltering visitors. As soon as the trees grow, things should be better. Early morning or evenings are best. The park is open from 9 am to 6 pm.

OUT OF TOWN

A few kilometers out of Kuala Lumpur and easily accessed by public transport (bus N° 66, N° 78 or N° 77 from Pudu Raya us Station) is **Templar Park**, 1,214 hectares (3,000 acres) of jungle and park land which offers many different types of activity. Pools fed by natural waterfalls, peaceful walks in the forest, birds of many species, caves and cliffs are just a few of the attractions here. The area is sufficiently large that a good amount of time can be spent here without seeing very many other visitors. Most people tend to collect at the swimming pools which have been created at various points along the fall of the river, but during weekdays even these areas are sparsely populated. There are some food stalls near the entrance to the park, ample parking, and easy access to the main road, where one can find a cab or a bus heading into Kuala Lumpur.

Other out of town spots are best seen as part of a countryside tour. There are many such tours easily booked at your hotel and they tend to all visit the same places for the same price ($8). The trip will include the **Selangor Pewter Showroom and Factory**. This is one of the largest pewter (97 percent tin and three percent copper and antimony) factories in the world, and while there are shops everywhere in Malaysia selling pewter ware, you can be assured of legitimate prices here, as well as having the opportunity to view the factory and a large showroom.

The tour should also include the **Batu Caves**, 13 km (eight miles) north of Kuala

Lumpur. These sacred Hindu caves contain various shrines, and the relatively easy 272-step ascent should not dissuade anyone from visiting the cathedral-like main cavern. During the Thaipusam festival the caves attract well over half-a-million devotees in the space of 48 hours. This is the time to visit if you want to view the penitents skewering their flesh and walking on fire. The caves are millions of years old, and tigers and bears once prowled the ground now trod by devotees. During the Japanese Occupation, a mass execution of communists took place here.

Local buses leave from the Pudu Raya terminal in town.

Countryside tours are a good value if you're on your own or have limited time, and some include a visit to a wretched factory where butterflies and scorpions are crucified and framed before being dispatched to tourist shops around the country.

A nice day out for the children is a trip to **Mimaland**, an amusement park about 15 km (nine miles) out of Kuala Lumpur and accessible by the N° 174 bus from Leboh Ampang or by cab. Built on a hill, it is about a kilometer (just over half-a-mile) from the

bus stop and uphill all the way, but there are usually people with transport waiting to strike a deal. On weekends this place is very crowded with local people who stay at the motel or the bungalows built over the lake. It has the longest water slide in Malaysia, a huge swimming pool and boat rides and one or two other things to amuse the children. Hardly a tropical Disneyland, as it is claimed, but pleasant enough.

Further afield is **Genting Highlands**, a rather brash and unpeaceful gambling resort with its own 18-hole golf course and bowling alley. It has, as well, the only casino in this predominantly Muslim country. If you want to play blackjack or baccarat, remember to pack a long-sleeved shirt and tie in order to gain entry to the casino. Genting operates its own daily coaches from the Pudu Raya bus terminal and the journey takes over an hour. The best deal is to arrange a package with any travel agent in town.

Fraser's Hill is infinitely preferable as an out of town trip although, because it can take three hours to drive the 100 km (62 mile) journey, you might want to plan to spend at least one night there before returning to the capital. See INTO THE INTERIOR, page 114, for more details on Fraser's Hill.

OFF THE BEATEN TRACK

Contact the Malayan Nature Society, ((03) 775-3330, to see if any interesting trips are being organized. At **Batu Caves**, for instance, there is a network of caverns not open to the public, but the Nature Society has permission to organize visits. There is also a reputable tour company, Asian Overland, ((03) 292-5622, that specializes in out of the ordinary trips like a one-day cave exploration that involves wading through waist deep water, a day's basic rock climbing or a trip involving rafting along rapids. It also conducts jungle walks and various nature tours that all start from Kuala Lumpur.

Only half-an-hour's drive west of Kuala Lumpur, out toward the airport, is the new town of **Shah Alam** and the **Sultan Abdul Aziz Shah Mosque.** This new mosque is stupendous in size and design, with a

ABOVE: Most people go to the Genting Highlands for its casinos and cool air, but this pagoda provides a scenic diversion.

prayer hall that accommodates over 12,000 worshippers. Although only Muslims can enter the actual chambers, the mosque is still worth viewing because of its commanding presence and the way that its sparkling blue color somehow avoids being garish.

A whole day could be planned in Shah Alam by combining a visit to the mosque with a longer stay at the 1,330-hectare (over 3,000 acres) **Agricultural Park**. The most successful and unique feature here is the paddy field with six plots in various stages of cultivation and the rice mill nearby. The whole process of rice growing can be observed in progress, and the rice mill is a little museum in itself with a guide who will be happy to talk about agricultural matters. The park has many other features, including a terrific suspension bridge.

There is no entrance fee, just M$2 for the regular buses that traverse the area. Hiring a bicycle would be more fun, though this wouldn't get you to the top of the 788 m (2,585 ft) Sapu Tangan Hill. This requires a stiff walk and is more fun early in the morning. Chalet accommodation is available in the park from $12 up, but you need to bring your own food to make use of the cooking facilities. More luxurious accommodations ($75) are planned. To make reservations, call ℂ (03) 550-6922; fax: (03) 291-3758. At weekends and public holidays the park and chalets are full but during the week the place is your own.

From Kuala Lumpur take the Sri Jaya Nº 338 bus, or the Klang bus Nº 222 or 206, from the Kelang Bus Terminal. A taxi would cost about $10, but getting one back could be tricky. A car would be best and it would also allow you to take in the nearby mosque. The mosque is right next to the Holdiay Inn, ℂ (03) 550-3696; fax: (03) 550-3913, and the hotel would provide the ideal place for a decent meal in the vicinity as well as an alternative source of accommodation to the park chalets. A double in the Holiday Inn is $82 and the amenities here are above average. A meal for two in the hotel's Sichuan restaurant would be around $20.

Further afield is **Carey Island,** , home to the Mah Meri aborigines, the *Orang Asli.* This site, near Klang, takes nearly two hours by car from Kuala Lumpur.

NIGHTLIFE

The best clubs, pubs and discos are scattered around the area surrounding the racecourse and known as the Golden Triangle. Discos there don't begin to fill up till after midnight, and on Saturdays they'll stay open until five in the morning. A house once belonging to Malaysian royalty has been converted into the **Phase 2** disco, ℂ (03) 248-2063, out on Jalan Tun Razak. Under the same management, down at the town end of Jalan Ampang, is **11LA**, ℂ (03) 232-4721, another converted old building with an equally young crowd flooding the place in the early morning hours. The Merlin, Park Avenue, Hilton and Shangri-La hotels have their own, pricier, discos and there are plenty of others to choose from. **Legends** has a good reputation, as does **Beetlejuice**, a '60s pub Next to the Ming Court Hotel is **London Pride**, a small pub that attracts expatriates. More recently Kuala Lumpur's satellite town **Petaling Jaya** has acquired a reputation for a lively nightlife. **All That Jazz**, ℂ (03) 755-3152, at Nº 14 Jalan 19/36, no longer plays jazz but is still popular. So too is **Jazz Boulevard**, ℂ (03) 719-9018, at Nº 65 Jalan SS21/1A. **Piccadilly**, in the Kimisawa complex, is a popular spot among singles.

After a long night, if you'd like a real massage (as opposed to one of a more questionable nature), visit the **Professional Blind Service Centre** at Nº 4A Jalan Thambapillai, Brickfields, ℂ (03) 274-1337. Blind masseurs charge $25 for an hour-long service.

WHERE TO STAY

TOP CLASS

For unashamed luxury, sheer class and history, the **Carcosa Seri Negara** wins hands down. In 1896, the first resident-general Sir Frank Swettenham began the construction of his official home in what is now the Lake Gardens, and it remained the residence of the highest British representative until 1941 when it became the Japanese Senior Officers' Army Mess. It has only recently been converted to a hotel and the price of a suite starts at over $300. The address is Taman Tasik Perdaqna, 50480 Kuala Lumpur, ((03) 230-6766; fax: (03) 230-6959.

A cluster of five-star hotels can be found along Jalan Sultan Ismail, among which the **Shangri-La**, ((03) 232-2388; fax: (03) 230-1514, most consistently and deservedly wins awards for its standard of service. Ask for a room ($137) fronting the racetrack for pleasant views of the hills in the background. The **Hotel Equatorial**, ((03) 261-7777; fax: (03) 261-9020, is close by and offers

less expensive ($90) but more homely rooms plus a coffee house that is very popular with locals. The **Hilton**, ((03) 242-2222; fax: 243-8069, is next door and the **Holiday Inn**, ((03) 248-1066; fax: (03) 248-1930, in Jalan Pinang, P.O. Box 10983, is just behind the Hilton with good doubles for $86. The advantage of staying in this area is your proximity to the largest shopping area in Kuala Lumpur, and there are numerous classy restaurants and nightclubs in the vicinity.

Well located for access to the airport and a large shopping complex (but with a small pool) is the **Pan Pacific**, ((03) 442-5555; fax: (03) 441-7236, adjacent to the Putra World Trade Centre and easily recognizable at night due to the lifts that climb the exterior wall like caterpillars. The postal address is P.O. Box 11468, 50746 Kuala Lumpur.

The airport area itself has a number of similarly priced hotels of which **Holiday Villa**, ((03) 733-7449; fax: (03) 733-7449, possesses the best sport and recreation fa-

cilities of any hotel in Malaysia, including an olympic-sized pool and open air jacuzzi. The nearby lake was once an open tin mine. This hotel with doubles for $82 is a good value for any temple and market-weary traveler who feels like a few days of healthy recreation. It has a special area for children, with films, video games, and a bowling alley. The French restaurant here has the Tatler tick of approval, and you could also use the outlets at The **Subang Merlin** next door, ((03) 733-5211; fax: (03) 733-1299. Rooms here are costly at $75, and the **Petaling Jaya Hilton**, ((03) 755-9122; fax: (03) 755-3909, is a far livelier place for the same price. On the same road as Holiday Villa is **Remmes**, an excellent South Indian and Moghul restaurant. Well worth a visit.

MODERATE

The **Kowloon Hotel**, ((03) 292-6455, is well situated at the town end of Jalan Tuanku Abdul Rahman (Nº 142–146) and has modern, good rooms at $30. The **Asia Hotel**, ((03) 292-6077; fax: (03) 292-7734, is similar but at the other end of the same main road at Nº 69 Jalan Haji Hussein. **Kuala Lumpur Mandarin**, ((03) 274-7433, Nº 2–8 on Jalan Sultan, has singles and doubles at $32.

Other well established hotels in this category are **Hotel Malaya**, ((03) 232-7722, on Jalan Hang Lekir in Chinatown, the **Lodge Hotel**, ((03) 242-0122, on Jalan Sultan Ismail and the **Champagne Hotel**, ((03) 298-6333, well situated in the downtown area off Jalan Masjid India. But for sheer good value, a wide choice of rooms and excellent location, it is difficult to beat the **Hotel Pudu Raya**. This modern hotel is located on the fourth floor of the Pudu Raya Station in Jalan Pudu near Chinatown. Their basic standard single at $32 is roomy enough for two and their deluxe twins at $43 come complete with a room fridge. The hotel has most of the services you would normally associate with room rates double those of the Pudu Raya. The set meals are also a good value and if you are leaving by taxi or bus for other parts of Malaysia, then this hotel is perfect: the bus and taxi stations are literally below the hotel in the same building.

INEXPENSIVE

Always worth trying is the historic **Coliseum**, ℂ (03) 292-6270, but with only 10 rooms ($10 and shared bathrooms) it takes some luck to get a room. Just a little further up Abdul Rahman is the **Rex** ($8), but while the restaurant serves decent, inexpensive western food the rooms are depressingly bare. The **Meridian International Youth Hostel** is situated on the walkway that runs alongside the Central Market ($7 to $20) and reservations can be made in advance, ℂ (03) 232-1428; fax: (03) 293-4792. **Paradise Bed & Breakfast**, ℂ (03) 293-2322, offers very spartan but clean rooms ($9) with continental breakfast included, but I would much prefer the new **Ti Lodge**, ℂ (03) 293-0261, at N° 20 Lorong Bunus Enam just off Jalan Masjid India. For $12 it offers an air-conditioned double with breakfast thrown in. The **Station Hotel**, ℂ (03) 274-1433, situated within the railway station, is presently undergoing a renovation that might affect its former budget status, but it would be well worth checking out because the rooms used to be huge. The Tourist Information Centres have a useful booklet listing budget accommodation in Kuala Lumpur and other regions of Malaysia.

WHERE TO EAT

Unlike in Singapore, many colonial-style buildings have survived in Kuala Lumpur. One such building is the restaurant **Le Coq d'Or** at N° 121 Jalan Ampang. (Taxi drivers are more likely to be familiar with the Angkasa Raya building next door.) The restaurant was originally the home of a tin millionaire who, story has it, stipulated in his will that his home could only become a restaurant if the interior remained unchanged. When you see the place you may think this interdict has been taken too seriously for the one-time elegance is now fading to the point of disintegration. Reservations are useful, ℂ (03) 242-9732, for the very economically priced set lunch ($3) though in the evenings they are not essential. A good meal can be enjoyed by two for

less than $15 and a drink on the verandah is pleasant at any time. Don't forget to view upstairs and check the powder room with its antiquated plumbing.

Another classic restaurant and bar is **The Coliseum**, situated at the town end of Jalan Tuanku Abdul Rahman, not far from the Masjid Jame and next door to the cinema of the same name. While Le Coq d'Or is going to seed, The Coliseum seems relatively alive and well and the place attracts a healthy mix of locals, expatriates and tourists. It was opened in 1921 and, despite a brief hiatus

during the early days of the Japanese occupation, it has remained open for business ever since. The framed drawing on the wall is an original by Malaysia's most famous cartoonist, Lat, and the artist can sometimes be seen at the bar. The ancient fans on the ceiling are purely decorative, for the place is pleasantly air conditioned and makes for a lovely watering hole. The restaurant is a separate area and the menu offers sound western favorites, including sizzling steaks at $6. Open from 10 to 10, a decent brunch can be enjoyed here at a price that would shame the big hotels. Reservations are not essential, ℂ (03) 292-6270.

For something authentically colonial and classy try the **Carcosa Seri Negara Hotel**, ℂ (03) 230-6766, in Lake Gardens. The afternoon tea, curry tiffin on the lawn, is highly recommended for anyone wanting to indulge in a mild splurge. The Mahsuri

OPPOSITE: Popular Eden Village restaurant offers airconditioning or *al fresco* dining with a cultural show. ABOVE: Or you can try the fare at one of Kuala Lumpur's many hawker stalls.

restaurant serves continental and Malaysian specialties and this is for a real splurge.

Just past The Coliseum is the shabby **Rex Hotel** but the western menu here is very decent. Next door is a clean, modern Malay establishment offering excellent *murtabaks*, curries and lighter snacks.

All the big hotels have fancy restaurants ranging from Malay-style buffets through to continental, Japanese and Chinese cuisine. The **Holiday Inn on the Park** has the best Italian place while the **Shangri-La's** Cantonese restaurant regularly wins acclaim as the city's best Chinese restaurant. In this part of town, the Golden Triangle, there are a number of classy restaurants but **The Ship**, just past the Hilton, offers good western food at decent prices. And if you fancy a cultural show with your meal try **Yazmin**, ((03) 241-5655, for Malay food; the buffet here is really quite good and vegetarians won't be disappointed either. For $34 you can enjoy the food and the show to the accompaniment of traditional Malay instruments. **Eden**, ((03) 241-4027, has a dance show, seafood and western fare, and it's a great value for the money, but reservations are very necessary. Two people can wine and dine for under $20, and the show includes a Filipino band that you could dance to through till midnight. If you want to avoid the floor show (and it won't be everyone's cup of tea), reserve a table indoors.

At the bottom end of the main Tuanku Abdul Rahman road there are two North Indian restaurants cheek by jowl: **Omar Khayam** and **Shiraz**. Prices are reasonable ($12 for two) and while the food is a lot tastier than the decor at both places I much prefer Shiraz. Another good Indian restaurant is **Bangles** at N° 60A Jalan Tuanku Abdul Rahman, ((03) 298-3780, within walking distance of Merdeka Square and serving authentic but mild North Indian food at very reasonable prices. There are two very individual places serving the best vegetarian food in Kuala Lumpur. One is the Indian **Annalakshmi** at 44/46 Jalan Maroof, Bangsar Park. Just a couple of ringgit (Malaysian dollars) by taxi from the railway station, this restaurant is one part of the commercial wing of the Temple of Fine Arts, a charity organization linked to an offbeat Hindu sect. An average meal will cost $12 for two, reservations not needed, and smoking or alcohol is unacceptable anytime. There is also a Devi Annapoorna in the city, very close to the Omar Khayam and Shiraz restaurants in Lorong Medan Tuanku Satu, ((03) 291-2705, but it is closed on Sundays. Another excellent place is **Gandhi's Corner**, near the junction of Jalan Thambypillay and Jalan Berhala in Brickfields. Local gourmets travel from far and wide to savor vegan kebab, "Bruce Lee" rice and other unique dishes created by a chef born on the day Mahatma Gandhi was assassinated. Open from 6 pm to 4 am, a delicious meal for two can be enjoyed for $5.

Chinatown has plenty of Chinese eateries that serve beer, rubbing shoulders with neighboring non-alcoholic Malay street cafes along Jalan Cheng Lock. Jalan Petaling is the main street and you should try some *ye tang* (coconut candy) here. McDonald's and close relations are also in evidence.

For inexpensive local food try the top floor of the Central Market where excellent Indian curries are available at the **Kampung Pandan** restaurant. On the fourth floor of the Mall, next to the Pan Pacific hotel and the Putra World Trade Centre, is the **Medan Hang Tuah** food court. Lots of local favorites here: *bak kut teh* (pork ribs soup) and *tom yam* (hot sour) soup from Thailand, to name just two.

Below Parkson's in the basement of **Bukit Bintang Plaza** is a supermarket and air-conditioned food court which might be a good way to try local food. About 15 stalls each offer a different type of local food, from banana leaf curries to noodles or *yong tau fu*, a delicious local soup made from vegetables and tofu fishballs.

SHOPPING

A dedicated Singaporean consumer might well turn their nose up at the shopping possibilities in Kuala Lumpur, but don't let that put you off because there are plenty of stores to visit. The biggest cluster with the widest

OPPOSITE: At the National Day celebrations in Kuala Lumpur, schoolgirls swop their uniforms for colorful national dress.

range of shops is at the junction of Jalan Sultan Ismail and Jalan Bukit Bintang. **KL Plaza** is a showplace of designer clothing with some nice shops and the Japanese Isetan department store. It also has a Delifrance for pastry addicts. On the other side of J. Sultan Ismail are a whole network of interconnected plazas within which you will find many good-priced clothing and shoe stores and two good department stores, MetroJaya and Parkson's Grand. Another good shopping mall is called The Mall, close by the Pan Pacific Hotel, with many small shops and a large department store.

The countryside tours that operate from all the big hotels may include a shopping trip as most usually stop at a batik/souvenir shop as well as the Selangor pewter factory. **Central Market** and **Infokraf** (see above) are both useful places for local items like silk batik scarves, carved wooden ornaments or pottery, and of course, the many night markets sell pseudo-designer items.

If you are keen on art and antiques, pay a visit to the wonderful **Loke House**. This mansion was built in 1904 by Loke Yew, one of Malaysia's first multimillionaires, a man so rich he had his own bank note printed. His house was the first brick mansion in the city and the first home to have electricity. Left empty for years, it was used by the Japanese during the Occupation and later by the police during the Emergency. It is now reopened under the name **Artiquarium**, Nº 237A, Jalan Medan Tuanku, 50300 Kuala Lumpur, ((03) 292-1222, fax: (03) 717-2110, and is a cross between a museum and an antique shop. You can wander around the many rooms admiring the beautifully restored pieces, and if one particularly appeals to you they'll gladly pack it up and sell it to you. How many times have you wished you could do that! The house itself is museum piece and if you can't afford the Melaccan dressers or chairs, there are lots of smaller craft items for sale. Artiquarium is open from 10 am to 6:30 pm Tuesday to Friday, and 10 to 5 on weekends. It is closed all day Monday.

GETTING THERE AND AWAY

BY TRAIN

From Singapore there's a night train that leaves at 10 pm and arrives at Kuala Lumpur at 7 am, and a day train departing at 8 am and arriving Kuala Lumpur at 2:30 pm. A similar service operates in the opposite direction.

From Thailand, the International Express departs Bangkok at 3 pm, arrives at Butterworth around midday the next day, where a connection can be made with the afternoon train leaving at 2 pm and reaching Kuala Lumpur at 8:30 pm the same night. To leave Kuala Lumpur for Thailand, catch the 7:30 am train for the first leg of the journey. Phone the railway station for details, ((03) 274-7435.

BY BUS

Coach buses arrive and depart from Kuala Lumpur's Pudu Raya Bus Terminal near Chinatown. This is the station for buses to Singapore, the north and the west coasts and the fast ones leave early in the morning. For details, phone (03) 230-0145. For buses to and from the airport and places in the vicinity of Kuala Lumpur you need the Kelang Bus Terminal on Jalan Sultan Mohammed. Buses to and from the east coast use more than one location, the most common station being the Mara on Jalan Medan Tuanku.

BY LONG-DISTANCE TAXI

The taxi station is also in the Pudu Raya Station so you can compare prices and times of departure. Basically, a taxi will leave as soon as one to four people are prepared to pay or share the cost. Do consider a visit to the taxi station as they are very efficient. The taxis occupy a floor of the car park and there are clear signs indicating the various destinations. Just front up and engage the drivers in discussion; politely ignore the touts who may approach you outside the station.

BY AIR

OPPOSITE: Kuala Lumpur's many celebrations attract huge crowds to Merdeka Square.

See the GETTING THERE section under TRAVELERS' TIPS (page 185).

The East Coast

THE EAST COAST, with its magnificent beaches, tiny fishing villages and resort hotels can be a fine introduction to Malaysia. There are an increasing number of excellent resorts that do not suffer from the kind of over-development found in comparable parts of Thailand. The local people are gentle and helpful, often to the point of tolerating visitors whose dress defies Muslim sensibilities. This section of the book will assume a journey northward from Johore Bahru, but the trip can be and is often done in the reverse order by tourists traveling south from Thailand.

There are excellent tourist offices in Kuala Terengganu and Kota Bharu, but most of the journey is through very small towns. It is well worth stopping in some of the smaller places and experiencing a little discomfort in order to experience the culture and lifestyle of this part of Malaysia.

JOHORE BAHRU

Johore Bahru is not the most picturesque town in Malaysia, but it is very interesting nevertheless. Although little now remains of its rich past, when it was an empire that governed the southern half of the peninsula including the then unimportant island of Singapore, the main road running along the waterfront houses a number of impressive buildings that convey an air of majesty quite appropriate to its past history and present importance to the national economy.

If you are staying in Singapore, a day and a night in Johore Bahru is an essential complement. It provides balance, a therapeutic antidote to the excessive cleanliness and moral rigor of Lion City. Singaporeans come to Johore Bahru, or JB as it is commonly called, in droves, they say, because the seafood and the shopping is cheap. Don't believe them. They come for a good healthy dose of chaos. Gone, for them, are the carefully regimented and well-drained pavements, the numbered and pruned trees and the well-ordered traffic flow. A Singaporean writer once wrote an amusing story about the government of Singapore buying a piece of JB to send its stressed-out executives to when things get too much for them in over-regulated Singapore. At this rest home for over-organized government servants they would be able to spit on the ground, jaywalk, drop litter, pick the flowers and then return to squeaky clean Singapore refreshed and ready to start anew.

GENERAL INFORMATION

The tourist information office is on the ground floor of Komtar on Jalan Wong Ah Fook, ((07) 223590, and there is also a tourist police station near the Causeway,

((07) 232222. Car hire firms have offices in the Holiday Inn, ((07) 323800, and the Tropical Inn, ((07) 233325. Taxis are readily available, and while inexpensive, expect to pay M$4 for any trip around town. They are not metered, so agree on the price before setting off. Travel agents in Johore Bahru offer sightseeing tours around town, as well as trips to the fishing village of Kukup and a rubber plantation. Contact the tourist information office for details. One company, S.S. Holidays ((07) 230491, also handles cruises to the Indonesian island of Batam.

WHAT TO SEE

In January 1942, after withdrawing steadily in the wake of the Japanese advance down Malaya, the last Australian and British

OPPOSITE: Women preparing crops on Malaysia's east coast. ABOVE: Johore Bahru, the second largest city in Malaysia, has a flourishing nightlife, drawing many people over the causeway from Singapore every night.

troops crossed the **Causeway** at 5 am, with the remains of the 2nd Argyll and Sutherland Highlanders playing their pipes behind them. Once the pipers had crossed, explosives were laid and detonated and after the roar and smoke of the explosion settled, a 20-meter (66-foot) gap was awash with water. Somehow no one remembered until it was too late that they were cutting off their major water supply at the same time. The **Istana Besar**,the main palace of the Johore royal family, was where General-Yamashita installed his advance headquar-

SHOPPING

Holiday Plaza is immensely popular with Singaporeans who flock here to take advantage of the exchange rate between the Singapore dollar and the Malaysian ringgit. An hour spent here does throw up some interesting differences between the two countries and the noise that seems to be an essential accompaniment to the shopping is very typical of life in Malaysia. There are also various craft stalls plying

ters. He used the palace tower as an observation post where he sat with a large-scale map of Singapore to direct operations. The palace now houses the **Royal Abu Bakar Museum**, a collection of royal treasures from all around the world, open daily except Friday. The entrance fee is $7.

Johore Bahru really comes alive at night. Restaurants and street stalls are crowded and a random walk often turns up something unexpected: a salesman with live snakes demonstrating the virtue of snake blood and selected organs, transvestites in their home ground near where the Pan Pacific stands, food stalls tucked away in alleyways serving delicious roti at 1 am or 2 am.

wares, and some nice leather items are available.

One specialist bit of shopping that will interest some people is computer software. Although Malaysia has copyright laws just like Singapore, they just don't seem to have the same effect. Most of the video tape shops you see everywhere are regularly raided when an American company organizes a confrontation with the authorities but the next week they are back again. Pirated computer software is not quite so blatantly on sale, but it is readily available and the interested reader should shop around in the recesses on the higher floors. Holiday Plaza is not in the main town near the Causeway and it is too far to walk to. It is next to the

Holiday Inn Hotel and is best reached by taxi or on the shuttle train from Singapore which has a station next to the Holiday Inn.

NIGHTCLUBS

The nightclubs in the Wisma Abad Complex, just across the road from the Holiday Inn and Holiday Plaza, offer Chinese night entertainment at its very best, and outside of Hong Kong, places like the **Golden Palace** cannot be seen elsewhere. As you step into the place it's the sheer size of the interior that takes your breath away. It's cavernous and electric, with a rooftop that stretches away into the distance with not a single pillar supporting it. This is what allows for the uninterrupted space and the tremendous atmosphere of the place. All down the left side, as you stand by the entrance gazing in awe, are the private rooms that can be hired for 20 ringitt. Take a walk down the side; it's impossible to resist glancing in at the cameo scenes: lush hostesses playing up to their customers, bottle of brandy on the table, the glint of jewelry. Outside all is music and more atmosphere. There is a great million-dollar sound setup with a flying saucer light system that sprinkles light and color everywhere. Looking across to the other side there is a large stage with dancing space in front. And everywhere are hostesses; escorting customers, carrying drinks, mingling at the tables. The electronic board keeps tab on the supply and demand, and the frequent change of numbers bears testimony to the business-like fervor of the place. The shows begin at 11:40 pm, 12:40 and 1:45 am and you won't see them anywhere else in Malaysia or Singapore. A strip show usually accompanies the show, with the main one at 12:40. In between there will be songs and dances. No matter that they sing in Mandarin or Cantonese. The style is what counts and the Golden Palace has that in plenty, and at reasonable prices. There is no cover charge (except when a big star from overseas is brought in) and a tourist could expect to pay $12 for a drink and a show. A half bottle of brandy will cost $60. Weekends are the best time to visit (it will be full up by midnight) but the Golden Palace, ((07) 312077, is open throughout the week and

you could have just as good a time on a quiet mid-week night. To reach the Golden Palace, use the lift and press the P button. It's a smelly old lift, but there's a terrific scene waiting for you once you step out of it.

The **Metropolis** is in the same building and has a similar setup — no cover charge and similar prices to the Golden Palace, but you would be advised to get the prices settled clearly. Negotiation might be called for and the cost of brandy varies between weekdays and weekends. The shows begin around 11:30 pm, 1 am and last show at 2:45 am. The

atmosphere at the Metropolis is just as frenzied as the Golden Palace but the feel of the place is more Chinese. Well worth a visit though non-oriental visitors might blend in more easily at the Golden Palace.

The **Great Eastern**, ((07) 316094, is situated in the basement of the building and as you travel downstairs you could be forgiven for thinking the place is going to turn out to be some real sleaze pit. One couldn't be more mistaken. The place is friendly and cozy, not too crowded and with a quaint English/American feel to the music. This is the place to visit if you fancy dancing to some oldies and watching a modest show. A jug of beer is $15, a bottle of whiskey around $70. The Great Eastern is a delightful place and closes at 12:45 am most nights, around 2:30 am at weekends.

OPPOSITE: Johore Bahru, the sultan's palace, now houses the Royal Abu Bakar Museum which displays some of the sultan's many treasures. ABOVE: Tourists are always greeted with a smile on Malaysia's east coast.

Star Karaoke is situated near the Sentosa complex, not far from the Holiday Plaza-Holiday Inn area. The exact address is N° 60A–B Jalan Sutera Tiga, Taman Sentosa, 80150, ((07) 329705. If you want to try out *karaoke* without having a live audience grimace at your efforts, then head for Star Karaoke. The private rooms are hired at around $10 an hour and come with their own bathroom. Once ensconced in your room order a jug of beer ($10) and look through the album of songs. There are hundreds of English ones to choose from. Having written your choice down on a slip of paper you ring the bell and hand it over to one of the girls. Minutes later the monitor will come to life with your song and the words as subtitles. Take the mike and let rip for the rooms are mildly soundproofed. There are two microphones in each room so a small group can have fun. Downstairs is a seafood restaurant and you can even have the food brought up to your room. You could have a lot of fun at the Star Karaoke in a small group or even with the family. Early on in the night you'll see children with their parents having a sing-along. Later in the night couples and small groups turn up. Recommended.

The shows at the **Mechinta** nightclub are at 7, 8, 9:30, 10:45 pm and 1 am, with an extra midnight show on Friday and Saturday. The later you go into the shows the more raunchy they get and the more crowded. Early on, there's not much atmosphere and you feel a little bit like a voyeur, but by about the third show things start to take off. The leather and thong macho stuff is kept to a minimum and you have to admire the expertise with which the men throw the women around the tiny floor space. The price of the show is around $15, more or less, depending on your negotiating skills, and it can be worth ringing to make a reservation and settle on the price, ((07) 231400, especially if a dinner is going to be included. Mechinta is well worth a visit. It is well run and not out to fleece the customer, nor is it a hideously male joint. Couples, young and not so young, are welcome and common. There is no good reason why unattended women shouldn't go there as well.

WHERE TO STAY

The newest and poshest hotel is the **Pan Pacific**, ((07) 233333; fax: (07) 236622, with deluxe rooms at $120 and within walking distance of the Causeway. The **Holiday Inn** is on Jalan Dato Sulaiman, Taman Century, ((07) 323800, and is right next to the popular Holiday Plaza. A double is $94 and before the opening of the Pan Pacific this was the only international hotel in town. The Malaysian owned Merlin chain have two hotels: the **Merlin Inn**, situated near the Causeway at N° 10 Jalan Bukit Meldrum, ((07) 237400; fax: (07) 248919, and the **Merlin Tower** in Jalan Meldrum, ((07) 225811. The $62 rooms at the Merlin Inn offer views of the Causeway and the friendly staff make the place more attractive than it seems from the outside. The Merlin Tower is located in the noisy downtown center and has little to recommend it. Rooms are $50 at the **Rasa Sayang**, N° 10 Jalan Dato Dalam, ((07) 248600; fax: (07) 248612, and the location is a pleasantly quiet one but requiring a walk to reach any shops. The **Tropical Inn**, N° 15 Jalan Gereja, ((07) 247888; fax; (07) 241544, is a popular place at $54, but like many of the hotels in Johore Bahru it lacks architectural charm and the immediate environment is uncongenial. The best of the rest is the **Hotel Malaya** with rooms at $18, ((07) 221691, located near the Merlin Inn on Jalan Bukit Meldrum and a few minutes walk from the causeway.

WHERE TO EAT

The **Straits Garden Restaurant**, ((07) 375788, is situated in Jalan Scudai, along the coast road from the town center and a taxi should cost M$4. It is open from 3 pm to just after midnight, and from 8 pm to 11 pm there is live music in the form of a Filipino band on stage. Ask for a seat near the fishing ponds at the back if you want a quieter meal (an air-conditioned room is also available). The ponds, incidentally, are merely decorative, for the live seafood is delivered daily by lorry. The menu is extensive, and two people could eat well for $20. Before you leave, make sure you view the Silver Dragon in its aquarium near the entrance to the kitchen.

This is a very special fish from Indonesia, worth almost $10,000, and would never be eaten. If you examine its forehead closely you will discern little lines that quite clearly spell out a four digit number — 5253. The numbering is quite natural.

Christine's Place in Jalan Tebrau, ((07) 248891, has almost everything. A hairdressing salon, sauna, baths, massages, gym, restaurants, *karaoke*, lounge bar, disco, hostesses. A whole night could easily be spent here or, alternatively, just pop in for a drink and a seafood or Sichuan meal. Start the night looking good. Visit the unisex salon here and have a cut and wash for $6 and/or a facial for $10. Or skip that and go straight to the health center: $6 for the unisex sauna or herbal bath and $17 for the Executive Service Massage! The health center is clean, posh and well run. The massage rooms are the best you'll see in Johore Bahru and the gym and rest rooms are free of charge. There are two restaurants: a posh one inside that is fine if its raining, but the al fresco **Seafood Garden** is the one recommended. There is a Sichuan menu but the seafood is the main attraction. Barbecued crabs, roasted over charcoal, are very popular though the item doesn't appear on the menu. So too are the drunken prawns which are dunked in wine and shaken dizzy before being unceremoniously immolated in the alcohol over an open fire. A match is put to the wine and *voilà* — flaming drunken prawns, which taste sweet and quite different from the drunk-on-brandy version. The price of a meal will depend on what items you select but a very good meal, including a jug of beer, could be enjoyed by four people for around $30. Another good seafood restaurant is **Jaws 5** situated on the main road that heads out west from town along the seafront. At weekends the place gets so crowded it's positively uncomfortable if you are looking for a quiet meal.

Just up the small road that runs alongside the Jaws 5 restaurant there is **Mechinta**, an old-style colonial house once owned by royalty and now housing an entertainment center. The open air restaurant is called **Ani Ani Seafood** and its prices are quite reasonable. Dishes cost $4 on average and they are available in two sizes. A mouthwatering meal for two could begin with the

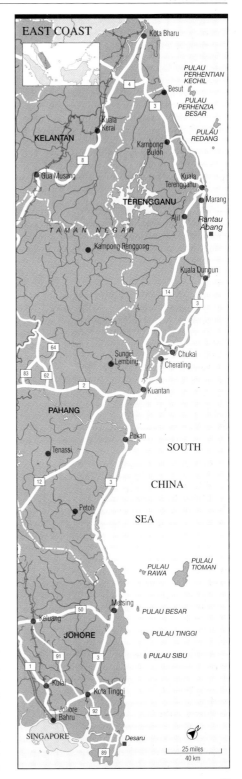

buttermilk prawns, a house specialty, deep fried with curry leaves till crunchy and swimming in deliciously cholesterol laden buttermilk sauce. Follow this by the special beancurds, ground with fish, sotong (cuttlefish), and prawns, fried to perfect crispness on the outside while melting inside. Don't forget the sambar vegetables mixed with spicy gravy and seaweed and some Sichuan chicken. On weekends a reservation, ((07) 231400, is a good idea.

In Holiday Plaza the **Yussof Restoran** is a huge Indian restaurant but it's horribly clinical and the food hardly compensates for this. If you do want to eat, or just have a drink and maybe a snack, then travel up to the third floor at N° F12 and partake of a quiet meal at **Plaza Corner**. The other place to eat in near Holiday Plaza is the Holiday Inn Hotel. There is a good **Sichuan restaurant**, ((07) 323800, as well as a reasonably priced coffee shop serving light meals.

The best Indian food in Johore Bahru is to be found in the small cafes in the vicinity of the Pan Pacific. It would be unfair to recommend one rather than another, as the food is equally delicious. A meal for two should cost less than $5.

GETTING THERE

Singapore's proximity has helped to make Johore Bahru a major interchange for coaches to and from every part of Malaysia. Along Jalan Meldrum there is a whole chain of agents handling bus and coach tickets. Johore Bahru's airport is 20 minutes out of town and flights connect with Kuala Lumpur, the East Coast towns and Sarawak and Sabah. From Singapore bus N° 170 leaves Queen Street or Bukit Timah Road every 15 minutes and the daily shuttle train departs at 7:00 and 10:00 am, 12:30 and 5:00 pm. The return journey departs at 8:40 and 11:35 am, 2:15 and 6:40 pm. As well as stopping at the main station in town the shuttle also serves Holiday Plaza. It is also possible to drive between Johore Bahru and Singapore but the regular traffic jam on the Causeway is no joke. An hour's wait is not uncommon during the evening rush hour, and the weekend is always best avoided. It is often quicker to just walk across, as many people do.

DESARU

Desaru is the nearest beach area to Singapore and **Johore Bahru**; consequently, it attracts a large number of local visitors, especially during school holidays, weekends and public holidays. The beach is large enough to still give you the space to wander off and find your own patch but finding accommodation at these times can be tricky. The beach itself is glorious but not suitable for swimming because of the fierce currents. Children will have fun ducking the big waves but you do need to keep an eye on them all the time. The biggest hotel is the **Desaru View Hotel**, P.O. Box 71, 81907 Kota Tinggi, ((07) 821221, with doubles starting at $60. The **Desaru Golf Hotel**, P.O. Box 50, 81907 Kota Tinggi, ((07) 821107; fax: (07) 821480, named after the 18-hole golf course, has doubles that start at $80. Unlike most other places in Malaysia there is no neighboring food center so you are very much dependent on the hotel outlets.

Desaru is just under 100 km (60 miles) from Johore Bahru and can be reached by taxi: at least $23 for a cab, unless sharing. From Singapore there are various companies offering packages that include transport and these are a better value than traveling by yourself in a taxi. Just turn to the back pages of the *Straits Times* newspaper for the phone numbers of different agencies.

MERSING

Mersing is most well known as the place where ferries leave for the smaller islands off the coast of Johore and this is why the majority of visitors are here. But Mersing has a pleasant atmosphere, some good seafood restaurants and a charmingly dilapidated government resthouse at very reasonable prices and some decent beaches of its own.

WHAT TO SEE

Not much here in the way of sights but there are two good beaches, one south of the town and the other, more popular one, to the north at Air Papan. It is about 15 km (nine miles) north of Mersing, past the Merlin Hotel, and well signposted. A taxi will take you there for a few dollars and there is also a bus service. The beach to the south of town can be reached by driving up the hill past the mosque along the coastline until you see some old brick kilns where you can park your car. Locals tend to shun the place, but it has an enormous expanse of shallow gentle water, white beaches and interesting plant life, including some mangroves. On foot, the beach can be approached from the resthouse,but it is quite a long walk. It is a shorter walk from the Puteri Inn Resort.

WHERE TO STAY

Just a little way north of Mersing is the **Merlin Hotel**, at 2 km, Jalan Endau, 86807 Mersing, ((07) 791313; fax: (07) 793177, with comfortable rooms at reasonable prices ($30). It has a small pool and restaurant and is very quiet. Just a little way south of town is an eccentric little resort owned by the Sultan of Johore and built entirely from converted containers. They have been prettily converted into thatched roof cabins, are fully air-conditioned and very neat if you don't mind a long narrow room. The beach is nothing to scream about but you can walk along a little way to an almost deserted beach with soft, white sand. There is a tiny restaurant but they don't cook regularly and require advance notice for meals. The place calls itself the **Puteri Inn Resort**, ((07) 334669, and the containers go for around $20 a night.

Alternatively there is the wonderfully shabby **Government Resthouse** at N° 490 Jalan Ismail, 86800 Mersing, ((07) 792102, standing on its own on a long-abandoned and water-logged golf course. The vast rooms are air-conditioned and many open onto the garden with fine views over the bay. There are only 18 rooms, a terrific value for $15, but reservations are often essential. The resthouse has its own heliport, but I've only seen it used once by the Sultan. In Mersing town itself, there are a number of inexpensive hotels, all equally unattractive, with the Embassy, ((07) 793545, being the best of a bad bunch.

WHERE TO EAT

Mersing's seafood restaurants are regularly patronized by Singaporeans on their way to and from the islands and there are a couple of Muslim places doing *murtabak* and curries. My favorite is the one directly opposite the only supermarket in town. It is clean and modern and always full of locals and visitors. The restaurant at the government resthouse serves inexpensive but disappointing western, Malay and Chinese food. But you can have the food served on the open verandah and the view helps compensate.

GETTING THERE

It takes three hours by taxi from Johore Bahru and usually it is not difficult to share the cost of a taxi. Buses and coaches also ply the route, but not on a very regular basis, so it is best to check-out the times and fares from various coach operators in Johore Bahru.

Ferries to the Islands

Several ferries leave here for the many islands off the coast of this part of Malaysia and it is best to just turn up at the jetty and make inquiries. All the ferry companies and most of the island resorts have offices near the jetty so it is easy to compare prices and times of departure. Apart from weekends, and especially holiday weekends, there is usually no problem in just booking passage and accommodation there and then. There is a **tourist center** near the jetty, ((07) 791204.

TIOMAN ISLAND

Despite its high profile, Tioman is still the best of the islands off Mersing, if only because it's larger and there is more to do there. There is also a greater range of accommodation and places to eat. The smaller islands are fine for very short visits, or if you want that Robinson Crusoe ambience, but Tioman has a modest infrastructure for the visitor.

Tourist information is a little haphazard on the island. At the new ferry terminal, by the airport at Tekek, the ticket booths will dispense information regarding the sea bus and accommodation, but life on the island is so simple that really there is little information to get.

WHAT TO SEE

Marine life is the most interesting sight on the island and that abounds just about everywhere. If you want to see marine life that other people don't see, you can go to an inaccessible beach, but the same fish and coral are lurking about right in front of Swiss Cottage or the Merlin Hotel. Boats can be hired by the hour or for the day and there are a number of very deserted beaches to spend the day on.

A sea bus travels around the island several times daily. Fares are minimal but you must be aware of the times if you want a ride back. It will take you to Juara village on the east side of the island where there are a few fairly simple places to stay and food is available. There is no snorkeling or scuba equipment to hire there though. Alternatively you can trek across the island's mountains to Juara and get the boat back. It is a pleasant walk through *kampongs* at first and then through primary rain forest where you will see lots of jungle creatures, including some spectacular lizards.

The sea bus will also take you from Tekek to Ayer Batang, where there is a good selection of places to stay, or further along to Salang where there is accommodation and a scuba center. In the other direction the sea bus stops at the resort's jetty and Genting Village which has a pleasant beach.

Starting from the north of the island, **Monkey Bay** is a regular stopping point for chartered boats. It has a good beach and snorkeling is possible. Traveling clockwise from Monkey Bay another pleasant stopping point is **Teluk Dalam** where there is an abundance of marine life to see. Good snorkeling is also possible off the beach at Juara. Traveling south a good stopping point is the **waterfall at Mukut**, location for much of the filming of South Pacific, the cause of the island's development as a holiday spot. Close by Tioman are two smaller islands to visit, **Tulai** and **Renggis**. Hiring a boat for the day can be an expensive business, but the resort that you stay at can arrange it for

you. A half day trip to Tulai will cost $56 per boat. Many resorts also offer scuba instruction packages and equipment rental.

For dyed-in-the-wool landlubbers, the resort hotel has a glass-bottomed boat which goes out daily for hour-long trips.

WHERE TO STAY

At the top end of the market is the vast and growing **Tioman Island Resort**, P.O. Box 4, 86807 Mersing, Johor, Malaysia, ✆ (09) 445445; fax: (09) 445718, which has looked like an enormous building site for several years but now appears to be reaching its expansion limit. Getting around the resort requires a small golf cart, and room service is delivered by bicycle. The resort offers the only luxury

accommodation in the area and is frequently full, so book ahead. It has a golf course, sea activities, horse riding and so on. A double room here costs S$90. Chalets are nicer but more expensive at S$120.

Down-market a little is the relatively unknown **Paya Beach Resort.** Bookings for this resort can only be made through **Giamso Tours** in Singapore, ((02) 534-1010, who arrange the whole trip. It is further south than the Tioman Island Resort.

The rest of the accommodation, and there is an almost uncountable amount of it, is spread along the beach from the Tioman Island Resort northward to Ayer Batang. Beyond that is a smaller and more primitive range of accommodation relying on generators for electricity.

Next to the Tioman Island Resort is **Swiss Cottage** which can be booked at N° 236F, Fourth floor, Gin Shew Building, Jalan Tun Abdul Razak, Johore Bahru, ((07) 248728; fax: (07) 232293. It is pleasantly small, has a very well organized scuba shop and training center and has rooms with a fan at $21. Chalets cost a little more. Swiss Cottage is regularly full up and has no intention of expanding, so if you want to stay there you should book well in advance.

A little further north is **Sri Tioman Chalets**, ((01) 711256, with similar rooms for $13. It has a good restaurant, a little shop selling many of the things that you forgot to bring

A glorious sunset on the east coast of Malaysia.

and some locally painted t-shirts, but it lacks Swiss Cottage's community atmosphere.

Beyond the new jetty, about 15 minutes walk, is **Ramli's House, (** (09) 445347, with pleasant large rooms with fans and bathroom at $11. Next door is a diving shop, **Dive Asia,** which offers a five-day diving course at $90. The beach here is a little scruffy and you are right under the flight path of the four flights a day.

Further north again is **Manggo Grove,** set on a rise in the ground above the beach, with lots of shade and cool breezes. It started as a restaurant and has now expanded into chalets with fans and little shower rooms for about $9. It sells batik t-shirts which are made while you watch.

Still hiking northward is **Nazri's,** Kampong Air Batang, Pulau Tioman, Pahang, **(** (01) 349534, which is highly organized and very popular. It offers a whole range of chalets and longhouse rooms with varying prices depending on proximity to the sea. Sea view bungalows go for around $22 and offer four beds, fans and bathroom, nicely decorated. The beach here is good, particularly if you walk a little way south through the trees. Right outside Nazri's it looks a little like Kuta Beach on Bali.

Along the beach all the way to the last of the tourist ghettos are any number of small settlements all of which have just acquired electricity and are likely to be improving their facilities accordingly. The **ABC**, at the very end of the strip, has large three-bed rooms with a fan and bathroom for $11. They also have plans for expansion now that electricity has arrived.

WHERE TO EAT

Only the monopolistic **Tioman Island Resort** hotel can offer international standard cuisine, and at a price. But if you come to Tioman prepared to live fairly primitively, the quality of the local food available is remarkably good. Each of the sets of chalets has its own restaurant, serving western breakfasts and Malay dishes. Sri Tioman has a particularly nice restaurant with remarkably quick service. **Swiss Cottage** serves food until about 8:30 in the evening. Its menu is limited but it has a good-value special each

night and often does barbecues. Best of all is **Liza Restaurant**, beside the police station, some five minutes north of Swiss Cottage. It serves a vast array of dishes to suit all tastes and does it quickly and at very reasonable rates. Two people could eat here for $13.

GETTING THERE

Tioman is accessible by air from Kuala Lumpur and Singapore. These are probably the wildest planes you will ever fly on so consider the expense well worth the adventure

and the time saved. Locals affectionately call Tradewinds' Dornier D08 the flying box and it certainly doesn't look aerodynamically designed. The plane makes the half-hour flight daily from a small air base in the north of Singapore. Watching it land, one worries about the coconut trees it neatly skims but they are all still intact. Pelangi Air's Fokkers' look a little more sophisticated but whichever way you choose to fly, it's an amazing experience, particularly landing at Tioman. Tradewinds, **(** (02) 221-2221, has flights daily from Seletar Airport in Singapore, while Pelangi Air flies daily from Kuala Lumpur, **(** (03) 770-2020; fax: (03) 746-2958. Pelangi Air can be contacted in Singapore at **(** (02) 481-6302.

By sea the journey can be made from Mersing by ferry; either by regular boat, which takes about two hours, or on the Tioman Island Resort's hydrofoil, which is more expensive but halves the traveling time. This can be a rough journey if you encounter a Sumatra, one of the storms which hit this part of the coast during May to October. There is now also a ferry service from Singapore which takes almost five hours, ℓ (02) 278-4677, and offers a package trip.

Tioman is pretty short on shops so bring anything unusual that you need with you.

tion Centre in Mersing, there will be details of other possibilities.

Do not confuse Pulau Besar with **Pulau Sibu Besar**, often just referred to as Sibu island, another delightful tropical isle with white beaches and coral reefs that make snorkeling irresistible. Waterfall Hillside Chalet Sibu Island Resort is the too-long name for a company that operates packages from Singapore, ℓ (02) 532-2920, and accesses the island not from Mersing but from the fishing town of Tanjung Sedii, which is just one hour away from Johore

On the island you can buy regular things like mosquito coils, suntan cream, etc., but they are more expensive than on the mainland.

OTHER ISLANDS

Pulau Besar is about an hour's journey from Mersing, $12 fare, and the accommodation scene here has grown in the last two years. The White Sand Beach Resort can be booked from Johore Bahru, ℓ (07) 334669, or Singapore, ℓ (02) 532-2920. The Hillside Beach Resort, ℓ (07) 236603, offers Malay-style chalets and can also be booked from Singapore, ℓ (02) 336-8855, and at the Informa-

Bahru. The island resort number is ℓ (01) 711790. Sibu Island Resorts is a different company operating from Johore Bahru, ℓ (07) 231188, and also departing from Tanjung Sedii. A two-room chalet currently costs $45 per night and the return boat fare is $15. The island can also be reached from Mersing.

About 16 km (10 miles) from Mersing lies **Pulau Rawa** with bungalows and chalets for hire. Reservations are made through Rawa Safaris at the **tourist center** in Mersing, ℓ (07) 791204. No other accommodation is available on the island.

ABOVE: Horses and ponies for hire on the beach at Terengganu.

Some 32 km (20 miles) southeast of Mersing is **Pulau Tinggi**, a largely uninhabited island but once a stopover point on the East West spice route. Accommodation is available at the luxury Smailing Island Resort and there is a range of packages from Singapore, ((02) 733-3555, Johore Bahru, ((07) 246490, or Kuala Lumpur, ((03) 298-0772. The island resort can be contacted at ((01) 763166. A two-night complete package from Singapore would cost $170 for two people.

KUANTAN

Kuantan is the beginning, or the end if you are coming down from Kelantan in the northeast, of the long beach strip that stretches along the east coast of Malaysia. Although it is the capital of the state of Pahang, the town of Kuantan itself is pretty nondescript. Kuantan's popularity with tourists is in its beaches at Telok Chempedak, about four kilometers (two-and-a-half miles) from the main town. The town itself is hardly worth a visit but you will arrive there if you come by bus. The actual beach area is a short taxi ride away. The tourist office is at 15th floor, Kompleks Teruntum, Jalan Mahkota, 25000 Kuantan, Pahang, ((09) 505566.

WHAT TO SEE

The beach is pleasant and the strong waves make for happy frolics, but are not very safe for swimming. There are several jungle walks to be done here, notably the 45-minute walk which goes behind the Merlin Hotel to a mini zoo on the hillside. If you are staying at one of the hotels, there are several day trips which you can take which the hotels regularly organize.

Beserah is a small fishing village 10 km (six miles) north of Kuantan where you will be able to watch the activities of the local fishermen, arrange a fishing trip for yourself, watch batik being made and possibly watch top spinning and kite flying competitions. Accommodation here is rudimentary so it is best done as a trip out of Kuantan. Local buses pass through and can be boarded at the bus station in Kuantan.

A day's trip out from Kuantan are two interesting sights, the **Panching Caves** and, 13 km (eight miles) further on, the **Sungei Pandan Waterfalls**. The road passes through rubber and oil plantations. To get to the caves one has to climb an external stairway of 170 stone steps. The caves are Buddhist, unlike the Batu Caves outside Kuala Lumpur which are Hindu. Inside among other statuary is a nine-meter-long (30-ft) reclining Buddha. Torches are necessary. To get there on public transport, you should take a bus to Sungei Lembing, home of the world's largest underground tin mine, and hitch a ride for the last three-and-a-half kilometers (two miles). From Panching, the Pandan Waterfalls are reached by taking a turn-off back on the road to Kuching and then a 13-km (eight-mile) journey along a laterite road. A picnic area is laid out by the falls, which are 150 m (500 ft) high. Many of the local hotels will organize trips to these two spots, lasting usually about five hours.

Fifty-six kilometers (34 miles) west of Kuantan on the Temerluh road, a small side road south brings you to *kampong* Chini from where you can cross the Pahang River to trek the rest of the way to **Lake Chini**, a lotus-covered lake said to contain a monster guarding a sunken Khmer city. There are Orang Asli settlements around the lake and some chalets and camping spots. Many of the hotels do a much easier trip there up the Pahang River through rainforest where, with some luck, many of the inhabitants of the forest will be spotted.

WHERE TO STAY

The **Hyatt Hotel** at P.O. Box 250, 25730 Kuantan, Pahang, ((09) 525211; fax: (09) 507577, provides all the luxury you could ask for (at $70) in a beach resort, including beautifully designed surroundings which somehow suggest primitive jungle conditions while simultaneously providing every amenity. There are three restaurants including a rooftop steamboat, a converted Vietnamese refugee boat offering drinks on the beach, a nice pool and a great beachfront view which becomes magnificent in rough weather when the waves are high.

Down-market a little is the **Merlin Inn**, designed primarily as a motel and with pleasant family rooms with verandas leading straight on to the gardens and the pool on the beach. Standard doubles, at $60, are smaller and further away from the beach with less pleasant views. The hotel has a restaurant serving western and local dishes and organizes coconut collections by monkeys and a weekly cultural show.

Less expensive is the **Samudra Beach Hotel**, Jalan Besar, P.O. Box 239, 25000 Kuantan, ((09) 522688, with air-conditioned double rooms at $20. Opposite the Hyatt is the **Kuantan Hotel**, ((09) 524755, with doubles

GETTING THERE

Kuantan can be reached by air on Tradewinds from Singapore, ((02) 3-226881, or by Malaysian Airlines from Kuala Lumpur. There is an Malaysian Airlines office in town, ((09) 521218. Roads link Kuantan with Mersing, Kuala Lumpur and Segamat. If you choose to drive or get a bus you will find the roads are pleasant enough, even if a little short on places to stop for a rest. Once lined on either side by rain forest, the roads now

at around the same price. This is an excellent hotel with a good restaurant and clean if unspectacular rooms. **Asrama Bendehara**, tucked in between the two resort hotels, has non air-conditioned rooms at $25 and below. It has a small inexpensive restaurant.

WHERE TO EAT

Besides the two resort hotels there are a number of rather tatty looking restaurants doing mostly Chinese seafood and a smart modern food center on the beachfront which seem to be mostly shut except at weekends when the beach fills up. The **Seaview Restaurant** on the beachfront does local and western dishes but the best food is to be had at the Hyatt.

have vast devastated strips where the forest is being cleared for oil palm plantations. The long-distance bus station is in Jalan Besar, from where buses leave for towns to the north. Nearby is the long-distance taxi station.

CHERATING

GENERAL INFORMATION

The name Cherating applies to an extremely large area covering several miles of beach and three or four large resorts. The village

ABOVE: Windsurfing, one of the many seasports along the east coast of Malaysia, is particularly suited to this coastline.

after which the area is named is in fact a tiny place which seems to make its living largely from the many budget homestays and chalets scattered around it. Cherating experiences the monsoon season during November to February so prices are seasonal at the small locally owned places.

WHAT TO SEE

From the hotels and resorts in Cherating the same visits can be made that were described in the Kuantan section, page 62. In addition you can visit a nearby island called **Pulau Ular** (Snake Island), which is about 20 minutes away by boat, for some unspoilt scenery and clear blue seas. In the village itself you can watch some hand-drawn batik being made and even have a go yourself at some of the homestay places. Some of the guest houses also arrange trips up the river to visit a tiny kampong followed by a nature walk. If you are not planning to stop again before Khota Bharu then you should consider making the trip to **Kapas Island** from here (see MARANG, page 66). Most of the hotels arrange trips, although from here it will involve a long bus ride north and then back again. If you don't stay in one of the budget places in Cherating village, then you could spend a day in the village itself just soaking up the laid-back atmosphere, watching the craft work going on, visiting the craft shops that spring up and eating very fresh seafood at very reasonable prices.

WHERE TO STAY

From Kuantan northward, there are a number of beach resorts offering sports and facilities typical of beach resorts and at typical prices, or there is the far more primitive accommodation at Cherating Village which offers a lack of luxury but local flavor.

Starting from the south, at Balok beach there is the **Coral Beach Resort**, ℂ (09) 587544, which offers sea-facing rooms at $48 to $78 and suites at $152. It has a pretty beach, safe for children although the waves can be quite strong. Further north about four kilometers (two-and-a-half miles) south of Cherating is the **Cherating Holiday Villa**, Lot 1303, Mukim Sungei Karang, Cherating, Kuan-

tan, ℂ (09) 508900, which offers rooms overlooking the pool at $40 or chalets with a sea view at $52. Each chalet is fashioned after a style indigenous to a Malaysian state. The beach is excellent, there is a supply of gadgets and equipment for sea sports, and a good tour agency within the hotel. The disadvantages of both these places is, of course, that unless you have transport of your own, getting to other places can be difficult, and so holidaymakers tend to stay where they are. From the Holiday Villa it is possible to walk along the beach toward Cherating Village, but do so only when the tide is out as the Cherating River can only be waded across at low tide. Right next door to Cherating Holiday Villa is another resort, **Palm Grove**, Kampong Baru, Cherating, 2608, an even more luxuriously appointed resort where a double room with a sea view is $82. North of the village is the **Club Med** at Cherating Lama, 26080 Kuantan, ℂ (09) 591131, which offers packages at $128 a day per person including meals and sports facilities.

In Cherating Village itself what you are likely to find is a chalet with a fan, mosquito net and primitive bathroom. The **Coconut Inn**, ℂ (09) 503299, is right on the beach and has pleasant rooms with fans and bathrooms at around $7. There are many more places, very small and without telephones, and more are opening up all the time, each one offering slightly more than its predecessors in comfort and facilities. If you intend to stay there, the best thing to do is walk around and choose a place which suits your mood.

On the main road are two places which are highly recommended by those who stay there, **Mak Long Teh** and **Mak De**, boarding houses with a family atmosphere.

WHERE TO EAT

Eating at the resorts is a comparatively expensive business. Breakfast at the Cherating Holiday Villa is about $4 while a meal for two would work out at about $18. The restaurant serves a variety of local dishes and western items. The Coral Beach Resort has two restaurants, both with good reputations, serving Chinese and Japanese cuisine. In Cherating Lama itself there are many restaurants which spring up and disappear.

The **Sayang Inn** serves Indian food, and a meal for two would cost about $7. **Mimi** restaurant serves *roti canai* when it feels like it, as well as many tourist staples like boiled eggs and fish and chips.

GETTING THERE

Buses to Cherating depart from the bus station at Kuantan, and if you are staying at any of the resorts south of the kampong itself, the local bus, run by a company called Sihat, reputedly travels in that direction at half-hourly intervals. Other means of transport are car hire and taxi hire. Cabs have no meters, and fares seem to depend on how rich you look. Your hotel will be able to tell you how much you should pay.

KUALA DUNGUN AND RANTAU ABANG

The town of Dungun itself is a pretty depressing place, but nearby are some lovely beaches and some pleasant resorts.

TURTLE WATCHING

The most famous activity not to be missed along this stretch of coastline is, of course, getting up at two in the morning to watch giant leatherback turtles heave themselves up on to the beach to lay their eggs. The beach along here is marked out into territories of individuals responsible for collecting the eggs and for the behavior of the many people who like to watch. Reports on the pleasure to be gained from this are varied, some visitors are put off by what they regard as the indignity of the turtles' treatment while others find it a mystical experience. In the past it was unpleasant to see the way some local boys behaved and there was a lack of respect for the rights of the animals, but it has now struck everyone that the number of turtles visiting the beaches has dropped alarmingly and there is a real danger that the turtles will stop coming altogether. This has helped raised the consciousness of local people but you will still hear cases

about stupid boys riding the turtles and shining torches in their eyes. At Rantau Abang all eggs are protected and allowed to hatch out in special hatcheries. You may have to pay a fee to the collectors for watching the process.

The peak egg laying time is August but turtles come ashore from June onward. Leatherbacks are a seriously endangered species which have only a few locations worldwide where they choose to lay their eggs. If you are visiting Sabah you will have another opportunity to watch the turtles.

WHERE TO STAY

Thirteen kilometers (eight miles) north of Dungun is the magnificent **Tanjung Jara Beach Resort**, 8th mile of Dungun, Terengganu, 23009, ((09) 841801; fax: (09) 842653, built in the style of an eighteenth-century Malay sultanate, and recipient of awards for architectural design. Accommodation is in two-story buildings built entirely of wood with beautiful moldings, every convenience and a great view of the sea from the large balconies. There are the usual beach facilities, lovely gardens, a lagoon and a pleasant pool, although not as big as the publicity material suggests! The restaurant is adequate although expensive for what it offers. A double room here costs $45.

A few kilometers further north is the **Merantau Inn**, Kuala Abang, Dungun, 23050, Terengganu, ((09) 841131, which has

ABOVE: On the east coast, turtles' eggs are lovingly collected and protected in hatcheries until the newborn are ready to return to the sea.

which do tasty dishes catering to the budget traveler.

GETTING THERE

Getting there from Cherating involves changing buses at **Chukai**, a one horse town about half-an-hour north of Cherating, just inside the Terengganu border. The only tourists that see this place are those getting buses to

an interesting fish farm on its premises, a small restaurant and clean air-conditioned bungalows right on the idyllic, if shadeless, beach. The beach is deserted for most of the day though you are likely to have gigantic turtles lumbering about it in the early hours.

Further north again is Rantau Abang, the location for most of the turtle watching organizations, and the **Visitor's Centre**, 13th mile of Dungun, 23009, Terengganu, ((09) 841533. It is built in a similar style to Tanjung Jara, with a museum, restaurant and chalet accommodation, but since it is only partly functioning at the present due to some structural problems, it would be advisable to ring ahead if you want to book rooms here. All around this part of the beach are many small budget bungalows built on to the beach, which is however quite untidy and crowded, particularly in the turtle watching season.

Terengganu and the rest haven't missed much. If you want to go to Tanjung Jara, the bus to Terengganu will drop you off a sweaty 500 m (550 yds) up the road. For the other places to stay, the bus will stop on the main road close by your destination. Getting away means flagging down another Terengganu-bound bus. Or flag down a relatively empty cab and ask for an estimate.

MARANG

Heading further north from Dungun and Rantau Abang you can hail any of the buses marked Terengganu, negotiate a cab from your hotel or just flag one down. From hotels, cabs are expensive; if you stop one on the road which already has someone in it you can travel a long way for very little, per-

WHERE TO EAT

Not much joy here. Tanjung Jara has an adequate but unexciting restaurant, there are some depressing Malay places in Dungun or several very cheap stalls in Rantau Abang

ABOVE and OPPOSITE: Beautiful faces of young Malays from the east coast of Malaysia.

haps M$4 per person for a one-and-a-half-hour journey. Avoid mentioning the name of the hotel you are traveling to if it is an expensive one until after you have negotiated the price.

Marang is the next interesting stop on the journey north. If you didn't stop at Cherating or if you found there that you love the small-town life of Malaysia, Marang is a must. Almost too cute to be true, Marang offers that scruffy but relaxing quality that only a small town in Malaysia seems to possess.

WHAT TO SEE

What to see in Marang is chiefly the town itself. It is built along a river which runs through the village, separating the one road from the beach. At one end is the hub of life of the village, where the boats hang out waiting for the good weather, longhaired young

men lounge about pretending they can play the guitar and listening to heavy metal music or oldies from the seventies like Hotel California, and the newly built market and hawker centers confront the crumbling and crazily leaning wooden buildings of an earlier era. Unlike many of the small towns further south, this is almost like Malaysia proper, the Chinese running the small stores

catering mainly to the many backpackers hanging out in the Marang Inn or Kamal's, the Malays manning the fishing and tourist boats. But there are some other sights to be seen from Marang and all the hotels organize trips.

One good half-day's adventure is to take a boat up the river and go **wildlife spotting**. The boat travels up the river to a tiny kampong where a brief walk will show you local women making *attap*, the rows of thatch which cover many of the roofs in the village, and men making *gula melaka*, a gorgeously sweet sugar made from boiled-down coconut water. Along the way the keen-eyed boatmen will spot monitor lizards, monkeys and other wildlife and there will be a trek to a batik factory. The trip costs around $5 per head from the smaller hotels in Marang but much more from the upmarket hotels.

Another reason for a stay in Marang is the trip out to **Pulau Kapas**, about half-an-hour out from the village. This is a small but unspoiled island with its own fairly simple accommodation, beach bungalows with a fan and shared bathroom and limited restaurants. The island is good for snorkeling and even non-swimmers can wade out and see some marine life. The trip will cost $5 per person return. If you intend to stay over-

night, you should arrange with the boatman when you wish to return. Bookings for the island can be made at either of two offices in Marang. Several boats go over to the island daily except in bad weather, when many frustrating days can be spent getting up at 7:30 am to find the boatmen sagely shaking their heads and looking at the sky.

Another trip which might be nicer made from the calm of Marang is a trip into **Kuala Terengganu** which is a noisy place to stay in but has some pleasant sights. A bus purportedly travels through Marang every half hour on its way to and from Terengganu but I have my doubts about it. Alternatively you can walk to the far end of the village where it meets the main road and flag down one of the express buses which don't seem to need an official bus stop to pull into. Or again flag down an already occupied cab or just look pathetic and somebody will offer you a lift.

WHERE TO STAY

Most of the accommodation in the village of Marang itself is very simple and inexpensive. South of the village, but away from the atmosphere that makes this place so interesting, are one or two resorts which approach a comfortable style. As in Cherating, here one has to decide between luxuries and atmosphere.

At Kampong Rhu Muda, two kilometers south of the village, are the **Mare Nostrum Beach Resort**, Nº 313 Jalan Pantai, Seberang Marang, 21600, Terengganu, ((09) 681322, which has air-conditioned chalets at around $15, and the **Beach House**, 12th mile, Kampong Rhu Muda, Marang, ((09) 681322, with air-conditioned chalets at the same price.

Back in the village, the best accommodation is a fan-cooled chalet with a fairly primitive bathroom and mosquito nets. The nicest is at the **Marang Guest House**, Lot 1367–8, Kampong Paya, Bukit Batu Merah, Marang, 21600, Terengganu, ((09) 682277, which, as its address suggests, is on a small hill which gives great views over the beach. It has a tidy and very flexible restaurant, fascinating travelers' comments books and extremely helpful staff. Loved by shoestring travelers but lacking fans, which can be disastrous on a hot night, is **Kamal's**, Nº B23 Kampong Paya,

Marang, 21600, Terengganu, which is friendly but primitive. In the village itself is the **Marang Inn**, Nº 132–3 Bandar Marang, 21600 Marang, ((09) 682132; fax: (09) 632191, offering rooms with a fan but shared bathroom for $3. The Inn is the most popular place to stay since it is centrally located, making boat trips easier and also because it serves alcohol, a rare event in a largely Muslim community. It also has lots of information, a good notice board, some pretty batik items for sale and organizes trips to suit its customers.

TERENGGANU

GENERAL INFORMATION

Terengganu is a bustling little town, about 15 minutes north of Marang, made rich by the discovery of offshore oil but still retaining some of its original fishing village charm. Travel within the town is largely by trishaw; all the taxis you see are long distance ones. Terengganu has its own beaches and many interesting places to visit but many travelers prefer to stay out of town and make visits to the town itself. The very new tourist office is directly opposite the central market.

WHAT TO SEE

The waterfront presents an interesting walk around Terengganu, starting at the central market, a newly built place with both fresh produce and craft ware, including locally made brass ware, cane items and woven and printed cloth. Right outside the market is the jetty from where fish make the journey on to the market stalls, still flapping in some cases. After exploring the market, a pleasant walk is along Jalan Bandar, which follows the curve of the river and has many old fashioned shops along it selling fishermen's gear, spices, Chinese medicines and other unusual items. Between the buildings quaint little alleyways lead down to the river. You might like to break for a while at Nº 224, **Kedai Kopi Cheng,** which serves excellent

OPPOISTE: Making kites and flying them is a serious business on Malaysia's east coast.

Chinese food or just coffee or soft drinks if you need a rest. At the end of this road is the outstation taxi rank where you can negotiate a cab to Kota Bharu or south to your next destination. Since the new bus station was built, though, cabs tend to lurk around there collecting enough passengers to make the long journeys profitable. At the junction of Jalan Bandar and Jalan Sultan Ismail, the old town merges into the new so if you hate traffic and noise, turn back here past the central market to the jetties and the tourist office which has now moved closer to the center.

Close by here is **Bukit Puteri,** a small hill on which stands the remains of a nineteenth-century fort, some cannons and a bell whose function was to warn the town of any approaching danger such as an *amok,* and a lighthouse marking the entrance to the Sungei Terengganu. Entry to the fort is 50 cents and it is open until 6 pm.

Gelanggang Seni is a center for the display of Terengganu's recreational and cultural activities. It is on Pantai Batu Buruk, the esplanade in front of the beach south of town and close by a hawker center. Shows of *seni silat* (self defense), dances, top spinning, and other pastimes can be seen on Thursdays, Fridays and Saturdays from 5 pm to 6:30 pm. Check at the tourist office, particularly during Ramadan, since these performances are often canceled on public holidays or other festivals.

The State Museum, Jalan Cherong Lanjut, 20300, Kuala Terengganu, ((09) 621444, is a trishaw ride away from the tourist office and other attractions. It has many interesting exhibits, the most notable being one of the bicycles that the invading Japanese used to travel down toward Singapore on.

In the river estuary are several islands, one of which, **Duyong,** the largest, is the home of the local boat-building industry. Ferries regularly go over to the island and you can watch boats being built using techniques which have changed very little in generations.

Rhusila is a small village about 12 km (seven-and-a-half miles) south of Terengganu where a handicraft center has been set up. Here you can watch basket-weaving demonstrations. Close by in Permint Jaya

are two small batik factories, and at Kuala Ibai is a silk factory where you can watch silk in all its stages of manufacture and printing. Also in the area are many manufacturers of wooden carvings and brass ware. These are carried out in people's homes and so there are very few, if any, signs pointing out their presence. The excellent tourist office in Terengganu will be able to give you addresses. *Songket* weaving is also practiced in the area. This is a cloth with intricate patterns woven into it using gold thread, and the *songket* is traditionally worn by Malay men for formal occasions. If you just want to buy the stuff and not watch it being made, there is **Desacraft** at Tingkat Bawah, Wisma Maju, Jalan Sultan Ismail, 20200, Terengganu, ((09) 636627, close to the outstation taxi rank.

WHERE TO STAY

Poshest of all hotels in Kuala Terengganu is The **Pantai Primula Hotel,** at Jalan Persinggahan, Kuala Terengganu 20904, P.O. Box 43, ((09) 622100. It has all the accoutrements of the resort hotel but its situation is close to the town and, in particular, very close to the town's sewer which flows odorously out onto the beach about a hundred meters from the hotel beachfront. How the people living in the quaint fishing village nearby survive is beyond me. A double room with all mod cons here is $56.

Back in the bustle of town there are some good-value hotels which offer good room facilities. The **Hotel Seri Hoover** at N° 49 Jalan Sultan Ismail, 20200 Kuala Terengganu, ((09) 633833, offers a basic double for $18, or for a little more, a double room with hot showers and television. It is very centrally located. The **Seaview Hotel** at N° 18A Jalan Masjid Abidin, 20100 Kuala Terengganu, ((09) 621911, offers air-conditioned doubles for $19. It is very pleasant, has nice views of the Istana, and is close to the tourist center, central market, etc. Again, though, nice as Terengganu is, if you are going to spend any time in the area, Marang would be a better choice.

WHERE TO EAT

Terengganu has the usual quota of small, very reasonably priced restaurants and coffee shops. If by now you are a *roti canai* addict, the **Taufik Restaurant** in Jalan Masjid is good. The **Rhu Sila** coffee house at the Pantai Primula has good buffets of Malay food in pleasant surroundings. If you are desperate for fast food, there are a couple of copy places, one called the **Whimpy Fried Chicken Restaurant** in Jalan Air Jernih, and another called **MacDota Fried Chicken Restaurant** in Jalan Kota Llama, but somehow fast food doesn't seem to take to Malaysia too well and ends up neither fast nor finger lickin' good. There is also a genuine **A&W** near the bus station, but only go there if you're really desperate.

OUT OF TOWN

Redang Island
This is about four hours by boat from Terengganu town and is actually a whole group of tiny, largely uninhabited islands, Redang Island itself being the home of a fishing village built on stilts over the sea. It is excellent for jungle wandering, snorkeling, swimming and scuba diving, but unfortunately there is little there in the way of accommodation. The big local hotel in Terengganu, the Pantai Primula, organizes day trips there, or camping trips can be arranged by some of the tour groups. **Camping Holidays**, Nº 16A Jalan SS2/103, 47300 Petaling Jaya, ((03) 717-8935; fax: (03) 717-3033, organizes three-night stays for $146 including scuba diving instruction, transport from Kuala Lumpur and back, all meals and camping equipment. Otherwise you could try asking around for people willing to put up travelers. A shorter boat journey can be made from Merang, further north, or from Besut, the stopping-off point for Perhentian island. These journeys are about one to three hours.

Kenyir Lake
Fifty-five kilometers west of Terengganu, this is a man made lake and hydroelectric dam. It is about 369 sq km (142 sq miles) and has many newly created islands. It is rapidly turning into a leisure center for boating, fishing and trekking and has some pretty waterfalls. Driving yourself, take the road to Kuala Berang, then turn west for another 15 km (nine miles) to reach the lake. There is

accommodation at the lake in the form of houseboats or floating chalets at **Kenyir Lake Resort**, Kenyir Dam, Kuala Terengganu, ((01) 950609. Package stays here consist of a three-day trip for $62 including full board and organized trips to the waterfall, jungle treks and fishing. The resort has its own floating restaurant, a television room and just what you'd want in an idyllic country retreat — a *karaoke* set.

Sekayu Waterfall
At the southern end of the system which

feeds Kenyir Lake is the Sekayu Waterfall, another point from where you can approach the interior of Malaysia. Both the waterfall and the lake are on the borders of Terengganu's segment of Taman Negara, so if you aren't making the trip to the National Park this might give you a good, if slightly commercialized, picture of what a stay there would be like. The waterfall is situated inside a recreational forest, has a government resthouse, some fairly well equipped chalets, including electricity and regular bathrooms, a mini-zoo and bird park. Some walks are marked out, and rumor has it that tigers have been seen in this area. To get there, take the same road toward Berang but take the left fork, following signs for the waterfall. A regular bus service goes to Berang from Terengganu. The chalets can be booked by phone at ((09) 811259. They are about $11 a night.

ABOVE: One of the myriad of traditional dress styles, this one is from the east coast of Malaysia.

Perhentian Island

On the very border of Terengganu and Kelantan is the small village of Besut, from where ferries travel regularly to the two islands, **Perhentian Besar** and **Perhentian Kechil.** These islands are much closer to the coast than Redang and offer simple but adequate accommodation. Like all the other islands along this east coast there is an abundance of marine life to observe, and unlike Tioman, which really is reaching capacity in tourist development, these islands are still unspoiled, to the point where it is advisable to bring some supplies just in case the few places preparing food decide to take a holiday at the same time. Accommodation here is provided by several small resorts, most of them on Besar, the larger island, but some are also on the smaller of the two. There is quite a sophisticated resort, the **Perhentian Island Resort** on Besar, offering chalet accommodation at around $22 which can be booked in advance at ((03) 248-0811 (a Kuala Lumpur number), or just take your chances and turn up at the beach like everyone else, wander around until you find the place that suits you and lie about for a few days. Not enough people go there to make accommodation a critical element. Getting there is fairly simple and getting easier all the time as the place develops more and more tourist-orientated services. The bus to Kota Bharu will stop at Jerteh where you can either get another bus to Besut or negotiate a cab. From Besut, fishing boats or ferries leave regularly throughout the day for the two-hour trip to Perhentian. Getting back, just wait for an incoming ferry. If, during your visit to Malaysia, you plan to stay at only one of the offshore islands, then you should choose this one. It is more primitive than Tioman and a longer journey than Kapas, but as yet is unspoiled and not as dependent, as is Marang, on the tiny fishing boats that get shorebound in bad weather. If you are staying at any of the budget places in Kota Bharu, Terengganu or Marang, you will find that each of them will recommend a place to stay and even arrange the details of the trip for you. If you need an even easier trip, many of the big travel agencies will organize the whole trip for you including, scuba equipment and instructor — for the right price of course. There can't be many nicer places to learn scuba diving.

GETTING THERE

Most express buses terminate here, and bus users should note that two bus stations have recently been established, one for express buses and the other for local bus services. So if you are traveling north to Kota Bharu from Marang on a local bus, you must go to the other bus station in order to continue your journey.

KOTA BHARU

BACKGROUND

The coastline from Besut northward is in the state of **Kelantan**, a very traditionally Malay and strongly Muslim state. The state has had a checkered past, finding itself under the influence of assorted foreign states from Majapahit, a Javanese kingdom in the fourteenth century, Thailand during the nineteenth century and Britain until 1948, when it became part of the Federation of Malaysia. These varying influences can be seen in many aspects of present day Kelantanese life, from the shadow-puppet shows which are still shown at festivals and weddings, to the batik printing and silk weaving whose influence is that of Thailand. The countryside, as you will notice on your journey through Kelantan, is decidedly different from the oil palm and rubber plantations further south and west. Bounded on three sides by the sea and mountains, Kelantan has retained its culture in a way that cannot be seen anywhere else in Malaysia. Top spinning, kite flying and traditional dances are not just things that get trooped out for the tourists. They are a genuine part of daily life. At the last general election in 1990 the Muslim fundamentalist party won control of Kelantan and they have made their presence felt. Restrictions on alcohol are becoming more and more severe, and it seems obligatory for Malay women to keep their heads covered.

General Information

The Tourist Information Centre is a good one and has lists of accommodation as well as some very useful leaflets about the area. It is at Jalan Sultan Ibrahim, ((09) 785534 or 783543, beside the museum. It is closed on Fridays and public holidays; on other days, it keeps office hours. Finding your way about town is fairly easy, partly because the tourist office has decent maps and partly because a good effort has been made to erect large maps in public places.

If you are going from here to Thailand, the Thai Consulate is on Jalan Pengkalan Chepa, ((09) 72545.

What to See

Merdeka Square

Kota Bharu has grown a little too large to be a real pleasure to walk around in and Merdeka Square is in the busiest quarter of the town. The square has a long history predating its new name which it was given in 1957. In 1915 the body of the Malay freedom fighter, Tok Janggut, was displayed here after being executed by the British. Around the square are some other buildings with tales to tell. The old Hongkong and Shanghai Bank, now a craft shop, was built in 1912 and served as the headquarters for the Japanese army during the Occupation. The Istana Balai Besar is nearby, built in 1844 as a palace for Sultan Muhamad II. Also nearby is the Istana Jahar, recently the home of the state museum but now a royal museum. It was built in 1887 and only part of it still stands.

Gelanggang Seni

Gelanggang Seni is situated in Jalan Mahmud, opposite the Perdana Hotel, and is the venue for many interesting sights. It is open between February and October, with a break during the fasting month, and puts on assorted shows on Mondays, Wednesdays, Saturdays and Sundays. (Check with the tourist office.) Here you will be able to see top spinning, self-defense exhibitions, cultural dances, giant-drum playing, displays of kites and shadow plays.

Wat Phothivihan

Reputedly the longest Buddha in Southeast Asia, Wat Phothivihan was built in 1973 and is 40 m (131 ft) long. Possibly more interesting than the statue itself is the journey out to it. The road passes through many small villages, strongly influenced by their proximity to Thailand and the importance of rice to the local economy. Water buffalo lounge about, beautifully tended rice paddies add color, and the houses are up on stilts to protect them against flooding during the rainy season. If you are in the area in April or during the national holiday for Vesak day, inquire about festivals that are held at the religious center. There are also other smaller Buddha statues in the area. The statue is situated about 12 km (seven miles) north of Kota Bharu near to Kampong Berok. Buses N° 19 or N° 27 from the central bus station go to Chabang Empat, from where you can walk or take a taxi for the final two kilometers. From town a return cab will cost about $11 including waiting time.

Where to Stay

If you want to make the town your base of operations, there are many good hotels to choose from at rates ranging from luxury to shoestring. But if you prefer beach life, you should be aware that there is accommodation out at Pantai Cinta Berahi from where you can make the trip into town on the local bus, which is very reliable, or on the organized buses from the hotels.

At the top of the range is the **Perdana Hotel,** at Jalan Mahmud, 15720 Kota Bharu, ((09) 785000; fax: (09) 747621, which offers a good range of recreational facilities as well as a pool and a coffee shop. It is nicely situated close to the cultural center and some hawker stalls and within easy walking distance of the center of town. A standard double is $63. No alcohol is available.

In the very center of town is the **Hotel Murni,** at Jalan Dato Pani, Kota Bharu, Kelantan, ((09)782399; fax: (09) 747255, where a standard double is $39.

In the middle range there is the **Temenggong Hotel,** at Jalan Tok Hakim, 15000, Kota Bharu, ((09) 783481, where a deluxe twin is $30, well worth the extra cost over a standard double. Opposite Merdeka Square is the **Hotel Indah**, at N° 236B Jalan Tengku Besar, 15000 Kota Bharu, ((09) 785081, where a double room is $18. Rooms are air-conditioned, have hot water, television on request. There is also a coffee shop in the hotel.

Of the middle range hotels the nicest has to be the **Tokyo Baru**, at N° 3945/6 Jalan Tok Hakim, ((09) 749488, where rooms are large and comfortable and recently renovated.

At the budget range there are many small places to choose from. Opposite the Thai consulate is **Mummy Brown's** which has a good reputation and has rooms for $3, breakfast included. Nearby is **Rainbow Inn Hostel**, N° 4423A Jalan Pengkalan Chepa, 15400 Kota Bharu, with rooms at the same price.

WHERE TO EAT

Kelantan, and Kota Bharu in particular, have some culinary delights not available anywhere else in Malaysia. Some of the best Malay food is to be found in Kota Bharu and the best place to try some is the **night market**, beside the SKMK bus station on Jalan Tok Hakim. There is a terrific range of seafood, *murtubaks*, satay and lots more (see WHERE TO EAT, below). A good meal for two couldn't cost more than $10 and it would be silly to visit Kelantan without having at least one dinner here in the open.

For a small outlay here, you can eat the weirdest things this side of Singapore and try different dishes each night for a month. Instead of trying the old favorites of *roti* or satay go for some of the stranger items like *nasi kerabau*, rice cooked with ground coconut, fish, and local herbs and spices, *ayam percik* the local specialty which is chicken marinated in coconut milk and spices and then roasted over charcoal and served with thick gravy. Especially local are the many sweets such as *akok* cooked from duck and chicken eggs, brown sugar and flour.

If you want air-conditioning with your meal, try the **Perdana's** Chinese restaurant which serves Cantonese food.

There are also some reasonable banana leaf restaurants in Jalan Gaja Mati, a Kentucky Fried Chicken if you've got several hours to kill, and an A&W by the bus station.

OUT OF TOWN

Pantai Cinta Berahi translates as the Beach of Passionate Love, although this should definitely not be taken as any kind of suggestion in this staunchly Muslim area. This is very much a local holiday resort, and during weekdays when the schools are operating, it is almost uncannily deserted. This is quite a pretty beach, although compared to beaches further south it's pretty average really. All the way out from town there are many batik factories and shops selling *songket*, silverware, and other handicrafts. The beach itself is the site of a historic occasion in the annals of the British Empire. It was on this stretch of beach that on December 7, 1941, the Japanese landed and began their blistering movement south that was to end in the dramatic surrender of Singapore. There is little evidence of the historic battle that was fought here, since all the earthworks and gun emplacements have long been swept away by the encroaching sea, but the Perdana Beach Resort, built on the actual site of the landing, has a display of memorabilia and some interesting photographs.

There's not much to do here besides battle it out with the ultra violet rays on the beach and wander along back toward town looking in the craft shops, but if you like beach life this is as good as any. Foreigners tend to get ignored here so if you really want to experience life in a beach village you should try one of those further south.

Where to Stay

The **Perdana Beach Resort** at Jalan Kuala Pa'amat, Pantai Cinta Berahi, P.O. Box 121, 15710 Kota Bharu, ((09) 785222; fax: (09) 747621, is the most recent and poshest of the resorts here. It has a pool, a lagoon with boat rides for children, tennis courts, wind surfing and other water activities, beautiful chalets built in a traditional Malay style and a good but pricey restaurant which is frequented by townspeople who come for the buffets which are quite a good value. A standard double chalet has all mod cons and costs $52.

Just along the beach further south toward town is the **Resort Pantai Cinta Berahi**, at P.O. Box 131 Kota Bharu, Kelantan, ℭ (09) 781307; fax: (09) 781307, which has double rooms at $22 and up but no swimming pool. The restaurant there is much cheaper than the Perdana and offers a good breakfast and snacks.

On the other side of the Perdana heading further away from town is **H.B. Village**, ℭ (09) 744993, offering lots of fun things like a mini-zoo, horse riding and a boating lagoon at prices ranging from $5.

FURTHER AFIELD

From Kota Bharu it is possible to explore the interior of **Kelantan** by taking a boat along the Sungei Kelantan to visit various points along the river. Most of these journeys are rarely done by tourists and involve some planning on the visitor's part. The tourist information office organizes a number of tours, one of which is a trip by train to **Gua Musang** followed by a two-hour river trip into the National Park to a waterfall. The return trip takes about nine hours and costs $22. Children under 12 go free. If you feel like a trip on your own steam, you could try getting bus N° 5 to Kuala Krai from where a boat near the police station will take you to Dabong through thick jungle. Three kilometers east of Dabong is **Gua Ikan**, some caves and a waterfall. There is a government resthouse at Dabong. If you stay on the boat past Dabong, you can visit **Kuala Balah** where you will be one of very few western visitors. You can also now travel to the outskirts of Taman Negara by train or express bus to Gua Musang, where accommodation is available at the **Kesedar Inn** ℭ (09) 901226. There you will encounter the entirely Chinese settlement at Pulai, and the hotel can make travel arrangements for a camping trip into the National Park. This area is really only opening up to tourism now and efforts to make this kind of a journey are difficult. The Tourist Information Centre at Kota Bharu will give you assistance.

GETTING THERE

If you are coming from the south it will take about three hours in a taxi from Kuala Terranganu, longer on a bus of course. From Penang a bus will take about eight hours. The bus travels through some interesting countryside which only ten years ago was home to communist insurgents left over from the troubles of the fifties. Now it is living testimony to the disappearance of the rain forest, the only signs of wildlife being the signs warning motorists against passing herds of elephants. The route also takes you past an enormous hydroelectric dam project where you can see the efforts being made to shore up the road against sliding away into the dam, and where dead trees stretch their branches out of the water where once was virgin jungle. The bus stops once at Grik, so bring food and drinks with you but don't bring any illusions about comfortable, smart buses. On one journey the decrepit and poorly air-conditioned SKMK bus I was on broke down halfway, leaving passengers to find their own way.

Kota Bharu is another town with a confusing network of bus stations. South of town are two bus stations, one in Jalan Hamzah for southbound buses, another in Jalan Pasir Puteh, where SKMK buses depart both south and west, and two in town, one at Jalan Pendek for travel inside Kelantan and the other for more local buses. How definite that description is is debatable. In theory, to get to Penang you should go to Pasir Puteh but the bus station in town also has buses going there. If you get confused, inquire at the Tourist Information Centre, where they are likely to know about any reorganization that may have taken place in what seems a chaotic system.

There are also trains going to Kuala Lumpur and points south. Tickets can be purchased up to a month in advance, and it is advisable to get them as quickly as you can after arriving, if not beforehand, in Kuala Lumpur since they regularly sell out. The railway station is at Wakaf Bharu, a short bus ride out of town on bus N° 19 or N° 27. Trains can also take you into or from Thailand.

The
West
Coast

LANGKAWI

Just off the northwest coast of Malaysia is a group of 99 islands, 104 if you include the five that disappear when the tide comes in, that are just beginning to make their presence felt. The whole group of islands is named after the largest and most populated one, Langkawi.

Compared to Penang or Thai island destinations like Koh Samui and Phuket, Langkawi offers solitude and quiet. At the moment there are just about the right number of resorts to cater to most budgets, but developments are on the drawing boards and in the future the ecology/tourism equilibrium could well be disturbed to favor the tourist. Hotels operated by two big chains will be opening in 1993, and a fancy promenade and shopping center is in under construction. At the moment though, Langkawi's attraction is its natural beauty and modest tourist infrastructure. If Penang strikes you as too commercialized, too noisy, or just too full of tourists, then Langkawi is the place to spend some time in.

BACKGROUND

Many legends are associated with the island, but the one that has a hold on people's imagination concerns Mahsuri, a young woman falsely accused of adultery and ordered to be punished with *sula* — burying the guilty up to the waist in sand and plunging a *kris* between the shoulder blades into the stomach. Protesting her innocence, Mahsuri was put to death, but the blood that flowed from her body was white and in her dying breath she cursed the island of Langkawi for seven generations. The legend was recalled when one of Malaysia's largest construction companies decided to invest millions in a giant tourist complex in the 1980s. The whole plan failed badly and was never completed.

Mahathir, Malaysia's prime minister, is from the state of **Kedah** under whose jurisdiction Langkawi falls, and the decision to turn the island into a tax-free haven in order to stimulate trade and tourism has been seen as one of his pet projects. Penang's economy was based on a similar concept, though

when the money was poured into Langkawi to build roads, an international airport and hotels, the economic boom that was expected never materialized. The curse of Mahsuri was blamed for the failure. The seven generations are now said to have run their course and there is optimism and confidence for the island's future.

GENERAL INFORMATION

The tourist information office is located in a small office at the jetty, ((04) 789789. As with the banks, Sunday is a normal working day, while on Friday, places like these are shut.

The island is best appreciated by traveling around it. Cars, motorbikes and bicycles are easily hired, the rates are reasonable, and petrol is tax free. Cars go for around $35 a day, small motorbikes are $10 and bicycles $5. Most of the big hotels will insist on seeing your license but the smaller places are not so fussy and will rent out motorbikes regardless.

If you are not staying at one of the big hotels it may be worth remembering that the local establishments are not likely to have a license to sell beer, and at Pantai Kok and Pantai Cenang there are no places selling alcohol. Remember to bring your own from Kuah or the airport shops. The airport shop also sells a useful tourist map of the island that is not available at the tourist information office.

WHAT TO SEE

Hire a vehicle and visit the beaches, stopping off to see some of the sights on the way. The following itinerary begins at Kuah and heads north through paddy fields and plantations to **Pantai Kuah,** 23 km (14 miles) away. The beach is stunning, though one should be somewhat wary of the current. The view is still worth the trip and there is a nice restaurant at the nearby Mutiara Beach Resort and there are several Malay stalls on the beach. Boats and snorkeling trips can be arranged here without having to pay the more expensive rates of the beach hotel. It

OPPOSITE: Sardine fishing and drying is a cottage industry in Tanjong Rhu on the island of Langkawi.

was here that work on the giant beach resort complex began and prematurely ended, and all that remains is an unattractive block of condominiums that are now inhabited but still look as if the workmen packed up and left suddenly. Carrying on west from Pantai Kuah will bring you to **Pasir Hitam**, a black sand beach.

To the west there is a road branching off to **Telok Datai**. It is a lovely new road with fine views of the sea but there are no accommodations or restaurants along the way. A resort and golf course is being built where the road presently ends. A 20 minute walk beyond this point will bring you to a beautiful and completely isolated beach. The main road carries on to **Pantai Kok**, the sort of place to stay in if you want an inexpensive and undisturbed vacation by the sea. The bay is beautiful and visitors have a habit of staying around here longer than they planned. Nearby is the small community of **Kuala Teriang**, from which one can walk to the waterfall at **Telaga Tujah**. The waterfall, which is featured in most of the organized scenic trips, is a freshwater stream that cascades through a series of seven (*tujah*) wells (*telaga*) or bathing pools. Bring swimming gear if you want to bathe.

From Kok Bay it is a short trip to **Mahsuri's Tomb** and the **field of burnt rice**. The tomb itself is not that memorable, but the journey there is an interesting one as you pass through the farm lands of the islanders and scenes of rural life surround you. The field of burnt rice is a site where villagers burnt their rice rather than allow it to fall in to the hands of invaders from Thailand.

The main accommodation area on the island is along the beach strip at **Pantai Cenang** on the southwest The beach lovely and sandy and quite safe for swimming. It is sometimes possible to walk across to the small island of Rebak.

Some of the hotels organize various boating trips around Langkawi as well as island-hopping cruises. Choose one that suits your interest because some are just for sightseeing while others focus on snorkeling or fishing. **Pulau Dayang Bunting**, a large island south of Langkawi, is a popular destination because of the **Lake of the Pregnant Maiden**, which takes its name from the legend

of a of a couple who, after 19 childless years, conceived a baby after drinking from this lake. On the same island is the **Cave of the Banshee**, inhabited by thousands of bats.

WHERE TO STAY

There are a few top-class hotels, but the best is easily the **Pelangi Beach Resort**, a gathering of wooden chalets decorated in traditional kampong style with modern conveniences. If you can afford the $100 a night, this is the place to stay, and rooms can be booked direct from the resort at Pantai Cenang, 07000 Langkawi, ((04) 911001; fax: (04) 911122, or through their office in Kuala Lumpur, ((03) 262-3888, or Singapore (02) 235778. The jeeps for hire at the Pelangi Beach Resort

are good for getting around the island, but their bikes are gearless and a better idea might be to walk down the road and rent a mountain bike if you're interested in anything more than local trips.

The next best bet is the **Burau Bay Resort** at Teluk Burau, ((04) 911061; fax: (04) 911172. This is a new resort, tastefully built in a lovely bay with rooms at $78. It is under the same management as the Pelangi Beach Resort, so reservations can also be made through the Kuala Lumpur or Singapore offices. If you like fishing, bring a rod to fish off the rocks of Anak Burau, a small rock of an island that can be waded or swum to. The resort will cook your fresh fish.

In the northern part of the island at Tanjung Rhu is the **Mutiara Beach Resort**, ((04) 788488, situated in a beautiful setting from which Thailand is easily visible in the distance. Unfortunately, the hotel's architecture fails to match the splendor of the natural surroundings and the rooms themselves lack long bathtubs and fridges. Rubbing shoulders with the hotel is an ugly set of condominiums that bears witness to an ill-fated development plan that went bust in the past. Standard rooms are $45 a night, and $10 more will give you a deluxe room with a television set.

The **Langkawi Island Resort**, ((04) 788209; fax: (04) 788414, is situated in the main town of Kuah, a very short taxi ride

ABOVE: On the west coast of Malaysia, boat building and fishing are traditional skills handed down from father to son for many generations.

from the jetty. The usual facilities for a place charging $65 (though long bathtubs are in only the deluxe rooms for $78) but ther are no decent beaches nearby. Standard rooms are $56 without a sea view. Rooms can be booked directly or through their Kuala Lumpur office, ((03) 291-4299; fax: (03) 293-7508. If you do want to stay in town, consider the **Captain Resort** at Lot N° 82 Jalan Penarak, 07000 Kuah, ((04) 789100; fax: (04) 788799. Chalets with and without air-conditioning are available from $18 to $32 and the place is pleasantly tucked away on the outskirts of town. If you ring from the jetty, you will be picked up for free. By comparison, places like the **Hotel Asia**, ((04) 788216, are nothing special at $25 for a double with air-conditioning.

Other accommodations are available at the main beach areas: Pantai Cenang and Pantai Kok. Pantai Cenang has the longest strip of beach resorts and huts. At the **Beach View Motel**, ((04) 91116, the small basic rooms with fans have nothing but their price ($10) to recommend them and the same goes for the similarly priced **AB Motel**, ((04) 911300. The older places tend to have Asian toilets and small rooms and even in places like the **Sandy Beach Motel**, ((04) 911308, for $30 can be claustrophobic.

The **Semarak Langkawi Beach Resort**, ((04) 911377, or ((03) 717-3650 at the office in Kuala Lumpur, is worth the $25 for big rooms with a fan, and from the chalets you literally step onto the beach. They have one air-conditioned room at $30 plus a decent restaurant, and across the road motorbikes can be hired from a friendly place that doesn't insist upon checking your license. Next to the Pelangi is the **Beach Garden Resort**, ((04) 911363; fax: (04) 911221, with modern air-conditioned doubles for $60, including an American breakfast. This German-run motel has no room service but it is modern and well run. At the end of the road, at Pantai Tengah, **Charlie's Motel**, ((04) 911200, has a few rooms with air-conditioning for $20.

At Pantai Kok, the **Country Beach Motel** is the best organized place and should be your first consideration. Rooms with air-conditioning are $22, without $10, and a sister resort is about to appear nearby under the name of the **Idaman Bay Resort**. Prices will be a little higher here, and at the moment the phone number of the Country Beach Motel should be used for booking either place, ((04) 911212/911066. What makes the motel a good place is the availability of good food, bikes, and fishing gear for hire, laundry and a place for keeping valuables. The management is friendly and will keep your beer in the kitchen fridge. A drawback at the Country Beach Motel is that the toilets are not of the western type.

All along Kok Bay there are a number of other beach motels to choose from. The **Coral Beach Motel**, ((04) 911000, the **Mila Beach Motel**, ((04) 911049, and the **Dayang Beach Resort**, ((04) 911058, are all fairly similar, and have rooms with fans for around $13. Most have their own restaurants, and none have western toilets.

Between the village of Kuala Teriang, near Kok Bay, and Pantai Cenang there is the **Muliana Resort**, out on its own. It is well looked after, and the rooms are clean and carpeted. At $15 for a double this is a good value and there is even a tiny pool near the Malay and Chinese restaurant.

WHERE TO EAT

What follows is organized around the various locations on the island.

Kuah

Located behind the modern block where the Bayview hotel is being constructed, you will find the modestly fronted **Domino Restaurant** at N° 10 Pandak Mayah Enam, ((04) 789214. The food is European, and New Zealand steaks are the house specialty at around $20 for two. A light lunch, say potato salad and beer, would be half that.

On the main road in Kuah, behind the government souvenir and craft shop, is the **Sari Restaurant**. The food is nothing special but there is a great view of the sea from the tables, and the menu is large enough to support snacks or dinners. Wine is available and a good seafood dinner for two would be about $15. Across the road from the Sari there are a couple of Indian cafes serving cheap but tasty food. I had a very good *roti canai* for lunch at the **Merdeka Coffee Shop**. The **Ports of Call** restaurant at the Langkawi Island Resort has a cultural show and simple meal for $12 every Saturday night. Other days of the week it opens only in the evenings, and a western grill for two will cost about $20.

Pantai Cenang

The **Spice Market Restaurant** at the Pelangi Beach Resort has good local and continental dishes, but the Resort's Thai restaurant is disappointing if you think closeness to Thailand is commensurate with authentic Thai cuisine. Next to the Pelangi, the posh **Bee Garden Resort** has a bistro and beer garden serving continental meals for $7 per person. Nearby, there is a seafood restaurant, and most of the other motels along the beach run small restaurants open to all. At Pantai Tengah there is **Charlie's Motel** where you can eat at one of the beach tables; sweet and sour fish with fresh orange is $3. Beer is not served, however.

Pantai Kok

At Pantai Kok, all the eating places are attached to the various motels and they all serve inexpensive local food. The **Last Resort** is recommended. On the northern end of the island at Pantai Rhu, the **Mutiara Beach Resort** serves a steak dinner for two at $20, a fish and chips lunch for $12.

GETTING THERE

By Air

Malaysian Airlines operates a regular service from Kuala Lumpur, Penang and Singapore. The airport number is ((04) 911322 and reservations can be made at ((04) 788622. A taxi from the airport into town will cost $4.

By Ferry

There is no shortage of boats crossing to and from Kuala Kedah and Kuala Perlis on the mainland. The 45-minute journey costs $4 and there are a number of boats each day. At the Kuah jetty the various companies, ((04) 754494 or 788272, have their sales offices and you can purchase tickets in advance. Boats to and from Penang cost $13 and take about three hours. There is also a daily ferry service in the afternoon to Satun in Thailand but there is little in Satun to attract the tourist.

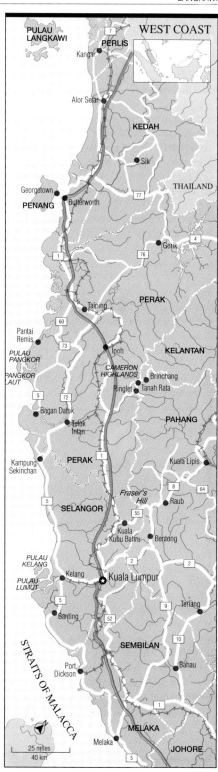

PENANG

BACKGROUND

Like Melaka and Singapore, Penang was recognized at an early stage in its history as a strategic point for trade. Occupied in the sixteenth century by the Portuguese, in the seventeenth by local pirates, and then in the eighteenth century by the British, it has witnessed many battles and played many roles. In 1786 Francis Light, working for a trading company, took control of the island with the permission of the local sultan. Later he had to defend the island from the same sultan who began to feel that he wasn't getting his money's worth out of the British. The British settled and prospered, finding rich deposits of tin in nearby states and making Penang the trading post for those wishing to buy and sell. Millionaire's row, a little shabby now, stands as testimony to the wealth created here.

By 1835 Penang was part of the Straits Settlements, with a large Chinese population as well as expatriates and Malays. Trouble between two different dialect groups of Chinese broke out in 1865 and lasted for a decade before it was finally settled. The motor car brought more wealth to Penang, boosting its port facilities with the massive demand for rubber and World War I brought even more riches to the traders. The depression also hit Penang, followed a decade later by Penang's abandonment by the British to the Japanese who took the whole peninsula in just three months.

Apart from the fact that Penang's occupiers were Japanese rather than English, business went on as usual here, the only difference being the destination of the rubber and tin. The Japanese left, and the British sheepishly returned, but it was never the same. By the fifties Malaya was independent, rubber became less and less profitable and now Penang is known more and more as a resort town with its Batu Ferringhi, a strip of beach hotels in the manner of Spain's Costa Brava.

RIGHT: Kek Lok Si Buddhist Temple, Penang.

GENERAL INFORMATION

Penang's climate is, if anything, a little cooler than mainland Malaysia and it is not affected by the rainy season, so visiting is fine all year round. In addition, its highly multicultural environment ensures that visitors can enjoy the delights of the local cuisine even during Ramadan. The island itself is about 24 km (15 miles) by 14.5 km (nine miles), smaller than Singapore and less built up. Transport around Georgetown is by local bus, which is quite efficient, taxi, which gets more expensive depending on the label on your luggage, or trishaw. Traffic in Penang is comparatively light, so a trishaw ride to places of interest is not the death-defeating activity carried out by the caravans of trishaws which duck and dive their way around Singapore each night. Bicycles can be hired at Batu Ferringhi and a possible day trip is a bike ride around the island. The ferry to Butterworth is a 24-hour service. The tourist office at Jalan Tun Syed Sheh, ℂ (04) 630066, is quite helpful and well situated next door to the booking office for boats to Langkawi and opposite Fort Cornwallis.

Before arriving at Penang, some decision making has to be done about what kind of a holiday you want to have here. Most of the medium-priced and budget accommodations are in town, and staying in town dictates that your holiday will urban, unless you bus out to the beach each day. On the other hand, staying at the beach leads you into the beach strip syndrome where most of the hotels are very definitely in the luxury class and the tendency is to make use of all the resort facilities you are shelling out for.

WHAT TO SEE

A Trip Around Georgetown

A pleasant two-hour sightseeing trip will show you the sights of the town and help you get your bearings. Starting from the tourist office, the first point of interest is right outside, the **Clocktower**. Erected at the personal expense of one of Penang's many millionaires, it marks the Diamond jubilee of Britain's Queen Victoria. Beside it is **Fort Cornwallis**, built in the early nineteenth

century by convict labor. One of the cannons, Seri Rambai, is said to grant fertility to barren women. Around the rest of the *padang* can be seen what were once the major municipal buildings. In Lebuh Farquhar is the **Museum and Art Gallery**, once an English school which now has fascinating old newspaper articles about clan wars and communist troubles. At the rear of the museum are interesting exhibitions of Peranankan life and of some lovely old cars. Next door is **St George's Church**, built by the same obliging set of convicts who built the fort. Carry-

ing on up Farquhar Street to Lebuh Leith you will come across a lovely old private house, **Cheong Fat Tze Mansion**, built in 1860 and surrounded by high walls. It doesn't welcome visitors and looks pretty shabby but it is one of the two remaining examples in Southeast Asia of Ching Dynasty architecture. Back up Lebuh Leith to Farquhar Street is the old Christian cemetery where Francis Light is buried alongside many of his countrymen. A slightly longer trishaw ride will bring you to **Khoo Kongsi**, an extremely ornate clan house in Cannon Square built by the Khoo clan in 1906. There are many clan houses in Penang, but this is the most ornate. The purpose of the clan house is to act as a meeting house for the extended family of that name and to extend charity and help to all other Khoos. Inside in the central room is an altar dedicated to Tua Sai Yeah, the family's particular deity, while other rooms bear the names of past members of the clan. The clan house is open to the public from 9 am to 5 pm on weekdays and 9 am to 1 pm on Saturdays. Before you finish your ride or walk around the town, you should go down some of the older roads such as Leboh Chulia, Muntri Street and Stewart Street where the old tile work, architecture and peculiar items for sale offer hours of interest.

more food than those deep in the park who only get the few leftovers. The gardens also have a small zoo and a waterfall. For $5, a cab will take you to the park and wait, or you can take bus N° 7 from the Weld Quay bus terminal. From the Botanic Gardens you can find your way up **Penang Hill**, but you should take the opportunity to ride up the funicular railway, built in 1899, with its carriages having the same angle as that of the hill slope. The railway works by the weight of the descending carriage pulling the ascending one up. After the funicular failed to

Out of Town

Further out of town are places which would take at least a half day to visit. The **Botanic Gardens**, on Waterfall Road, are a good wheeze. Much wilder than Singapore's tidy and well labeled park, the gardens are ruled by seven troupes of extremely sneaky macaque monkeys, each of which guards its own territory. They have a cute habit of coming close, pretending to take the peanut out of your hand, and while you are engaged in giggling at it, snatching the whole packet and biting you if you try to get it back. Going through the park empty-handed, especially if you are small, is asking for trouble. One tribe has been thrown out of the gardens by the others and hangs around outside getting

move on its maiden voyage, it took twenty years, until 1923, to get it actually started. The hill itself is very pretty and cool, with an aviary, lots of stalls selling fake designer things, and a hotel. The views from the hill are spectacular. To get to the funicular railway, take bus N° 91, from the bus terminal next to the Komtar building, to Ayer Hitam where you can change to bus N° 8, which will take you to the tram terminus. Alternatively, bus N° 1 from the jetty terminal will take you to the **Kek Lok Si Temple**, worth a visit in its own right, and from there bus N° 8 to the funicular station. This Buddhist temple's

Wat Chayamangkalaram Temple, Penang. Its huge Buddha figure is garishly painted and claims to be the biggest in the country.

architecture is a mix of Thai, Chinese and Burmese.

If you enjoy both wildlife and temples, an interesting visit might be made to the **Snake Temple** which is quite a way out on the way to the airport. It was built in 1850 and is dedicated to the memory of Chor Soo Kong, a priest who was said to have healing powers. Pretty tatty as temples go, its one distinction is that it is home to a whole gaggle of snakes of several different species, many of which may be extremely poisonous. They drape themselves conveniently

over some dead branches in pots in the main temple. Outside is the usual bunch of stalls selling "I've been to the snake temple" t-shirts, snake motif ornaments, etc. Yellow bus N° 66 goes to the temple.

Out at the far end of the strip of beach hotels is a **Butterfly Park** and an interesting **batik factory**. The butterfly park is 22 km (14 miles) from Georgetown, about $6 by cab, and has butterflies and other insects from all over Malaysia. Everything in its shop has a butterfly motif. Just before it is the batik factory, where one can witness this amazing and beautiful art created first-hand.

Batu Ferringhi is worth a visit. In the '60s and '70s this was an important stop on the route to Thailand and Burma for the many young people who sought alternative lifestyles. Now they've all grown up, and perhaps some return to stay in the expensive hotels built where they once stayed for next to nothing. More and more package-holi-

days from Europe are organized every year. The beach is quite pleasant, although sunbathers tend to get hassled by beach-boys selling rides on speedboats, massages, hairbraiding and even the odd bit of illegal substances. Keep in mind that there is a mandatory death penalty for anyone caught handling even small amounts of drugs.

WHERE TO STAY

Beach Hotels

Luxury hotels abound in Penang and the choice is almost as wide as that in Singapore. Your biggest decision is whether to stay at the beach or in Georgetown. At the far end of the strip of beach hotels, in a little kampong called Telok Bahang, is the **Mutiara**, at N° 1 Jalan Teluk Bahang, 1150 Penang, ((04) 812828; fax: (04) 812829. This has to be the most extravagantly luxurious resort in Southeast Asia. The basic double room will set you back $112, but if you arrive there after an eight-hour bus journey from the east coast, as I did, the magnificent bathroom makes it seem perfectly reasonable. The trouble is getting out of your room long enough to enjoy the other aspects of the resort which are also pretty impressive. They have a great service for taking young children off your hands, including camps, video games, a water slide and entertainment park. All the rooms look over the sea which is littered with the paraphernalia of the marina. The restaurants are good and feature a cultural show (in case you haven't yet had the pleasure!).

The best of the hotels, architecturally at least, is the **Rasa Sayang**, P.O. Box 735, Penang, ((04) 811811, where double rooms are $75. Rooms on the ground floor have tiny gardens opening out to the swimming pool and are excellent if you have children. The grounds are well laid out with a very large pool and all the regular beach facilities, and guests have access to the facilities of the other two places owned by the same hotel chain. The **Golden Sands,** ((04) 811911; fax: (04) 811880, is more of a family hotel, with room rates similar to the Rasa Sayang. All these hotels have pleasant gardens but face on to a public beach. Further along toward town is another hotel, the **Ferringhi**, at 12.5 km, Batu Ferringhi Road, 11100 Batu

ABOVE: Batu Ferringhi beach, Malaysia's answer to the Costa Brava.
OPPOSITE: A rooftop scene.

Ferringhi, ((04) 805999; fax: (04) 805100, rather less luxurious, but because of its isolation, less subject to crowded beaches or people hassling you to buy things. Its published room rates match those of the Batu Ferringhi Hotels, but it regularly offers good discounts if you ask at the reception desk. It is across the road from the beach, but has all the facilities of the other hotels.

Budget hotels are few now that the big hotels have moved in. The **Lone Pine** has spartan rooms at an asking price of $40 but goes lower after negotiation. Its rooms are barer than the Hotel Malaysia, but it is on the beachfront, has a tiny pool and a pleasant atmosphere. Below this is very primitive accommodation consisting of rooms with fans and shared bathrooms, e.g., **Ali's** at N° 53–4 Batu Ferringhi, ((04) 811316. For $5 you get lots of atmosphere, '70s music and the usual travelers' tales. Nearby **Beng Keat Guest House** offers similar but less pleasant accommodation for the same price or rooms with a bathroom, television and fridge for $13. A cooker and washing machine are available for guests' use. Out at Teluk Bahang there is even less to choose from. **Rama's**, ((04) 811179, is a tiny guest house run by an Indian family and has a couple of double rooms at $4, which have shared bathrooms, fans and are pretty cramped. Guests are treated as one of the family and can use the fridge and cooker. They have room for 12 people in all and are usually full. Near the Butterfly Farm and off down a side road is **Miss Lee's**, unsignposted, so look for a green house and spot the backpackers. Similar prices and facilities, also always full, not because it's particularly pleasant, but because of the lack of competition.

Town Hotels

The **City Bay View**, at N° 25A Farquhar Street, 10200 Penang, ((04) 633161; fax: (04) 634124, a good value at $62, has a pool, great views from the revolving restaurant, and is perfectly placed for trips around the city. An equally good value is the old colonial **E&O**, N° 10 Farquhar Street, 10200, Penang, ((04) 635322; fax: (04) 634833, which has deluxe rooms at $65 overlooking the sea. The standard doubles are $39, more in the medium-budget range, but they are in a modern wing

and lack the faded elegance of the deluxe rooms. The E&O was built by the Sarkie brothers, creators of such legends as Raffles in Singapore and the Strand in Rangoon. This hotel would be my personal choice to stay at in Penang because it has style, a nice garden alongside a small pool, good food, and a central location.

The hotels which offer more simple air-conditioned comfort are all in the area of Penang Road, and typical of these is the **Oriental**, ((04) 634211; fax (04) 635395, where a standard double is $38. At the **Hotel**

Malaysia, ((04) 363311; fax: (04) 371621, standard doubles are $39. These rooms are a little nicer than the E&O's standard doubles but lack the charm, gardens and pool.

At the budget level there are some excellent Chinese hotels redolent with the atmosphere of a long-gone age. In Leith Street is the **Cathay**, ((04) 626271. It offers huge high-ceilinged rooms at $21 for an air-conditioned double, spacious and airy lobby areas where food is served and an atmosphere somewhere between a nineteenth century railway station without the noise and an old mansion. Next door is the **Waldorf**, a good value at $21 but lacking the crumbling charm of the Cathay. It has a good restaurant serving Chinese and western food at very reasonable prices. Out a little way and nicely situated for nights in Gurney Drive is the **Paramount** at N° 8F Jalan Sultan Agmad Shah, 10050 Penang, ((04) 363649, where scruffy doubles are $15.

WHERE TO EAT

All the big hotels have good luxury restaurants offering a large range of cuisines. The **Mutiara, Rasa Sayang** and the **Bayview** all have good Japanese restaurants. The **Revolving Restaurant** at the Bayview is very popular, particularly for the evening buffet. At the Mutiara again, **The Catch** is popular with locals as well as guests, has a nightly cultural show and offers Thai, Malayan and European-style seafood. At Batu Ferringhi there are several places run by **Eden** restaurants, all of which are popular and offer either steaks or seafood at quite reasonable prices. They are mostly open air restaurants.

At 105 Penang Road is **Kashmir Restaurant**, ((04) 637411, serving North Indian food, tandoor-cooked dishes, with a pleasant atmosphere and live Indian music. Go later rather than at opening time, when the place goes from empty to crowded in a couple of minutes and everyone has to wait a little too long for their food.

Descending in price range, there are many places at Batu Ferringhi. One is the **New Last Drop**, ((04) 811325, which serves western, Chinese and Malaysian dishes in a little concrete garden opposite The Palm Beach Hotel. Steamboat here is $9 for two people.

In town there are excellent *roti canai* and *murtabak* places on Penang Road, offering the crispiest *prata* I can remember eating anywhere. The **Komtar Kompleks** has the usual range of fast food places and some local variants which should be avoided if at all possible.

Out at Teluk Bahang are two Indian Muslim places, seedy-looking but good for a cheap breakfast. The best one is on the other side of the road to the Mutiara. In the village itself, which you get to by turning left at the road junction, there are some seafood restaurants with their own boats parked in the back, so the food is pretty fresh.

Gurney Drive is really the place where the locals go. It opens only at night when it comes alive with hundreds of restaurants and hawker stalls set up in the road.

GETTING THERE

Penang's **international airport** has flights from Singapore, Kuala Lumpur, Johore Bahru, Kota Bharu, Kinabalu and Hat Yai in Thailand. From the airport, a cab to Georgetown is about $6.

Penang has a reputation as a source for cheap air tickets although you should take care when buying.

There is a regular **ferry** service to Langkawi which can be booked at the office next door to the tourist information center.

By **train**, a service goes from Butterworth to Kuala Lumpur and Singapore daily.

Buses go daily to all destinations in Malaysia, Thailand and Singapore. Along Lebuh Chulia are many travel agents offering good prices for all means of transport out. Hotels will also arrange travel for you.

There is a **road** link back to the mainland along the ever-long Penang Bridge, but it doesn't seem to be used very much because of the toll fee and because it is quicker to use the ferry. A cab from Georgetown to the railway station via the bridge is about $11 whereas the trip to the ferry terminal is $1 to

$2, followed by 30 minutes on the boat and a five-minute walk to the station. The ferry service is a regular 24-hour one. There are also ferries for cars.

IPOH

BACKGROUND

Like many other towns in the area, Ipoh owes its existence to tin mining, and crumbling mansions of tin millionaires dot the

GENERAL INFORMATION

There are two tourist information offices in Ipoh. One is in the Royal Casuarina Hotel's shopping complex at N° 18 Jalan Gopeng, ((05) 532008, extension 8123. The other is in Jalan Dewan, ((05) 532800, extension 301.

WHAT TO SEE

The old town is situated around the railway station, with its impressive colonial archi-

townscape, suggesting a little of the life of the past. Nowadays it has the best Chinese food in the country; add some startling cave temples, a pretty *padang* and some beautiful colonial architecture, and you have many good reasons to make your stop a little longer than overnight.

The best and most spectacular way to see Ipoh and its surroundings is by approaching it from the air. What stands out is the scale of the tin mining and its effects on the landscape. Almost like a moonscape at times, the bare earth is scored with water-filled pits. The extraction process unfortunately involves the loss of much of the fertile quality of the soil, accounting for the wasteland visible from the sky.

tecture. The *padang* is still intact as are the law courts and government offices.

Outside the town are the well known Buddhist temples built into limestone massifs. The pillars are honeycombed with caves, and into these caves have been built temples and monasteries. Six kilometers south of the town in Gunung Rapat is the **Sam Poh Kong Temple**. The inside of the limestone tower is hollow, so one enters the caves and comes out into a garden completely enclosed by a towering wall of rock. Back inside the temple, alongside statues of Buddhist mythology

OPPOSITE: Lunar landscapes, the result of Ipoh's extensive tin mining. ABOVE: Perak Tong Temple, one of several in caves above the naturally occuring limestone pillars around Ipoh.

and a Buddha, are staircases carved into the limestone going up to lookout points in the rock. Outside there is a pretty Chinese garden and a vegetarian restaurant.

North of the town is the **Perak Tong Temple**, built into the caves inside Gunung Tasek. Altogether more impressive, this set of caves holds two massive Buddhas and many smaller statues. The walls of the caves have been painted by the many artists who still come to fill the caves with Buddhist images. A climb of 385 steps brings you to the top of the rock with some magnificent views of the countryside. Should you choose to make a contribution to the temple, the huge bell will be sounded.

WHERE TO STAY

Top Class
The most luxurious and conveniently located for the airport and roads to Kuala Lumpur and Penang is the **Royal Casuarina** at N° 18 Jalan Gopeng, ℂ (05) 505555; fax: (05) 508177. It offers all the amenities of a top-class hotel, including two restaurants and a pool. A double room costs from $83, going up to $188 for an executive suite.

In town is the pool-less **Excelsior Hotel** at Jalan Clarke, ℂ (05) 536666; fax: (05) 2307268. Rooms here are around $56 for a double. Around the hotel are some popular local restaurants and hawker centers. Offering very similar facilities, but again no pool, is the **Ritz Garden Hotel** at N° 79 Jalan C M Yussuff, ℂ (05) 30250; fax: (05) 545222. This place is right in the nightlife part of town and has its own disco which is very popular so it could be a little noisy, but at about $37 for a double room, it offers the best value in this range.

Moderate and Less
There are any number of hotels in the same area as the Ritz Garden, such as the **Hotel Mikado** at N° 86–88 Jalan Yang Kalsom, ℂ (05) 30250. No restaurant, but at $21 and up, it offers clean, rather over-furnished rooms with television and attached bathroom. Down-market again but in the same area is the **Kowloon** at N° 92 Jalan Yang Kalsom offering very basic accommodation with a double air-conditioned room with its own bathroom at about $11.

In the older part of town are several hotels, notably the faded and no longer splendid **Station Hotel** at the railway station, ℂ (05) 512588, which offers huge suites full of crumbling sixties furniture at $25. The restaurant does a good breakfast for about $3. The lift is a museum piece and so are some of the employees, but you get lots of atmosphere and a lot of space on the huge verandahs overlooking the other old colonial buildings. Closer to the new part of town are more hotels which are bland but reasonable. They all have restaurants and offer packages including breakfast or all three meals. One such is the **Hotel Eastern** at N° 118 Jalan Sultan Idris Shah, ℂ (05) 543936, with rooms at $22 to $33.

With all of the above, consider practicing the gentle art of negotiation; if business is poor, they'll be willing to bargain.

WHERE TO EAT

Chinese food in Ipoh is reknowned and a brief foray into the streets around Jalan Chamberlain will show you why. This is the nightlife area and there is no shortage of good places to eat at reasonable prices. For the reputed best *kway teow* (flat rice noodles fried in black bean sauce with seafood, eggs and bean sprouts) try **Kedai Kopi Hong Keng** on Jalan Leech, near to the *padang*. If you are an Indian food lover there are several good places, the best being **Restoran Pakeeza** at N° 15–17, Persarian Green, ℂ (05) 501057. It is slightly out of the bustle of town but within easy walking distance of the main hotels and serves moghul food with a wide range of breads. Two people can eat here for about $11.

Another excellent and very inexpensive Indian Muslim restaurant is **Rahman Restaurant** on Jalan Chamberlain which does the typical *murtabak* and biryani range, as well as some *kurma* and *rendang* dishes. This place is very clean and is completely devoid of the cigarette advertisements that most of these places adorn their walls with.

A very popular Chinese restaurant is the **Oversea Restaurant** at N° 57–65, Jalan Seenivasagam, ℂ (05) 538005. Decorated in traditional deep reds with the supper selection swimming about in tanks, this restaurant requires reservations and can be best enjoyed with a large group.

Many of the hotels have good restaurants, the Royal Casuarina having a reasonably priced Italian restaurant, **Il Ritrovo**. At the Excelsior is **The Palace**, serving Cantonese and seafood dishes. The **Ritz Garden** has an inexpensive 24-hour coffee shop serving western and local dishes.

For vegetarians there are some pleasant places, not all as far out as the cave temples. In Jalan Yang Kalsom is the **Bodhi-Lin** restaurant ((05) 513790, which is very reasonably priced.

GETTING THERE

Ipoh is on the main routes to and from Kuala Lumpur, Penang, Kuantan and the islands of Pangkor and Pangkor Laut. From Ipoh you can get the train to Thailand or Kuala Lumpur. Express buses go from the main coach station in Jalan Kidd to all destinations at regular intervals and are very inexpensive. Buses to Lumut, for Pangkor island, have a separate bus station across the road from the main one, also in Jalan Kidd.

From Ipoh, Malaysian Airlines has direct flights to Kuala Lumpur and Johore Bahru.

PANGKOR AND PANGKOR LAUT

Pangkor and its smaller sister island are places to enjoy a beach holiday. Both are tiny islands, situated close to the mainland, offering crystal-clear water, excellent and empty beaches (as well as a crowded and rather dirty one), good food and high quality accommodation.

BACKGROUND

For many years Pangkor Island has been a holiday resort because of its proximity to the mainland and pretty beaches. But Pangkor's history goes back a long way. In the sixteenth century a battle was fought here between Sumatran invaders and local people. The Sumatran leader was killed on the beach and the story goes that his fiancee came to Pangkor to find his remains. Not finding them, she stayed on the beach to pine away and die for love of him. The beach Puteri Dewi is named after her.

In 1663 when the Dutch arrived they found a wilderness of mangrove swamps. By 1670 they had taken Pangkor as a storage depot and outpost against pirates. It was abandoned in 1748, and after that, the pirates ruled Pangkor, which was the scene of battles between the Bugis, Indonesian pirates and the Malays. The little island visible out at sea between Pangkor and Pangkor Laut is called Pulau Simpan, which means "storage island" and legend has it that pirates kept their stolen treasure there. After the Dutch came the British, and in 1874 the island hosted the Treaty of Pangkor, giving the British the sole rights to mine tin in Perak.

Nowadays Pangkor's main industries are shipbuilding and fishing, but increasingly tourism is taking up more and more of the life of the island as young people turn to the hotels for employment.

GENERAL INFORMATION

Cabs on Pangkor are ancient and expensive by Malaysian standards: about $10 from the Pan Pacific to town and back. There is a bus service running from Pasir Bogak, the main tourist beach, to the ferry and on to the northernmost village. Bicycles are for hire in town and from The Pan Pacific if you are a guest. Motor bikes can also be hired in town. The Pan Pacific organizes boats from its jetty to Pangkor village once a day. Having a good time on Pangkor is largely a question of timing. School holidays (mid May to early June and late October to December 1) are not a good time unless you plan to stay at the luxury resorts, and even then they will make bookings difficult. If your stay is going to be a short one you should try to avoid weekends. There are two other shorter school holidays in August and February so it is best to check with the Tourist Board before you plan your trip.

WHAT TO SEE

If you want to spend some of your time exploring the island, there is the **Dutch fort** to visit at the south end of the island near to kampong Teluk Gedung. The fort has been rebuilt using what bricks could be found. Ten soldiers, a corporal and a slave were stationed on the island. In 1690 the fort was attacked by locals and destroyed, to be rebuilt in 1743 with a garrison of 60 soldiers. It was abandoned in 1748 and gradually fell into ruin.

The two villages on the island are dominated by the Chinese community and provide an interesting picture of small-town Malaysia. Between the two villages is the **Fu Lin Kung Temple** with a miniature Great Wall of China in a garden. Further along toward Sungai Pinang Kechil is an Indian Temple, an ancient Dutch tomb and one of the island's two mosques. All the sights of the island can be easily done in a two hour cab trip which will cost around $12. Cab drivers don't speak much English though.

WHERE TO STAY

There are two luxury resorts, the **Pan Pacific** at Teluk Belanga on Pangkor and the **Pansea Resort** on the nearby island of Pangkor Laut.

The Pan Pacific is isolated from the rest of the island by a crumbling tarmac road, which the cabs barely make it along. The resort is beautifully designed to blend in with its surroundings and offers a range of accommodation, from double rooms at about $100, to chalets and honeymoon bungalows at the end of the beach. The beach is an idyll of white sand and palm trees backed by a golf course, and all the sea sports expected of these types of resorts are available. Many other activities are organized by the resort including jungle walks, trips by boat into the village and a boat tour around the island. Or you can lay about by the pool and swim over to the bar for a drink while the hornbills squawk overhead. Bookings for the Pan Pacific should be made at Lot 9, Shopping Arcade, Pan Pacific Kuala Lumpur Hotel, Jalan Putra, P.O. Box 11468, 50746 Kuala Lumpur, ((03) 441-3757, fax: (03) 441-5559.

Pansea, the other resort hotel, is, if anything, even more exclusive than the Pan Pacific. At one time it was common for holidaymakers on Pangkor to hire a boat and go over to the beautiful Emerald bay on Pangkor Laut for the day, but now security guards patrol the beach, keeping out the riffraff. Pansea offers traditional-style grass-roofed chalets and rooms, most of them clustered around the reception area, but a whole new and beautifully designed group of bungalows has been built along the next bay. Some are built into the hillside on a stilt arrangement while others are out in the water with walkways connecting them with the land. Guests are transported by minibus from one site to the other or the 10-minute walk is pleasant enough. There are no televisions here, so it really is a getaway holiday. If you want to just visit the island there is a $10 fee which includes a meal at the restaurant. Prices vary depending on where your room is: $62 for a double/family room at the original site to about $90 for the newer, prettier rooms at Coral Bay. Reservations can be made at Pansea Pangkor Laut, 32200 Lumut, Perak, Malaysia, ((05) 951375 or 951973; fax: (05) 951320.

After the two resorts, prices and exclusivity move rapidly down-market. A good place to stay is **Nippah Bay Villas**, Lot 4442, Teluk Nippah, 32300 Pangkor, ((05) 951430 (between 10 pm and 7 am), which lies out of the main hotel area in Nippah Bay, two bays round from the highly populated and, at peak times, dirty Pasir Bogak Beach. This is a tiny settlement of 10 bungalows and a restaurant; no pool or water sports but lots of quiet and a completely deserted and idyllic beach. Rates include all meals, and the rooms are air-conditioned and comfortable, although there is no hot water. A room and meals for two people here is $45, with a little extra per meal for children. You should try to book if you want to stay here because it is often fully occupied. Cabs charge $8 to bring you there and back.

Back on Pasir Bogak, which these days looks a little like the Costa Brava, or even worse, there is a very new resort sponsored by the government which should rival the two big resorts in facilities if not in seclusion. Called Sri Bayu, it will offer villas, a pool,

OPPOSITE: A young boy dressed in traditional Malay costume.

and all the facilities of the mega-hotels, as well as a limousine pickup service and butlers. At the time of writing, room rates had not been established.

There are two other good hotels close together at the start of the Pasir Bogak Beach strip. **Beach Huts** is the smaller and quieter of the two establishments and has air conditioned chalets fronting the beach with a verandah, large single beds, a television and fridge for about $43. They can be contacted at their management office, N° 7 Jalan Datuk Ahmad Yunus, P.O. Box 7, 32000 Sitiawan, Perak, ((05) 911142, or at the hotel itself, ((05) 951159. **Sea View** at Pasir Bogak, 32300 Pangkor,Perak, ((05) 951605, is much bigger and has a range of room types, but the nicest are the chalets on the beach front at about $30 including breakfast for two. This place has a large Chinese/Western restaurant and a pretty garden along the beach front but gets noisy at peak times and the chalets are unimaginatively arranged, closely packed and not all of them are near the sea. Further along the main strip are two older and very popular places, **Khoo Holiday Resort**, ((05) 951164; fax: (05) 951164, and **D'Village** at Pantai Pasir Bogak, Pangkor Island, Perak, ((05) 951951. Both offer a wide range of accommodation ranging from tents at $3 a night per person to air conditioned rooms at Khoo's at $39 or beach chalets with a fan and shared bathroom at D'Village at $56, including all meals for two people. They both stand at the noisiest part of the island with the most crowded and least pleasant beach areas.

WHERE TO EAT

If you're staying at either of the two resort hotels this problem is solved for you by the difficulty of getting into town. Both hotels have a choice of restaurants of international standard. Pansea's continental restaurant, **Sri Legenda**, is one of the most beautifully located restaurants you are likely to see. It is built on to a promontory of rock and uses the natural lay of the land in its construction. Its huge verandahs offer magnificent views of the beautiful Coral Bay, and a meal for two here with wine will cost about $35.

Back in town, many of the hotels offer meals and accommodation packages but there are plenty of reasonably priced local restaurants along the beach area.

In vogue right now is the **Restaurant Number 1,** which is part of a collection of huts near the Sea View Hotel offering seafood dishes. The Sea View itself has a pleasant restaurant with a garden overlooking the beach. In town there are more restaurants, including Indian Moslem places.

GETTING THERE

Pangkor is approached from the small town of Lumut from where ferries leave to Pangkor regularly. Journey time is about half-an-hour. There is a separate service to the Pan Pacific Resort which goes less often. Pansea also has its own ferry service which takes an hour, so if you miss one is faster to take the ferry over to Pangkor and get a cab round to the Sea View Hotel from where a smaller ferry makes the five-minute journey over to Pangkor Laut and the resort.

Getting to Lumut is chiefly by express bus or taxi from Ipoh. Planes from Singapore, Malaka and Kuala Lumpur, on Pelangi Air, fly to Sitiawan airport and from there it is a 15-minute drive to Lumut. Sometimes heavy rains put Sitiawan out of action, so contact **Pelangi Air,** ((03) 746-4555, to see if Ipoh is being used instead. Pangkor should be getting its own airstrip soon, so Pelangi Air will have information about that also. You can also fly from Kuala Lumpur and Singapore to Ipoh and catch the two hour express bus from there.

The bus station at Lumut is within sight of the jetty, and close by are some good hawker stalls and low priced restaurants to hang around in if you have missed your ferry or are waiting for a bus. The ticket offices for the buses are situated around the bus station, so all you have to do is wander round looking for the name of your destination above a booth and find out the times. There are also small offices of the Malaysian Tourist Board and Pansea Resort close to the jetty.

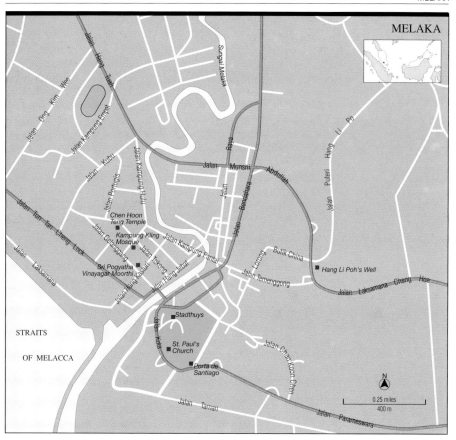

MELAKA

There is nowhere quite like Melaka anywhere else in Malaysia and a visit there is highly recommended. It is the most historic town in all of Malaysia, and though the effects of tourism are beginning to be felt here, the heart of Melaka remains untouched, and the town retains a distinctive idiom of its own, with the Chinese and Malay character each making its own mark on the feel of the place.

BACKGROUND

According to legend, a late thirteenth-century fugitive prince from Sumatra was resting under a tree at the mouth of the river when one of his dogs attacked a mousedeer. The deer drove the dog into the sea and the prince was led to exclaim, "This is a fortunate land where even the deer are full of

courage!". He decided to found a new city and named it after the tree under which he sat, the *melaka*. True or not, the story is immortalized on the crest of the municipality of the town.

Melaka gained the emperor of China, who sent Admiral Cheng Ho as an emissary there in 1403. The location of the town made it a natural entrepot, for Indian merchants could sail across the Bay of Bengal while their Chinese counterparts could come down from their land and the Spice Islands, and neither had to endure a long wait for the right weather that would have allowed them to make the entire India-China run. The trade with India facilitated the conversion to Islam of Melaka's rulers, and the city grew to be the most important and cosmopolitan port in the whole of Asia.

By the beginning of the fifteenth century, the Portuguese had heard enough to know that capturing this port would wrest control of the European spice trade away from the

Arabs. Under Alfonso de Albuquerque, Portuguese forces took control of the city in 1511.

Dutch imperialists captured the Portuguese fort in 1640 after a five month siege, but because their trade capital was Batavia (Jakarta) the economic importance of Melaka declined rapidly. From 1824 until Malaysia was granted independence in 1957, apart from a brief period of Japanese occupation during the World War II, the English controlled the city.

Such basic historical facts are woven into

the appeal of modern Melaka and it is impossible to ignore the past when visiting the city, not least when you hear a whole community of Malaysians speaking a language that has more in common with Portuguese than Malay!

GENERAL INFORMATION

The Tourist Information office, ((06) 236538, is just across the road from the Stadthuys,

ABOVE: Two of Melaka's older buildings. OPPOSITE LEFT: The Stadthuys, dating back to the Dutch era. OPPOSITE RIGHT: This roofscape shows the Kampung Kling Mosque and some of the many well preserved shophouses surrounding it.

and booklets on Melaka and other parts of Malaysia are freely available here. Cars can be rented from Avis, ((06) 235626, or through tour companies like Aquarius, ((06) 231876. Sightseeing tours are also available through a number of agencies like Atlas Travel Services (((06) 220777), Dynasty Tours & Travel (((06) 248888), or through any of the bigger hotels. There is a quite a choice: historic Melaka tours, countryside tours, night trips by trishaw and a mediocre river cruise which departs from the back of the Tourist Information office.

The *Visitor's Guide*, which is available from the information office, has full details on all the tours available.

WHAT TO SEE

There is plenty to see in Melaka. Its unique blend of Dutch and Chinese cultural influences makes it an interesting city for sightseeing and I suggest you begin by heading straight for the salmon-pink-colored **Stadthuys** and **Christ Church**, two buildings that have survived remarkably well from the period of Dutch rule. Built around 1650, the Stadthuys has all the solidity of a Victorian bank but with a grace and elegance that the nineteenth century rarely expresses in its architecture. Inside there is one room left with the authentic wooden ceiling of the Dutch, and the whole interior that once housed the Dutch governors is now a museum. The exhibits are representative of Melaka's cultural mix, with some fine furniture and porcelain from Portugal, Holland and China. Christ Church, just a little way up Jalan Gereja, was built a hundred years later and it is worth going inside just to see the original wooden pews and the 15 m (48 ft) rafters over the nave that must have been carved from single trees.

St Paul's Church. Or at least what remains of it, for the Dutch took the roof away when they converted it into a military post. They used the hill as a burial ground, probably because of its proximity to Christ Church. The walk up the hill is worth your time because the top affords picturesque views and inside the ruins are some remarkable tombstones.

Retrace your steps back to the tourist information office by the river and cross the bridge that leads to Jalan Hang Jebat. The small river has a still charm that invites repose and it may be difficult to imagine the

Porta de Santiago, only a short walk from the Stadthuys, is all that remains of the Portuguese fort that was laid siege to by the Dutch. But it wasn't the Dutch who destroyed the fortress, for even though it was damaged in the siege, they actually repaired the gateway, hence the date "Anno 1670" inscribed over the entranceway to the fort built which was actually built in 1512. It was the English who set about systematically demolishing the fort when they took control in 1807 and it was only through the intervention of Stamford Raffles (who had not yet stepped foot on Singapore) that the still remaining gateway was preserved.

Another Portuguese building, at the top of St Paul's hill and just a short walk away, is

flurry of commercial activity that must have once arisen from the coming and going of Chinese junks, Arab dhows and dealers from India and Java and Sumatra. **Chinatown**, across the river, has a real historical identity of its own and retains a feel for the past that is stronger than Chinatowns in neighboring countries, primarily due to the relatively languid intrusion of modernity. **Jalan Tun Tan Cheng Lock**, running parallel on the coast side to Jalan Hang Jebat, is a good example, for here you will find eighteenth- and nineteenth-century homes built for prosperous merchants. And at Nº 50, the site of the **Baba Nonya Heritage**, you can view the interior of one such home (two houses actually, linked by doorways). The term Baba refers to the descendants of inter-racial marriages between early Chinese set-tlers and Malays, and the resulting fusion of lifestyles was a unique blend of two quite different cultures. The Babas were prosper-ous merchants who could afford to be influ-enced by European styles, and the house that is now a museum is an excellent exam-ple of this. Renaissance-style Victorian col-umns, air-wells for the tropics and brightly colored tiles are the features that stand out most dramatically but there is also a wealth of fine detail to be admired inside. Make a

phone call, ℭ (06) 220777, to confirm the times of the daily tours. Incidentally, if you visit the museum you may wonder about the proportions — each house has a frontage of 7.3 m (24 ft) but a length of 36.5 m (120 ft) — a result of the Dutch property laws that cal-culated the house tax according to the length of the front.

Also in Chinatown is **Jalan Hang Jebat**, sometimes still called by its Dutch name, Jonkers Street, and famous for its antique shops crammed with what once made up the homes of the wealthy Dutch, Chinese and British. Bargaining is *de rigueur*.

In the same part of town is what is maybe the oldest Chinese temple in Malaysia, **Cheng Hoon Teng Temple**, founded during the Dutch period of control by a fugitive from China following the fall of the Ming Dynasty. The solid bronze statue of the Goddess of Mercy was brought from India, though the bulk of materials came in junks from China. Worshipers may be engrossed in prayer or quietly busy lighting joss-sticks, but you are free to discreetly wander around.

On the same road rests the unusually shaped **Kampong Kling Mosque**, another typical piece of poly-stylistic Melakan architecture: a Hindu-like roof, Corinthian columns, colored tiles from Portugal and Britain and a Victorian chandelier. The **Sri Poyyatha Vinayagar Moorthi** temple is just a few steps down Jalan Tukang Emas. The Indian god Vinayagar takes the form of a human body but with an elephant's head, hence the carving over the main altar.

Out of the Town Center

There are a few places worth seeing that are not exactly out of town, but walking there and back in the tropical heat can be exhaust-ing. Driving or hiring a trishaw or bicycle would be more pleasant options.

Bukit China has a notable history, being a gift from Melaka's Sultan Mansur Shah back in 1459 to his new bride, Princess Hang Li Poh, the daughter of the Chinese emperor Yung Lo. It was supposed to be her royal residence but *fung shui*, the Chinese art of geomancy, encouraged its use as a graveyard and the disintegrating graves date back to the seventeenth century. At the top of the hill which commands a fine view of Melaka, you can still find on the eastern side large flat stones, remnants of an old monastery and chapel built by the Portuguese in the 1590s.

At the foot of the hill is the **Sam Poh Kong** temple, built in 1795 and later dedicated to Cheng Ho, the famous Chinese admiral who first came to Melaka in 1409 and firmly es-tablished commercial and cultural links. Just next to this temple is **Hang Li Poh's Well**, also known as the Sultan's Well. Ad-miral Cheng Ho is said to have bestowed it with powers of purity, but that didn't pre-vent it from being poisoned by neighboring Malays when they attacked the town in 1551. When the Dutch took over they fortified it. The remains can be seen today in the crum-bling masonry around the well.

Further afield is **St John's Fort**, once an important Dutch fortification of which now only the walls remain. It is still worth a visit, not least because of the splendid views af-forded from the top of the hill.

St John's Fort might best be seen as a short stopover on route to the **Portuguese Settle-ment**. It is situated three kilometers, or nearly two miles, south of the town, accessible by the N° 17 bus from the bus terminal, at a cost of 40 cents, and since the 1930s has been home to Malaysians with names like Albuquerque, Santa Maria, De Costa, Dias — descendants of the Portuguese of the first quarter of the sixteenth century. When the Dutch community left Melaka in 1824, those remaining joined the Portuguese and gradually intermarried, which may explain some of the idiosyncrasies of the local dialect of Portuguese. Despite all the pressures to change, these people retain their Catholic religion and their unique Cristao language. Many of their words have become a part of the Malay language.

The community has its own school whose playground contains a statue of the Blessed Virgin, and while their language would not be readily understood by a tourist from Portugal, it is certainly not an Asian tongue. The land for this settlement was purchased by two Jesuit missionaries in the 1920s, and the movement of the disparate Eurasians in Melaka to this one area probably accounts for the successful survival of the culture and language of these people until today. In the 1930s this area consisted of *atap* houses, but it has gradually become positively suburban. In the early 1980s the Portuguese community was given the square, which is built in a Portuguese fashion on reclaimed land. The square, or **Medan Portugis**, is enclosed by buildings which house mostly restaurants and a community center. Inside the square is an open courtyard with a pier built out into the sea. The square holds performances of Portuguese folk dancing as well as Chinese, Malay and Indian dances on Saturday nights for guests of the restaurants, and particularly festive occasions are Christmas and the Festival of St Peter (June 29) when the local fishermen decorate their boats before they are blessed by the priest. Recent years, with their emphasis on all children learning Bahasa Malaysia, have made things difficult for these people. Call in at the **Restoran Lisbon** which has a collection of memorabilia and handicrafts of the Portuguese community, and whose owner, George Alcantra, is a local community leader and will be pleased to tell you about the Portuguese in Melaka. This community is in no

way a show for the tourists. Many of the people here live by fishing, and the music and dancing which you may see in the cultural shows are vital parts of the survival of these people's identity.

NIGHTLIFE AND SHOPPING

The Ramada Renaissance, Plaza Inn and the Emperor Hotel all have discos, but don't come to Melaka for a jet-set nightlife. A more pleasant evening could be spent shopping along the waterfront area near

Glutton's Corner where you will discover a whole bunch of handicraft and souvenir stalls which are open day and night. The cooler night air makes for easy strolling and this is a good opportunity to purchase locally produced items made from rattan and pandanus. There is also a good selection of pottery and as long as you don't pay the first price asked, you should pay less than regular shop prices.

In the same area, but only at night, there is a **Light & Sound Spectacular**

ABOVE: A traditional shophouse selling craft work from all over Malaysia.
OPPOSITE: Festival of the Hungry Ghosts, Penang. Food is left out for the wandering spirits and incense is lit.

presenting the city's historical and cultural background. It takes place on the green opposite St Paul's Hill and is well worth seeing.

OUT OF TOWN

If you have a car, the place to head for is **Tanjung Bidara**, a coastal location 35 km (21 miles) north of Melaka. Tanjung Bidara has a long beach with good shade and a resort hotel nearby with all the expected amenities.

Some 50 km (31 miles) from Melaka is **Mount Ophir**. The mountain requires no special skills to climb but you do need to be fit and climbing alone is not recommended. In 1988 a group from Singapore managed to get completely lost for days before stumbling into a loggers' camp. If you are seriously thinking of climbing, do consult the book on mountain climbing in Malaysia, under RECOMMENDED READING after the TRAVELERS' TIPS section.

Without your own car, an alternative way to see the everyday rural life of Malaysia is through a countryside tour. The

agriculture around Melaka is rich and varied and this can be a good opportunity to visit cocoa, rubber and oil palm plantations, as guided visits to the plantations are usually a feature of the countryside tours. Because of the relative prosperity of the area, there are some fine examples of authentic, traditional Malay homes and a late afternoon cycle tour would be a good way to take these in.

Air Keroh

Air Keroh is a very recently developed recreational area some 12 km (seven-and-a-half miles) east of the town and there are a number of new attractions here on either side of the main road. The **Recreational Forest** offers quiet walks through the trees and there are cabins for rent, ((06) 328401 or 591244). The **Mini Malaysia Cultural Village**, ((06) 32849, is a collection of thirteen houses representing the various regions of the country and sometimes shows are staged here. The appeal of this place has been complemented by the opening of the **Mini Asian Cultural Village**, in 1991 and now the thirteen Malaysian houses constitute just one of the twelve elements that together are being billed as a complete portrayal of Southeast Asian domestic architecture. If all the planned features of this project are implemented, this will be a place well worth visiting, and a quick check with the Tourist Board would do no harm.

Other attractions at Air Keroh include the **Melaka Zoo** which is situated near a lake with canoes and aqua-boats for hire. A visit to the zoo, which is open every day from 10 am to 6 pm, will allow you to see the increasingly rare Sumatran rhinoceros.

Air Keroh can be visited by bus (N° 19) or reached by bike along the main road running east out of town. The various attractions are spread out in green open spaces off the main road, but a few kilometers separate the first from the last, so a bit of walking is involved if you don't have your own transport.

Off the Beaten Track

Pulau Besar is a small island just four kilometers (just over two miles) off the coast of

OPPOSITE: The oldest hotel in Melaka, full of character and faded splendor. ABOVE: One of Melaka's many artists painting at Regency Hill.

Melaka and makes for a perfect retreat. Never occupied by the Portuguese, Pulau Besar is mentioned in old Chinese texts where Ming records refer to its use as a navigational aid for mariners. Nowadays, boats depart from the Pengkalan Pernau jetty or they can be chartered from Umbai jetty, just out of town on the coast road to Singapore. Check with the Tourist Information office because plans are well under way to build a holiday resort on the island and a more regular boat service will probably be introduced. Apart from the planned resort,

Top class

If you want the best hotel in town, head for the **Ramada Renaissance**, ((06) 248888; fax: (06) 249269, situated off the main road that runs through Melaka, Jalan Munshi Abdullah. The postal and booking address is Jalan Bendahara, P.O. Box 105, 75720 Melaka, although there is a sales office in Kuala Lumpur as well, ((03) 241401; fax: (03) 242-1498. Ask for a room ($60) high up and overlooking the town and sea for you will be able to trace the course of the river as it snakes through the houses. The **City Bayview** on

which will have five-star prices, accommodation could be arranged in one of the kampongs on the island. You would have to arrange this yourself on the island.

Even when the resort is operational, the island will still offer isolation to intrepid explorers who wish to go snorkeling and have a picnic by a beach campfire. As a one-day expedition, with a bit of organization, Pulau Besar would complement a visit to Melaka.

WHERE TO STAY

There are three accommodation areas: the town itself, the coastal area and an eastern strip at Air Keroh.

Jalan Bendahara, 75100, Melaka, ((06) 239888; fax (06) 236699, is in the same price bracket. Less expensive ($45) is the **Emperor Hotel** (formerly the Merlin), just behind the Ramada on Bangunan Woo Hoe Kan, Jalan Munshi Abdullah, 75100, ((06) 240777; fax: (06) 238989. If you want a beach on your doorstep, there is the five star **Tanjung Bidara Beach Resort**, ((06) 542990, at Tanjung Bidara, 78300 Masjid Tanah.

Moderate

In town there is the usefully situated and well kept **Plaza Inn** ($22 and more on weekends), located in a shopping complex at N° 2 Jalan Munshi Abdullah, 75100, ((06) 240881. Some of the rooms have views of the river, and amenities close by include bicycle hire, money exchange, a bowling alley, a disco and several food spots. The **Palace Hotel**, ((06) 225115, is on the same road at N° 201 and has cheaper rooms.

For space and greenery leave town and head for the **Air Keroh Country Resort**, ((06) 325212; fax (06) 320422, at Air Keroh, 75450 Melaka. There are good rooms ($32) and chalets with attached kitchens ($50). Although 16 km (10 miles) out of town, the N° 19 bus runs every 15 minutes and the place has its own 12-seater tripping into

a place with a well-established and well-deserved reputation with expatriates. Poolside chalets are $37 and the swimming pool here is a better bet than the polluted sea, but the beach is nice for a stroll. As with Air Keroh it helps a lot to have your own transport. The postal address is Batu 6 1/2, Tanjung Keling, 76400 Melaka.

Inexpensive

If you like an air of faded elegance and individuality, the **Majestic**, ((06) 222367, has good-value doubles for $13 — but skip the

town. If your reason for coming to Melaka is solely to explore the town and historical sights, then staying at Air Keroh is not a good idea, but there is the attraction of peace and quiet as well as non-historical places of interest. If you want to relax and make occasional trips into town, Air Keroh is perfect, especially if you have a car. The **Malacca Village Resort**, ((06) 323600; fax: (06) 325-9555, is also situated here at 6th Mile, Air Keroh, 75450: no chalets but plenty of rooms ($56).

On the coast at Tanjung Keling is **Shah's Beach Motel**, ((06) 511120; fax: (06) 511088,

outside rooms at the front. This 20-room hotel is at N° 188 Jalan Bungah Raya is tucked behind the Ramada Renaissance. The bar downstairs is open till midnight and it's a good place to meet fellow travelers.

The **Hotel Wisma**, ((06) 239800, is situated close by at N° 114A Jalan Bendahara. The rooms cost a little more ($15) and while they are more modern than anything the Majestic can offer, the drawback is that the room rates go up on weekends.

Budget accommodation (around $10) is available at the **Cathay**, ((06) 223744, and the **May Chiang**, both on Jalan Munshi Abdullah or the **Chong Hoe Hotel**, ((06) 226102, which is just opposite the Kampong Kling Mosque in Chinatown.

ABOVE: Children in traditional Malay dress, Terengganu.

WHERE TO EAT

I warmly recommend the **Banana Leaf** for an Indian breakfast. *Roti canai* or *dosa* with coconut sauce and curry sauce are served hot and fresh from early in the morning to the accompaniment of Indian music. Evening curries are also available and at any time the food is cheap and good. The place is conveniently situated on the main street of Munshi Abdullah, just past the Bungah Raya junction and the Ramada Renaissance.

Another inexpensive and pleasant little place that serves western and Asian food is **Kim Swee Huat** at N° 38 Jalan Laksamana. The average dish is $2 and the notice board bears testimonials from happy customers. The **Plaza Inn** restaurant offers inexpensive meals, including an American breakfast for $3. A **McDonald's** can be found along Jalan Tun Ali. All the bigger hotels have air-conditioned restaurants offering standard European fare, with the Ramada Renaissance being the best in this category, but if you want to go local, the most popular nightspot is **Glutton's Corner** along the waterfront, across from the Porta de Santaigo. There are a number of open air food stalls and you just pick out whatever takes your fancy.

Out at the Portuguese Settlement there are three restaurants claiming to offer "authentic Portuguese cuisine" but take it with a pinch of salt. At the **Restoran de Lisbon** or **Restaurant Santiago** in the square, $8 will cover a basic but tasty meal for two plus a view of the sea and a cultural dance. Do not be put off by dishes named "devil curry" because the food is just mildly spicy. The **San Pedro** restaurant, set back on a small road with all its tables inside, offers a more private atmosphere.

Out at Air Keroh the **Country Resort** has a pleasant restaurant and the Mini Asean Village includes food stalls featuring the various national cuisines.

Thai food is served at **My Place,** N° 537 Taman Melaka Raya, ((06) 243848, and there are two beach locations where seafood is available *kampong* style: **Serkam** and **Pengkalan Pernu**, 15 and 10 km (nine and six miles) from Melaka respectively.

One of the newest restaurants in Melaka is **Jonkers** and a visit here is recommended if you want to sample true *nonya* cuisine. The dishes are a mix of Chinese and Malay food, and Jonkers is the place in Malaysia to experience this type of food at its best.

HOW TO GET THERE

By Bus or Taxi

Express buses run from Kuala Lumpur, Singapore and other major towns. The departure point for coaches, in Melaka, is the Express Bus Terminal at Jalan Tun Ali. Contact the taxi station in Melaka, ((06) 223630, for details of long-distance taxis out of Melaka. See the TRAVELERS' TIPS section for more information on travel between Malaysia and Singapore.

By Air

Pelangi Air runs flights to and from Singapore, Sitiawan (close to Lumut, the jetty point for boats to Pangkor island) and Kuala Lumpur on Tuesdays, Fridays and Sundays. It has an office at Melaka Airport, ((06) 355784, though in Melaka it would be easiest to go through a travel agent to book a ticket. Pelangi Air is based in Kuala Lumpur, ((03) 770-2020; fax: (03) 746-2958, with a sales office in Singapore, ((65) 481-6302.

By Car

It takes 90 minutes from Kuala Lumpur along the Air Keroh expressway, passing thousands of rubber and oil-palm trees along the way. The car journey from Singapore takes more than four hours but this will be reduced when road works are completed.

By Train

You may take a train to Tampin and complete the 38-km (23-mile) journey by bus or taxi.

By Ferry

A fast passenger service between Melaka and Dumai in Sumatra now runs from Melaka harbor. The journey lasts about four hours and service is limited to once a week in each direction.

Into the Interior

MOST of the places that people visit in peninsular Malaysia are on the coastlines or just off them. Small towns, kampongs and beaches make up the familiar terrain. But if you ever travel across Malaysia in a plane, the most astounding and characteristic sight is the vista of rain forests and dense jungle that make up the interior. You should try to find time in your itinerary for a trip that takes you away from the coastline and into the true heart of Malaysia.

CAMERON HIGHLANDS

Four hours by car from Kuala Lumpur, Cameron Highlands is distant enough to deter day-trippers but big enough to absorb all the tourists and holidaymakers who choose to spend some time there. The Highlands offers a whole range of activities, all of them enhanced by the cool temperatures and burgeoning gardens of the area. There are many well-marked jungle walks here, a golf course, some tea plantations, a Buddhist temple and a good butterfly park with many interesting local plants and animals.

BACKGROUND

The place originally came into being when it was discovered by a surveyor called — you guessed it — Cameron, who first thought of the area now called Ringlet becoming a hill station. Further areas were cleared and now there are three distinct settlements in the Cameron Highlands all with a purpose and atmosphere of their own. **Ringlet** is now a center for flower nurseries, the next village, **Tanah Rata**, 13 km (eight miles) further up the road, is the tourist center and **Brinchang**, the highest of the villages, is a center for vegetable growing.

GENERAL INFORMATION

Readily available from most of the hotels in Tanah Rata are maps showing the main walks in the area. These vary from short, family-type rambles such as Walk 9 which goes to **Robinson Falls** or Walk 4 to **Parit Falls**, to longer and more strenuous ones. A good two-and-a-half hour walk covering a

variety of terrain and plant life would be Walks 10 and 12 which, when combined, take you through lowland forest, the fast disappearing rain forest vegetation and then into higher terrain where the vegetation becomes typically stunted and where many pitcher plants, the carnivorous plants native to Malaysia, can be seen.

You should take care in these jungle walks and always let someone know which walk you intend to take. One famous incident is the disappearance of Jim Thompson, the wealthy ex-CIA man who took a walk on March 26, 1967, and never returned, despite a search by police and the aborigines, the *orang asli*.

WHAT TO SEE

A visit to the **tea plantations** in the area is a fascinating experience. There are two Boh plantations in the Highlands and both welcome visitors and provide guided tours of the tea making process. The Boh plantation below Tanah Rata packs the tea as well as dries and ferments it, but the plantation above Brinchang is bigger. To get to it one has to travel through the barrack-like houses of the tea plantation workers. Tea gathering hasn't changed much since the British first began their tea plantations in India. It has become slightly easier on the workers now since they use a kind of hedge clipper to cut

OPPOSITE: The Golf Club, Cameron Highlands.

the new shoots rather than hand-picking each shoot, but they still carry the baskets on their heads and hand-pick shoots from the less accessible parts of the bush. Most of the workers at this plantation are Indians, descendants of the first wave of cheap labor brought over from Sri Lanka. You may notice that a very high proportion of the population in the Highlands is of Indian origin.

Another interesting sight is the **Cameron Highlands Butterfly Park** at N° 0–5 43rd mile Green Cow Kea Farm, 39100 Tanah Rata, ℂ (05) 90115, where many butterflies live and breed. Unlike most such places where the butterflies are shipped in and die without breeding because the climate is too hot, these are furiously fertile and often cause damage to the many rare and unusual plants growing inside. There is a section here where some of the local carnivorous plants are struggling to stay alive and another section for the poisonous plants that these butterflies need to breed but which are too dangerous to have out in the main park. There are also many of the indigenous insects, some of which look like extras from a '50s science-fiction movie, and a gigantic python which gets fed a whole live chicken once a month and then sleeps it off till the next month. Try to persuade the owner, Mr Patrick Chow, to give a guided tour. He knows a lot about the creatures he looks after. Also, look out for the green roses which flourish in here.

Other places to visit include the **Sam Poh Kong Temple**, about a kilometer (just over half-a-mile) off the main road to Brinchang, a strawberry farm in Brinchang, and further up, beyond Brinchang, some vegetable farms which grow cabbage and cress on precarious ledges. These ledges have cables leading up to the road to carry the produce to the lorry which collects it all once a day. Rose lovers might also like to visit the rose garden.

WHERE TO STAY

Accommodation covers the whole range of possibilities from self-catering apartments to luxury hotels. Starting at the poshest is **Ye Olde Smokehouse,** built in the thirties as a resthouse for weary planters and glowing with Ye olde English kitsch. As hotels go, it is very small but very exclusive, and will

cheerfully turn you away if you don't look like the right sort. Foster, the man who built it, was a sort of colonial Basil Fawlty and thought nothing of sending the dogs out to chase away the curious. If you don't stay there you should go in for tea. Room rates start at $68 for a single, including breakfast, and go up to $150. Each room is individual, very large and contains a huge four-poster bed. In the evenings they light log fires and residents sit about engaging in the gentle art of conversation. Reservations can be made at Ye Olde Smokehouse Hotel, By-the-golf-course, 39007 Cameron Highlands, Malaysia, P.O. Box 77, ℂ (05) 901214/5; fax: (05) 901214.

When Foster got fed-up with the tourists he sold the Smokehouse and built another similarly-styled hotel back down at Ringlet,

which is probably the only reason you'd want to spend any time there. Similar in style to the Smokehouse but with less kitsch, and its rates are slightly lower at $93 for a double with breakfast. Bookings can be made at **The Lakehouse**, 30th mile, Ringlet, 39200 Cameron Highlands, Pahang, Malaysia, ((05) 996152; fax: (05) 996213.

More mundane but serviceable are the **Merlin Inn**, ((05) 941205; fax: (05) 941178, where rates for a double are $76, and the **Golf Course Inn**, P.O. Box 46, 39007 Tanah Rata, Cameron Highlands, Malaysia, ((050) 901411, where a standard double room costs about $37.

In the medium price range there is the **Garden Inn,** at Tanah Rata, ((05) 941911, which has its own cinema, pool tables and a

restaurant and where double rooms cost about $23. Further up at Brinchang, several new hotels have opened, including the very neat **Hill Garden Lodge** at N° 15–16 Jalan Besar, 39100 Brinchang, Cameron Highlands, Pahang, ((05) 902988; fax: (05) 902226, where rooms cost $33 for a double. This is a pretty basic hotel with no restaurant. On the other side of the road is the **Parkland Hotel**, at Lot 5, 39100 Brinchang, Cameron Highlands, ((05) 901299; fax: (05) 901803, which has a tendency toward tudor beams and log fires, albeit artificial ones, and where doubles are $33. This place has a restaurant and competes with several other restaurants

ABOVE: Ye Olde Smokehouse. You can almost hear the planters' ice tinkling in their drinks as they relaxed after a hard day in the plantations.

in this strip to do the best and cheapest steamboat, a kind of fish, meat and vegetable fondue. This area, Brinchang, is a working town and the hotels look over the main road and wet market so there are no scenic views here.

At the budget rate there are many hotels in both Tanah Rata and Brinchang, the nicest being **The Orient** at N° 38 Jalan Besar, 39000 Tanah Rata, Cameron Highlands, Pahang, ((05) 901633. Rates depend on the number of people, the season and how long you intend to stay, but a double room with bathroom should be in the area of $13. Like many of the smaller places, prices are fluid. Downstairs is a very popular Chinese restaurant and down the road they have a coffee house which does a good breakfast.

If you are really on a shoestring (like $2 a night) head for the **Father's House**, which is a collection of ex-British army Nissen huts around the local priest's house. Head toward the convent and you'll see the priest's house from there. Accommodation is a bed in a dormitory with cooking facilities.

There are also self catering places, many of which are advertised in shop windows, or you can call in at the local travel agent, **C.S. Travel & Tours Sdn. Bhd.**, at N° 47 Jalan Besar, 39000 Tanah Rata, ((05) 901200; fax: (05) 902390, who manage several places for their owners. Since the information office spends most of its time closed these days, the travel agents seem to be doing most of their work for them. They also handle ticketing, tours of the area and hotel accommodation.

WHERE TO EAT

Eating out here is as expensive or unusual as you care to make it. The big hotels all have restaurants; at the Merlin the **Rajah Brooke** serves western and Chinese food at reasonable prices, the **Smokehouse** is quite pricey but does some dishes you won't find anywhere else, such as beef Wellington, which the local Sultan is pretty fond of, or steak and kidney pie for the homesick British. The **Lakehouse** also has a pricey western restaurant. In Tanah Rata the most popular place is the **Orient's restaurant**. Or there are two excellent banana leaf places serving

murtabaks and *roti canai* as well as curries served on a banana leaf. One is the **Restoran Kumar**, and next door is the **Restoran Thanam**, the only place where I have ever seen a woman making the *roti*. Up at Brinchang you should really try the steamboat. These restaurants are in fierce competition to do the cheapest and best, so just choose the one you like the look of. If you are eating on a shoestring, try the **Restoran Sentosa** at Brinchang which does Indian Muslim food at ridiculous prices. Very seedy looking but the food is good and there's lots of it.

GETTING THERE

Getting to the Cameron Highlands can be difficult. Trains stop at Tapah Road, 20 minutes from the town of Tapah at the bottom of the hill, and you can arrange a taxi up to Tanah Rata from there. There are also hourly buses from Tapah to Tanah Rata. There are express buses from most major towns to the Highlands or a taxi can be hired. The easiest mode of transport is of course by car, which

OPPOSITE: A tea plantation where Indian Workers still pick the crops that brought their ancestors from South India.
ABOVE: English country flowers abound in the Cameron Highlands.

Into the Interior

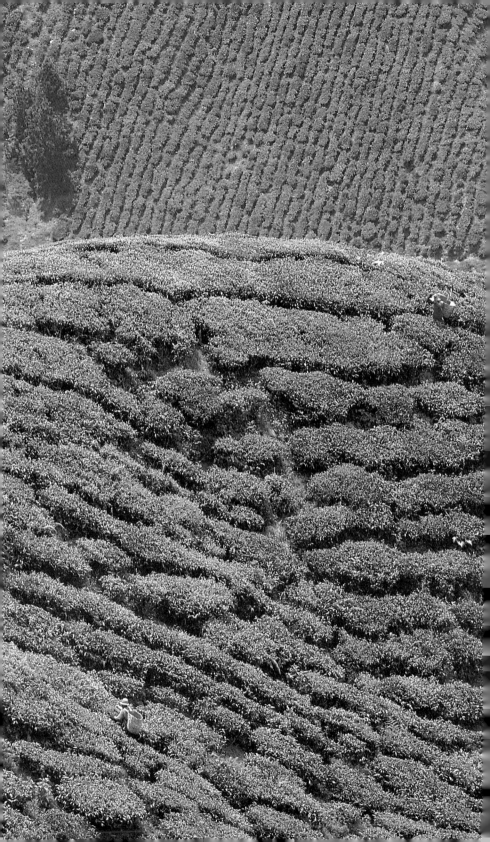

will make your stay at the Highlands easier since the three villages are some miles apart and a car is a useful means of transport if you wish to visit tea plantations or the temple. If you intend to go from here to Thailand, the train from Ipoh connects with trains to Thailand, although you should check timetables.

The government has great plans for this part of Malaysia and already a road into the area from Ipoh is partly built. Eventually this will form a new East–West Highway, making the journey from Ipoh to Kuantan a much shorter prospect. Hoteliers in the area are already planning for the days when the Highlands are a stopover for travelers on this road. This will change the nature of the Cameron Highlands radically, making it more accessible, with all the advantages and disadvantages that that brings, so if you like your holidays to be solitary, peaceful ones, see the Highlands before the road gets there.

FRASER'S HILL

Fraser's Hill is over 100 km (62 miles) from Kuala Lumpur, and the best way to get there is from the capital. Legend has it that a man called Louis James Fraser lived in the hills and ran mule trains of tin back to the nearest trading posts. In the early twentieth century he disappeared, and those who came looking for him found instead a perfect hill resort with a daytime temperature of around 24°C (75°F) and cool green hills to put up bungalows for the colonialists needing a rest from the boiling temperatures of the Empire. The place soon attracted other colonials who wanted a second residence to escape from the humidity of the lowlands. Today Fraser's Hill is hardly the idyllic mountain retreat that it was in the early part of this century, but it has many hotels and facilities like jungle walks, swimming, an open-to-the-public nine-hole golf course, tennis, fishing, boating and a sports complex with a heated swimming pool.

GENERAL INFORMATION

There is an information center just before the Merlin Hotel, ℭ (09) 382201, to help with the booking of rooms and providing of maps.

Because of its easy access and closeness to Kuala Lumpur, Fraser's Hill tends to get overcrowded on weekends, public holidays or school holidays. At other times the place is quiet and relaxing with few organized activities, and even the jungle walks are underplayed.

WHERE TO STAY AND EAT

Outside the peak periods, accommodation is no problem. The **Fraser's Hill Development Corporation,** ℭ (09) 382044, or (03) 804-1026, has chalets for around $18 but make sure you see what you are paying for, and don't expect any frills. Your best bet is the functional **Merlin Hill Resort,** ℭ (09) 382300, a good value at $63 for a double. It has good views, a coffee shop and a bar where people hang out at night around the fire. Very definitely upmarket is the super-kitsch **Ye Olde Smokehouse**, not a place for children who could do untold damage to the multitudes of flower arrangements, busts of Henry VIII, and other bric-a-brac littering the place. It has 12 rooms, all individually designed with four posters and all the trimmings. Rooms go for various prices, but the lowest is around $75. Lunch or dinner is available and the afternoon tea and strawberries are popular with local tourists who may be under the illusion that this is what life in Britain is like.

There is also the **Fraser's Pine Resort** which rents condominium-type accommodation. The apartments have two or three double bedrooms, a small kitchen and a balcony. It has a mediocre Chinese restaurant and at peak times is exceptionally noisy with little privacy. One unit can take up to 10 people and costs about $90. Bookings can be made at ℭ (09) 382122. There are several smaller places in the area — the **Tenerloh Bungalow**, for example, which has rather scruffy and basic rooms for $13. The best feature here is the attached **steak house** which offers decent meals at decent prices. Unless you have no choice, I do not recommend staying at the **Puncak Inn,** ℭ (09) 382201, where the rooms are basically unpleasant. At the bottom of the hill there is the old **Gap House** with more character and atmosphere than anywhere in Fraser's Hill itself. Rooms at $12 and a restaurant make this place worth a night's stay on your way there or back.

GETTING THERE

You really need a car to get there in comfort. Along the main Kuala Lumpur to Ipoh road there is a turn-off at Kuala Kubu Bahru which leads to a one way system up the steep winding hill. An alternative is to take up one of the many packages offered by tour operators in Kuala Lumpur and Singapore. There is a public bus to Kuala Kubu Bahru, but the connecting bus to Fraser's Hill only runs twice a day, at 8 am and 12 noon, so check your timing because you won't relish the eight-kilometer climb.

TAMAN NEGARA

BACKGROUND

Just imagine over 4,000 sq km (1,544 sq miles) of primeval, virgin rain forest, situated between four and five degrees north of the equator, and protected by statute from loggers and others despoilers of the environment. This is Taman Negara: Malaysia's greatest asset and one of the major natural wonders of planet Earth.

At a time when rain forests around the globe are being systematically destroyed (peninsula Malaysia alone destroys half-a-million acres of jungle every year as part of its role as the largest exporter of tropical hardwoods in the world) Taman Negara has become precious, and a visit there is a unique experience. It is a place for anyone who appreciates nature, and whether you're six or 60, or somewhere in between, this is a place you can handle because the choice of activities is up to the individual. At the moment Taman Negara remains sacrosanct; but there's no guarantee it will remain so. Plans to construct the Tembeling Dam will cause a large area of the park to be flooded, and who knows where the logging operations will stop.

GENERAL INFORMATION

Between mid-November and mid-January the monsoon rains present a danger and the Park Headquarters are closed to visitors, but at any other time of the year a little planning and preparation will ensure a rewarding and fascinating glimpse into the natural order of Mother Earth.

The accommodation and administration of the park has now been privatized under the name of the **Taman Negara Resort** and you can contact them direct at the park, Kuala Tahan, 27000 Jerantut, Pahang, ((09) 261500; fax: (09) 263500. There is also a sales office in Kuala Lumpur at Suite 1901, 19th floor, Pernas International, Jalan Sultan Ismail, 50250, ((03) 261-0393; fax: (03) 261-0615. If you are in Singapore reservations can be made at Room 3201, Overseas Union Building, 333, Orchard Road, (23577: fax: 235880. You can turn up at the jetty without a reservation but of course there's no guarantee of a place. It really is worth making a phone call beforehand.

WHAT TO SEE

The medium is the message and, unless you fly in from Kuala Lumpur, the experience begins on the jetty at Kuala Tembeling. There are no roads in Taman Negara and access is by means of the eight-seater *perahu*, a wooden boat with an outboard motor. The journey will take around three hours depending on the time of the year. The 60-km (37-mile) boat trip up the Sengai Tembeling is a memorable and glorious journey. At first you'll see signs of kampong life along the banks, women washing their children or their clothes and village buffaloes up to their necks in the water, but these give way to long stretches of inactivity when you're tempted to nod off and then wake with a shock as you gaze around. Occasionally a majestic flash of blue will signal one of the three types of kingfisher, or you'll spot a two-meter long monitor-lizard (*Varanus salvator*). Between April and July look out for the blue-throated bee-eater that will sweep across the water when disturbed by the sound of the motor.

By the time you reach the Park Headquarters the magic of the jungle should have started to play on your mind. Most nights a 16 mm film about Taman Negara is shown around 8 pm. Don't miss this. It's first-rate and concludes with a rallying call to get out of the Park Headquarters, get a sweat on, get tired, and experience Taman Negara. Spend your first afternoon relaxing by all means; purchase a copy of the excellent new guide and plan your stay. For the active and fit, the trails are just waiting for you, but if you wish to stay overnight in one of the jungle hides or go on a river trip, you will need to book ahead, ensure you have sufficient food and fuel and collect the necessary bed linen and accessories like lanterns.

Park Headquarters is where you book in, collect keys, study the maps and acclimatise yourself. Check out the inconspicuous glass cabinet that contains artifacts for sale, all made by the *Orang Asli* — the native non-Malay inhabitants of the area. Items include aphrodisiacs culled from jungle roots.

There is sufficient variety in the types of trails to suit all tastes and staminas. From the edge of the forest near the restaurant there is an 800-meter (874-yard) circuit path with points of interest marked and linked up with knowledgeable explanations in the guide book. Here's your chance to see, strangling figs, jungle epiphytes, giant termites' nests, the valuable *merbau* tree that has almost disappeared from other parts of Malaysia, 250-year-old tualang trees, rattan palms and lots more.

An even shorter walk leads to a *bumbun*, a wildlife observation post that looks out upon a natural salt-lick. If you're lucky, and perhaps very patient, you might spot mouse-deer, barking-deer or sambar, or maybe even the Malayan tapir or civet or the large black gibbon. Other walks of one to two hours and longer will take you to other hides deeper in the jungle.

An attractive feature of the park is the availability of boat trips that allow you to cut down on the leg work. Lata Berkoh, for instance, is a rock-fall area that marks the limit of navigability on one of the main river's tributaries. Trekking here will take you a healthy five hours but you can book a boat for the return journey or take a boat there and back. Either way, Lata Berkoh is a delightful resting place where you can swim or fish (rods can be hired from headquarters) or just relax and watch for those incredible hornbills that raucously announce their imminent arrival. A sight to behold.

Another river trip well worth booking ahead on the day you arrive is a journey upstream on the Sungei Tembeling to Kuala Trenggan. From here you can trek for 90 minutes to a Visitor's Hide and stay the night or just rest and watch birds. Unless the river is shallow at the time, you can expect fun on the way back as the boat rides the numerous rapids.

Consider a night out in the jungle. Taking a few basics (torch, mosquito coils, matches, candles, food, a novel to read perhaps) you can book a four-seater boat which will take you close to a lodge or hide and bring you back the next morning. The boatmen will probably stay the night as well. As dark settles in, light a small camp fire and sit back to enjoy the magical lights of the fireflies and the symphony of sounds. As you contemplate your insignificance in the black vastness that surrounds you, a primitive humility and awe will lull you to sleep. The light of morning will seem like one of nature's miracles.

Real enthusiasts may consider the eight-day round-trip to Gunung Tahan, the highest mountain in West Malaysia. Guides are compulsory and the whole thing is best arranged before coming to the Park. As the guide book says, "This is an arduous journey demanding physical fitness and mental determination, as well as good equipment, thorough preparations and sound leadership for large groups."

If you want to test your mental stamina I'd suggest a morning trip to **Gua Telinga**. This is a small but spectacular limestone cave that you thread your way through by following a rope. Not for the claustrophobic but terrific if you like seeing thousands of roundleaf bats, giant toads, harmless whip spiders and black-striped frogs. A more difficult-to-reach cave is Gua Kepayang where you can move around freely and search for elephant droppings. Don't let any of this scare you. No one has ever been trampled to death in Taman Negara or bitten by a poisonous snake. You may have a small amount of blood taken from your system by leeches but this is harmless and painless. All part of the fun. And if you don't want anything hectic and physically demanding just stay around the Park Headquarters and relax. Go for short walks and return river trips. You'll see and learn a lot wherever you go.

Where to Stay

Unless you're spending a night in one of the jungle hides or lodges, then Park Headquarters is where you stay. A new accommodation center has just been opened, offering private cabins with separate bathrooms as well as simple chalets and hostel rooms for backpackers. See below for the room rates.

Where to Eat

Park Headquarters has two restaurants; the **Tahan Restaurant** and the self-service **Teresek Restaurant**. At the Tahan an American breakfast is $6, a set lunch $8 and a buffet dinner $10. Picnics are around $6. At the Teresek restaurant a meal is about $5.

My advice is to bring with you as many eatables as you can because it's more fun stopping for a picnic on the walks. A small Gaz burner and plastic plates along with suitable picnic food will cheer up a lunch break in the jungle. The packed lunches available from the restaurants are satisfactory but you can get tired of chicken legs.

Costs

Since privatization, the costs have increased. A standard chalet is $12, a standard room $15, a superior $30 and a deluxe $63. A one bedroom suite is $103. Tents can also be hired and accommodation is available in the hostel at $4 per person. The boat transfer is $11 return per person.

Guides can be hired at $30 a day or $4 an hour and for the week's journey to climb Gunung Tahan would cost $150. The resort also organizes various trips into the jungle and the price usually includes a picnic and a guide. A four-hour trip to Lata Berkoh, for instance, is $13 per person, and the same length of time spent visiting the caves with a guide by boat is $15 per person.

Getting There

If you are traveling from Singapore, catch the night train that departs at 8:30 pm and arrives at Tembeling Halt around 6:30 in the morning. Tembeling Halt consists of a dilapidated crumbling shed and a concrete platform and the train will only be stopping for those visiting Taman Negara. From here you have to walk for half-an-hour to the jetty where boats leave at around 9 am and 2 pm.

Traveling from Kuala Lumpur means leaving the capital at 8:20 pm, arriving at Kuala Tembeling at 6:30 am the next morning after meeting the train from Singapore at Gemas in the early hours of the morning. Leaving the park means a boat down the river in the morning or after lunch. From the jetty you can walk to Tembeling Halt and catch the night train to Singapore (around 8 pm). This involves a long wait but you can drop in at the small village built on the river bank and find food there. You may feel a little uncertain as you wait on the platform in the dark, probably alone, wondering if the international express train really will stop just for you. I felt compelled to flag it down like a bus and was astounded when the train actually ground to a halt and the guard stepped down to politely inquire whether I was going to Singapore or not! It's more sensible to catch a bus or taxi to Jerantut from the jetty and spend the evening there waiting for the night train at a real station. The trains back to Singapore only have sleeping berths on certain nights of the week so check this beforehand. If you're traveling north you will have to spend the night in Jerantut and catch the train up the next morning.

Traveling from Kota Bharu means a long train journey with either a long wait at Gua Musang till 4 am or going on to Kuala Lipis and spending a night there in order to catch a morning train to Tembeling Halt.

Flights by Pelangi Air are available to and from Kuala Lumpur to the Park Headquarters on Tuesdays and Saturdays. The fare is $30 one way and Pelangi Air can be contacted in Kuala Lumpur, ((03) 770-2020; fax: (03) 746-2958, or in Singapore, ((65) 481-6302.

By road from Kuala Lumpur involves traveling along the main Kerak highway toward Kuantan and turning off at Temerloh for Jerantut. From here it is a 15-minute drive to the boat jetty where cars can be left in a compound. From the central Pudu Raya bus station in Kuala Lumpur a taxi could be hired for the three- to four-hour journey.

Sarawak

SARAWAK'S treasures are its national parks, which present amazing opportunities for viewing rarely seen wildlife and plants, and to be in contact with the state's fascinating mix of cultures. For anyone with an interest in nature and ethnic diversity this is Malaysia's premier destination.

BACKGROUND

From the fifteenth century Sarawak was part of the kingdom of the Sultan of Brunei. When antimony was discovered in the 1820s, the dependency began to attract attention. The Sultan's power was threatened by Malays and Bidayuh natives who were fighting for their independence. The Englishman James Brooke arrived at Sarawak in 1839 and was was rewarded for his help in putting down the rebel revolt. He was proclaimed the Rajah of Sarawak in 1842. The Astana in Kuching became his residence and seat of government. When he died in 1868, his nephew, Charles Brooke took over the throne and ruled till his death in 1917. His son, Charles Vyner Brooke, while holidaying in Australia, was dethroned by the Japanese when they arrived in Kuching. This brought the Brooke era to an abrupt end in 1941. The Australians received the surrender of the Japanese in 1945, and after the war Sarawak became a British Crown Colony. Civil unrest simmered and reached a climax in 1949 when the governor was assassinated in Sibu.

The struggle against the British was associated with the Brooke heir apparent, Anthony Brooke, the nephew of Vyner Brooke, but in 1951 he publicly disassociated himself from the campaign.

In 1962 a revolt broke out in Brunei, and a plan to unite with Sarawak and Sabah was formed. The fighting spread to parts of Sarawak, and British troops helped crush the rebellion. When Malaysia's independence was being negotiated, the idea of incorporating Sarawak and Sabah gained popularity with Malay politicians because it was seen as a way of reducing the numerically large Chinese element. In 1963 this became a political reality but was strongly contested by President Sukarno of Indonesia and an undeclared war — known as the Confrontation — lasted until 1969.

Peace now reigns and Indonesia and Malaysia are on friendly terms. For a long time it was virtually impossible to travel between the Indonesian part of Borneo, known as Kalimantan, and Sarawak or Sabah but this is now a thing of the past. If you fly to Bareo from Sibu it is easy to trek across the border into Indonesia and the army presence in Sarawak is now more concerned with the protests of the natives against the logging operations than any threat of political insurgency.

VISITING LONGHOUSES

It is difficult to imagine travel to East Malaysia without visiting a longhouse. Used as homes by the various ethnic groups that make up Sarawak's distinctive culture, an overnight visit to one is an experience worth treasuring. There are, however, a number of points worth considering. The tribes of Sarawak have a natural friendliness and are hospitable but the impact of tourism has turned some of the more accessible longhouse communities into something like tourist ghettos. This is especially true of those around Kuching. Some tour companies have even built their own guest houses alongside the longhouses so visitors have the benefit of modern conveniences while window-gazing on another way of life. I can imagine a time when the green American Express sticker will be posted on the door of

ABOVE: An Orang Ulu longhouse, Sarawak.
OPPOSITE: The highly ornate tribal dress of the Orang Ulu, Sarawak.

a longhouse. It is also true that the twentieth century is rapidly catching up with these isolated cultures, and when you see dancers in a longhouse performing their traditional dances but wearing Reebok trainers you might wonder just how real the whole thing is. But this thought need not linger; it would be an indulgence to suffer disappointment because so-called primitive people have conveniences you take for granted in your own life.

Having said this, there are ample opportunities to visit longhouses and the experience of hospitality and a window on another

and ask lots of questions beforehand. A detailed itinerary should always be available and, as a rule, the longer it takes to reach the longhouse the more authentic it is likely to be.

NATIONAL PARKS

These are the other principal attraction of Sarawak Near Kuching, there is **Bako National Park**, in some ways the most attractive park. It is easy to get there and doesn't involve any strenuous physical activity, yet

way of life leaves a deep impression. The Ibans in particular have a terrific sense of fun. An organized trip with a tour agency is recommended as the guide will speak the local language and you will have the opportunity to ask questions about the things you see around you. If you want, though, you can do the whole thing yourself. Take a boat up river from Kuching, Miri or Sibu and just front up at a longhouse. Come prepared with some token gifts and arrange beforehand to pay the chief for your night's lodging and food. $M10 for person per night is reasonable and you might like to bring along some food of your own.

If you are going on an organized trip with a tour agency it is best to know what you want

it is the best park for seeing wildlife like proboscis monkeys and hornbills. Near Miri is **Mulu National Park** with the world's largest caves, amazing flora and fauna and the opportunity to climb Mount Mulu (2,376 m or 7,800 ft). You need at least four days to make the return journey to Mulu but **Niah Park** is only a two-hour journey by road from Miri and once there you have the opportunity to see prehistoric rock paintings spread over 60 m (200 ft) of cave wall. None of these parks provide luxury accommodation or food but you won't starve and you will get closer to nature. Visits to Bako and

ABOVE: Niah Caves National Park, Sarawak brings you close to nature and to man's early history.

Sarawak

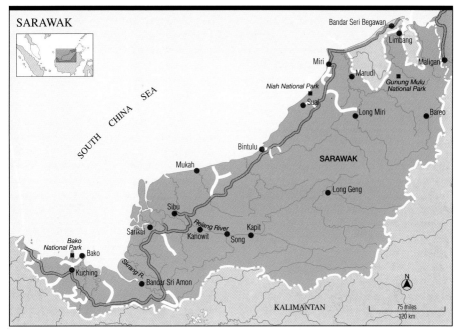

Niah can both be organized quite easily on your own, but traveling to Mulu Park is best done with a tour company.

Reliable tour agents are mentioned in below but if you are planning your trip from Kuala Lumpur the people to contact are Asian Overland Services, ((03) 292-5622; fax: (03) 292-5209. They specialize in packages to the national parks and longhouses.

TRAVELING IN SARAWAK

Travel in Sarawak is quite different from travel in peninsular Malaysia. Roads are of secondary importance to rivers and while it is not possible to make reservations for scheduled boat journeys it is advisable to always plan ahead and have a general idea of how you intend to spend your time in Sarawak. Plane journeys are sometimes necessary and these should be booked ahead. For instance, if you are intending to travel from Kuching to Miri, or from Sibu to Miri, a plane is the best way to cover the distance. A boat journey from Sibu to Miri will take days and it will not be much fun; the journey by bus will involve hours of uncomfortable driving over poorly surfaced roads. Malaysian Airlines has a good network of routes

and the prices are very reasonable, but if you don't have a reservation you may find yourself waiting around for hours or even days. And the key to a successful time in Sarawak is getting to where you want to go to with the minimum fuss. There is just no joy in hanging around in the towns waiting for connections. There is little to do and your time will be wasted. Decide on the places you want to visit and plan accordingly, making whatever flight arrangements are necessary. Bear in mind, too, that from July to October the dry season can often make the rivers difficult to navigate and a flight is the only way in or out. This is especially true along the upper stretches of the Rejang, from Kapit to Belaga, and reservations will then be essential.

KUCHING

One hour by air from Singapore and 30 minutes longer from Kuala Lumpur will bring you to Kuching, a wonderfully laid-back town which has managed to accept the modern world without being overwhelmed by it. All the modern hotels and shopping complexes are lumped at one end of town, leaving the old town to retain its identity and charm. The river and its banks are remarkably untainted by development, as you will quickly discover when you cross to the other side. Kuching is a town not to be missed and at least a couple of days are needed here if the place is going to work its magic. More time is required if you want to visit the nearby Bako National Park.

GENERAL INFORMATION

The **Sarawak Tourist Information Centre** is conveniently located down by the river on the Main Bazaar, ((082) 410944, and right next door is the state **Sarakraf** craft shop open from 9 am to 6 pm Monday to Friday and from 9 am to 3 pm on Saturday. **Sarawak Plaza** is the modern shopping complex next to the Holiday Inn and here you will find more shops selling native artifacts and handicrafts. A good local travel company is Saga Travel, ((082) 418705; fax: (082) 426299. Contact them if you want an organized trip to any of the places of interest including Bako National Park and longhouses on the Skrang River. Borneo Transverse, ((082) 257784; fax: (082) 421419, is another reliable company based in Kuching and good for river trips to longhouses on the Skrang and Rejang Rivers. A three-day / two-night complete package for visiting longhouses will cost in the region of $360 for two people. The top hotels should be able to arrange play on the Kuching 27-hole golf course if you have a certified handicap. Exercise can also be had by joining the Hash House Harriers, ((082) 421133, on their weekly runs. For reading material visit the bookshop in the Holiday Inn; it is open till 10 pm and you're unlikely to find a better selection of books on Borneo anywhere else. If you are traveling up-river consider purchasing here the 1:50,000 scale map of Sarawak.

Traveling around Sarawak and Sabah is very likely to involve flights, and Malaysian Airlines, ((082) 246622, has an office in Song Thian Cheok Road, in the Holiday Inn part of town.

WHAT TO SEE

Kuching suffered remarkably little damage from the ravages of World War II and a number of old colonial relics are well preserved and all conveniently located around the tourist office down by the river. The **Court House**, erected in 1847, housed the Brooke administration and its Romanesque style somehow blends in comfortably with the sleepy Asian setting. Around the corner in Jalan Tun Abang Haji Openg is the Post Office, and its mighty Corinthian columns seem equally at ease with their surroundings. A real treat is **Fort Margherita** on the other side of the river and not the least of its attractions is the journey there. Down by the river bank, just behind the tourist office, is the departure point where boatmen punt you across for the 20 cents that passengers unceremoniously leave behind them. Just follow their example. The fort, completed in 1879 by the second rajah, Charles Brooke, and named after his wife, is perfectly preserved for two reasons: it was strategically located to repel troublesome natives but trouble never came, and secondly, because of faulty marksmanship, the attacking Japanese dropped their bombs in the river instead of their intended target. The Fort now houses a **Police Museum** and is well worth a visit. The fort's watchtower is now home to six laughing skulls, collected in battle many years ago, but reported to have been heard laughing since then. The Astana is also on this side of the river but the original home of the white rajahs is now the official home of the state governor and is not open to the public.

One place that cannot be missed on any trip to Borneo is the **Sarawak Museum**, conceived during the reign of the second rajah. The co-author of Darwin's *Origin of Species*, Alfred Russell Wallace, played a vital role in its establishment. It now houses a fascinating collection of natural and anthropological exhibits that could well convince you of the need to take a trip into the interior. The museum shop is equally well stocked. There are now two wings to the museum and they are open daily, except Friday, from 9 am to

OPPOSITE TOP: Fort Margherita museum is well worth the trip to the other side of the Sarawak river. OPPOSITE BOTTOM: Kuching, the most Conradian town in the whole of Malaysia, is a cosy cluster of old shophouses nestled on the banks of the Sarawak river.

midday and again from 1 pm to 6 pm. Admission is free. If you are planning to visit the Niah Caves you may pick up your permit to see the Painted Cave from the curator here. Incidentally, the 1,200-year-old funeral boats discovered in the Niah Caves are on display in the museum, and these should be seen if you are planning to visit the caves themselves.

Every evening there is a **river cruise** that departs from behind the tourist office, with the option of a meal. Confirm the details with the tourist office, but usually the boat

architecture, as well as a Penan hut where blow-pipe making is demonstrated. Demonstrations of arts and crafts are on hand as well as a small theater showing different dances. Allow a whole morning or afternoon to see the place and catch one of the regular tours and cultural shows. Admission is $8. Like all such exhibitions, the place may seem too studied for some, but as an introduction to Sarawak's cultural diversity and a spur to visit the interior, this cultural village serves a purpose. Quite honestly, I would say a visit here is a better use of time

leaves around 5:30 pm. Walking from the Holiday Inn or the Hilton toward the tourist office will take you past the colorful **Tua Pek Kong** temple, built in 1876. On Saturday and Sunday nights there is a busy and interesting **market** on Jalan Satok.

OUT OF TOWN

Out at Damai beach, right next to the Holiday Inn resort, is the **Sarawak Cultural Village,** ((082) 416777. It takes up nearly eight hectares (17 acres) displaying the lifestyles of the various ethnic groups that make Sarawak such an exciting place. Longhouses from the Bidayuh, Iban and Orang Ulu have been reconstructed, all very different in their

than going on some of the local longhouse trips. A taxi from town will cost $9 but the 2B bus will also take you there for considerably less. **Santubong** is the name of the local fishing village and during the evening you can buy fresh prawns here and take them to one of the seafood stalls for cooking. Government chalets here can be booked and you should inquire at the tourist office.

If you are not visiting Sandakan in Sabah to see the orangutans being rehabilitated then try to see Kuching's equivalent at the **Semenggok Wildlife Rehabilitation Centre** about 22 km (14 miles) out of town. Here you can see orangutans, honey bears, hornbills and monkeys after a half-hour jungle walk from the road to the entrance.

Permits are available from the Tourist Information Centre but if you arrange a visit through a travel agent this will be handled for you. Go in the morning to catch the feeding time.

An interesting half-day trip can be made to the old gold-mining town of **Bau**. Nearby is **Fairy Cave** situated about 30 m (100 ft) above the ground and not a gentle stroll at anytime. An organized trip from Saga Travel, that includes a visit to a local pottery, costs $40 for two people.

Bako National Park

When the park was gazetted in 1957 it was announced that "Bako was picked ... as both the flora and bird life of Bako are of exceptional interest, the scenery beautiful and there are numerous bathing beaches." The simple truth still holds today, and while not spectacular Bako has the virtue of being easily accessible. What I like most is the fact that you can set off on a jungle trek, work up an almighty sweat, but then collapse in joy when you discover a beautiful beach that marks one of the trails' destinations. It was in Bako that I first saw pitcher plants with their cups suspended from the leaf-tips to trap and digest insects. A memorable experience that can be guaranteed on the Lintan trail that takes you up onto an open and barren plateau, quite un-Bornean until you realize the pitcher plants are all around you.

There are 16 clearly marked trails in the park and they range from a one-hour return trip to a seven-hour trek that requires overnight camping. Accommodation at the Park Headquarters is in resthouses that may be rented by the room ($12) or the whole bungalow ($23). Bedding and self-catering facilities are provided, including a fridge, and although there is a canteen at the park it is better to bring your own basic provisions. There are plans to renovate the resthouses so don't expect anything grand for the time being.

Getting to Bako is not as difficult as tour companies might suggest. Bus N° 6 leaves regularly every morning from the bus station and takes you to Kampong Bako (Bako village). The journey involves a short ferry crossing and the whole journey takes two hours. From Kampong Bako you must travel by longboat into the park. When you make

your booking at the National Parks Office on Jalan Gartak in Kuching, ((082) 2480, the official park boat will have a place reserved for you. You can also book through the tourist office on Main Bazaar. If you go through a tour company expect to pay at least $40 per person for a two day/one night package.

Skrang River

As said earlier, some of the longhouse trips on the Skrang River are badly commercialized but the tour companies mentioned are honest about this and if you make it clear

that you want something more authentic they will arrange it. Time is the factor because the interesting longhouses, at places like Murat or Mejung, are more remote and at least three days are needed for the return journey. A three-day/two-night trip will cost around $360 for two people, including all meals, accommodation and transport.

WHERE TO STAY

Top Class

At the moment there are two top-class hotels, very different in character, and a third one opening in 1992. For serenity and sedateness stay at the **Hilton** in Jalan Tunku Abdul Rahman, P.O. Box 2396, 93748 Kuching, ((082) 24200; fax; (082) 428984, and be sure to ask for a room overlooking the river if you want that Conradian view early in the morning. Rooms start at $80. The **Holiday**

OPPOSITE: Sarawak's Cultural Village celebrates the indigenous cultures of Borneo.
ABOVE: For a few cents this ferryman will carry you across the river at Kuching.

Inn, just a stone's throw away along the same road, lives up to its name and at night the place is alive with bustling groups. Rooms are $75, and for $10 more there's a river view room, ℂ (082) 423111; fax: (082) 426169. The new hotel will be called the **Riverside Majestic**, located in the same area and with similar prices no doubt. The local plush beach resort is the **Holiday Inn Damai Beach**, ℂ (082) 411777; fax: (082) 428911, with rooms that start at $80. It is about 45 minutes from Kuching town.

Moderate

Close to the Damai Beach Resort is **Camp Permai**, ℂ (082) 416777; fax: (082) 244585, where air-conditioned tree houses are available for $50 and log cabins for $35. The rates increase at weekends and lots of organized student groups invade the place then and during school holidays. Not a bad idea for families though, because there are lots of organized recreational activities and children under twelve can sleep in tents near the beach. If you want to stay in the modern part of town, a short walk from the Holiday Inn will bring you to the new **Motel Siangalila**, ℂ (082) 425221; fax: (082) 243567, with good modern rooms for $22, plus hot water courtesy of solar energy. An older hotel in the same area is the **City Inn**, ℂ (082) 414866, in Jalan Abell ($20). There is an open-air seafood restaurant next door as well. In the old part of town in McDougal Road is the **Fata Hotel**, ℂ (082) 24111; fax: (082) 428987, charging $30 for rooms with a fridge, less for smaller rooms. At the corner of the same road, in the direction of the museum, is the **Aurora Hotel**, ℂ (082) 240281; fax: (082) 425400, with similar rates. But a better value for the same price could be had at the **Borneo Hotel**, ℂ (082) 244122; fax: (082) 254848, just across the road from the Fata Hotel. Despite a silly pricing system (20 percent discount off the published rates but then 15 percent added for service and tax) this is a good tourist hotel, and breakfast is included. The modern **Telang Usan Hotel**, ℂ (082) 415588; fax: (082) 425316, is on Ban Hock Road, P.O. Box 1579, 93732 Kuching, with rooms around $40. A good value for the money, though inconveniently located 25 km (15 miles) out of town, is the **Buntal**

Village Resort with rooms at $25, ℂ (01) 212457; fax: (01) 212457. The beach here is about nine kilometers (five miles) past the Damai Beach Resort.

Inexpensive

Not far from the Sarawak Plaza and the Holiday Inn, on Jalan Padungan, is the **Kapit Hotel**, ℂ (082) 244179, with pokey air-conditioned rooms for $12. The **Kuching Hotel**, ℂ (082) 413985, is across the road from the Rex cinema on Temple Street and, while bathrooms are outside the rooms, it is well-kept and clean, and doubles with a fan are only $8.

WHERE TO EAT

Most of the best restaurants are in the two big hotels, and if Kuching is the first leg of your journey in Sarawak, make the best of it because there is more variety of food here than anywhere else in Sarawak. The Holiday Inn, ℂ (082) 423111, has excellent Chinese food at its **Meisan Szechuan** restaurant and a good meal for two would cost about $30. The **Hilton** has a daily lunch buffet for $7 and a steak house that opens in the evenings only. There is also a good Cantonese restaurant open for lunch and dinner. A evening meal for two would also cost around $30.

Vegetarians should head for the **Wan Fu Yen Vegetarian Food Centre**, located at 261 Datuk Wee Kheng Chiang Road, a short taxi ride from the center of town, ℂ (082) 427052.

The **Aurora Hotel** has a coffee shop serving featureless western and local food but at reasonable prices. Behind the Hilton the **Permata Food Centre** opens at night serving local food, including steamboat, at local prices. On Jalan Carpenter there is the tasty **National Islamic Cafe** and a walk here for breakfast will allow you to catch Kuching in the morning.

GETTING THERE

From Singapore, Malaysian Airlines flies twice daily to Kuching, and Singapore Airlines now has a limited service as well. Malaysian Airlines also has numerous flights from Kuala Lumpur and Johore Bahru. Flying from Johore Bahru is significantly cheaper than from Singapore, and

Malaysian Airlines has a coach that runs from the Novotel Inn in Bukit Timah Road in Singapore to the airport in Johore Bahru. Cheaper still would be to purchase the ticket in Johore Bahru. Sarawak has its own immigration control, so your passport will get stamped again when you arrive in Kuching.

SIBU

If you're visiting longhouses all the Rejang River, you have to pass by Sibu. The town itself has decent hotels but very few decent places to eat. There is no tourist office, but one lovely pagoda which at night provides an atmospheric view of the mighty Rejang River. It is advisable to have your travel plans made before arriving in Sibu because it isn't really the most interesting or exciting place to hang around. The most experienced local tour company is under the charge of Mr Johnny Wong, ((084) 326972; fax: (084) 323399. A three-hour tour of Sibu would cost $30 for two people and a complete three-day/two-night trip to two different Iban longhouses would cost at least $330 for two people. Another tour company is the Sazhong Travel Service at N° 4, Central Road, ((084) 338031; fax: (084) 335031, and it would be worth comparing prices and the details of packages. Ideally, you would have your travel plans already settled before actually arriving in Sibu.

BACKGROUND

Situated some 128 km (80 miles) from the sea Sibu has an interesting history. It was only in 1900 that a Mr Wong Nai Siong came exploring the Rejang basin looking for land suitable for development, and he returned a year later with about 70 farmers, all from the Hokkien province in south China. More followed and today the vast majority of Chinese in Sibu are descendants of these pioneers and Hokkien is the only dialect spoken when Mandarin is not used.

WHERE TO STAY

The best hotel is appropriately named the **Premier**, ((084) 323222; fax: (084) 323399,

and it is located on Jalan Kampong Nyabor, 96008 Sibu. Published room rates range from $30 to $100 but any independent traveler should expect a 20 percent discount. The location is a central one, near the night market and the Sunday wet market, and within walking distance of the wharf where the boats depart. The **Tanhames** is on the same road, ((084) 333188; fax: (084) 333288, and has a pool, but a standard double is $67. The **Centrepoint Inn** is a new hotel in the Jing Hwa Building off Central Road, ((084) 320222; fax: (084) 320496, and if the room

rates stay at $20 this is a good value for a clean and modern room with television and video, especially if you are just staying overnight and leaving on a boat early in the morning. Another new place, the **Hotel Bahagia**, also on Central Road, ((084) 320303, is an even better value if they don't revise their present charge of $15 for a double. There is also a coffee house here, unlike the Centrepoint. The Bahagia can be contacted by fax, (084) 311706, through a sister hotel called the Capitol. There are plenty of other hotels to choose from in the central town area but beware of the cheaper-looking ones: they charge by the hour.

ABOVE: The superb Chinese temple overlooking the mightly Rejong River.

An honorable exception is the Methodist guest house, **Hoover House**, next to the church on Jalan Pulau. No air conditioning or attached bathrooms, but at $5 that seems quite reasonable.

WHERE TO EAT

Sibu is a gourmet's hell. There are too many unpleasant Chinese cafes serving inexpensive but un-nourishing and un-tasty food. The Chinese restaurants are not much better. Your best bet is to head for the restaurants

views of the coastline and the network of rivers that define the topology of Sarawak. In Sibu the Malaysian Airlines office is at N° 61 Jalan Tuanku Osman, ℂ (082) 326166.

From Kuching the boat trip takes from three and a half to five hours and costs $12 upwards. Check the newspapers in Kuching for advertisements or ring Kuching Union Express (ℂ (082) 48424) about their early morning boat. There are buses from Sibu to Bintulu and Miri, but the journey is not recommended, as the ride is long and uncomfortable; the plane fare is well worth it.

and coffee houses at the **Premier** and **Tan-hames** hotels. The food is reasonable and so are the prices: a meal for two at the Premier coffee house will cost around $15. For recognizable western fast-food, which might seem tempting after a couple of nights in a longhouse, there is always the **Sugar Bun**, near the two main hotels just mentioned.

GETTING THERE

The best way of reaching Sibu is via Malaysian Airlines on a Fokker 50. From Kuching, the fare is currently $22. The flight gives terrific

ABOVE: Miri is a bustling little boom town but many of its Malay communities still live beside the river.

UP RIVER FROM SIBU

From the waterfront in Sibu, boats depart for Kuching and upriver to Kapit and Belaga. It is a five-hour trip to Kapit in a fast steel-bottomed launch that speeds through the water at more than 30 km (20 miles) an hour, generating a noise that drowns out conversation. If you are lucky it will also drown out the voices coming from the non-stop videos that are an obligatory part of the journey. The boats will stop briefly at a number of places along the way, including **Kanowit** which is 64 km (40 miles) from Sibu. Kanowit was where Charles Brooke built a fort to use as a base in his campaigns to suppress headhunting. But this is all there is to see and it hardly justifies stopping off. About two hours from Sibu will bring you to **Song** where, during the Second World War, the Ibans were given permission to renew headhunting, against the Japanese that is. Song is a typical river settlement where Ibans come to sell their produce and buy provisions. There are no good restaurants or hotels but at N° 6 Ling Hak Seng, ((082) 777228, there is a local guide and tour operator who could arrange a visit to Iban longhouses for a lot less than the agents in Sibu. Costs could be negotiated and they will depend on how far you wanted to travel and for how long. Expect to pay around $100 for two people staying two nights with full board.

Kapit is a typical town on the Rejang. It has a wooden fort that dates back to the time of Charles Brooke, and like the much smaller Song, the town itself attracts tribespeople from the interior who come here to buy and sell. Many Iban longhouses harvest pepper and cocoa which they sell to the Chinese merchants who monopolize the trade. The Malaysian Airlines office is with the Hua Chiong Company at N° 6 Jalan Temenggong Koh, ((082) 796988, just opposite the jetty. It is easy to arrange visits to longhouses in the immediate vicinity but they are urbanized and well used to visitors.

The best hotel in town is the centrally located **Meligai**, ((082) 796611, on Jalan Airport. A double room costs just under $20. The boats back to Sibu leave fairly regularly throughout the morning and you can take your pick.

If you have come this far consider going further upstream toward **Belaga**, from where you can arrange visits to Kayan or Kenyah longhouses which are far less patronized by foreign tourists and likely to be more of an authentic experience. On the way, by boat, you will experience the infamous Pelagus rapids which Charles Brooke and his expedition of Ibans successfully negotiated when setting out on their pursuit of the Kayan and Kenyah people in 1863. The territory around Belaga is still inhabited by these people, although they have been forced to come to terms with the logging operations that have become a permanent feature of life here. Accommodation in Belaga is dismal and only two hotels have air-conditioning: the

Sing Soon Hing and the **Belaga Hotel**. Only stay here if you have to. Trips to the longhouses can be arranged at the riverside. The Malaysian Airlines office is at N° 4 Sayarikat Awang Radin, Belaga Bazaar.

Officially, you are supposed to have a permit for travel beyond Kapit and this can be arranged at the State Government Complex in Kapit. In practice, however, it is a waste of time collecting them because they will never be asked for — as long as you go no further than Belaga. If you are going further than Belaga, and that would mean setting out to trek to Bintulu, it would do no harm to inform the police in Belaga. The trek to Bintulu will take at least three days and, although this is a route I haven't experienced myself, people I've spoken to say it is hard going but manageable.

Bintulu itself has nothing to recommend it. If you are traveling from Sibu consider instead heading straight for Miri from where the Niah Caves are just as accessible.

MIRI

Miri is an important town because it serves as a base for visiting some of the most interesting places in Sarawak. If you were short of time, Kuching and Miri are the only two towns you need visit in order to see most of what is best in Sarawak. Kuching accesses the Skrang River and the Bako National Park and Miri opens up the Niah and Mulu National Parks, as well as the delightful settlement of Bareo up in the highlands near the border with Indonesia's Kalimantan. From Miri you could also make a quick visit to **Brunei Darussalam**, an independent kingdom ruled by the richest man in the world.

GENERAL INFORMATION

Miri is a compact little town with one central block containing the Malaysian Airlines office, ((085) 414144, a number of good hotels and a supermarket. The top hotels, as well as the budget ones, are all within walking distance of this central block and so too is the bus station which is behind the **Pelita Wisma** tower block. In this block you will find bookshops and a couple of mediocre handicraft shops and on the fourth floor the government map department where you can purchase the detailed 1:50,000 scale maps of Sarawak.

There are two experienced and reliable tour companies in Miri offering more or less the same services and packages. Tropical Adventure, ((085) 414503; fax: (085) 414503, is at Lot 228, First floor, Jalan Maju, Beautiful Jade Centre, P.O. Box 1433. As well as standard trips to Niah, Mulu and Bareo, they have the expertise to design a one-off tour for anyone with special requests. The other recommended company is Borneo Overland Services, ((085) 30255; fax: (085) 416424, at 37, Ground floor, Raghavan Building, Brooke Road, P.O. Box 1509. The Plaza Regency Hotel is just next door. Both these companies offer excellent packages to Mulu National Park.

WHERE TO STAY

Top Class
The **Park Hotel**, next to the Pelita Wisma block, is one of the best at $58 for an ordinary double. It is often full, so reservations are useful. The postal address is Jalan Raja, P.O. Box 443, ((085) 414555; fax: 414488. The **Hotel Plaza Regency**, ((085) 413113; fax: (085) 41445, is on Brooke Road, P.O. Box 1323, and charges $60 for a standard double. The rooms are ok, though nothing special. I prefer the Park Hotel because the restaurant is far better. As the top two hotels in town they will both lose out to the new **Holiday Inn**, due to open in 1993, where a standard double will cost at least $75. With hope, the competition might improve the two existing hotels or make them competitive pricewise.

Moderate
The **Gloria Hotel** is also on Brooke Road, P.O. Box 1293, ((085) 416699; fax: (085) 418866 and their doubles start at $46. Across from the Malaysian Airlines office on South Yu Seng Road there are a few middle range hotels all offering clean, modern rooms at around $25. Typical of these is the **Million Inn**, ((085) 415077; fax: (085) 415085, but my first choice would be the **Today Inn** which is tucked behind the Maxim restaurant. There is no coffee house but the rooms are a good value for the money and their rates for overseas calls are very reasonable.

Inexpensive
The hotels in this category are mostly in Jalan China and the surrounding streets. The only problem is that Jalan China also has its fair share of brothels and there is no way of telling the difference just by looking at them from the pavement. The **Tai Tong Lodging House**, ((085) 34072, at N° 26, opposite the Chinese temple at the bottom of the road, is the cheapest at $12, but I persuaded myself to pay an extra $3 and stay at the **Thai Foh Inn**, ((085) 418395, at N° 19. This is fine if you arrive late and plan to leave early. Nearby at N° 7 Kingsway is the **Sarawak Lodging House**, ((085) 413233, often full but with clean rooms at $14. There is also a money changer here, open long after the banks have closed.

WHERE TO EAT

The Park Hotel has two very good restaurants: the **Kokchee** serving Cantonese dishes ($3 to $5 per dish) and the **Park View** providing continental meals. A three course dinner would cost around $35. The special coffee menu is interesting and the wine list has standard wines for around $20. The **Plaza Regency** Hotel has an open-air steamboat restaurant but the setting is not particularly attractive. When the Holiday Inn opens there is bound to be a Chinese restaurant worth a visit.

Outside of the hotels there are a few places offering good food. Near the Gloria Hotel the **Cafe de Hamburg** serves a set dinner for $10 but two people could eat a la carte for $20, not including wine. Next to the Tropical Adventure office, on Jalan Maju, there is an Islamic cafe serving Indian-style food and around the corner near the Bank Simpann National there is the **Restoran Jashimah** with a similar menu. For a good Chinese breakfast of *mien* (rice-noodle) try the **Toto Cafe** opposite the Kentucky Fried Chicken outlet. A breakfast and coffee will cost only a couple of ringgit. The **Maxim** restaurant, on South Yu Seng Road, is very good indeed, serving tasty curries and Chinese dishes at reasonable prices. Many locals consider it the best restaurant in town.

OPPOSITE TOP: Reaching the Niah caves if half the fun. OPPOSITE BOTTOM: A detail of the prehistoric cave paintings to be seen at Niah.

NIAH NATIONAL PARK

This park is most famous for its **caves** in which, some 40 years ago, archaeologists found a treasure-trove of human and cultural remains indicating that the caves were inhabited some 40,000 years earlier. The excavations have now come to an end and all the finds, save one, have been removed to the Sarawak Museum in Kuching. What they couldn't remove from the caves were the hematite rock paintings of coffin ships and skirted dancing figures. These are believed to date back a thousand years and although they have faded the shapes are quite distinguishable. To visit the Painted Cave you need a guide, or a permit, which is obtainable from the park office.

Speleologically speaking, the caves themselves are disappointing and cannot be compared with the splendor of the Mulu Caves. But apart from the wall paintings there is another reason for visiting the caves; the present-day human inhabitants who daily risk their lives to earn a living collecting birds' nests from every available nook and cranny. They balance themselves on bamboo crossbars 60 m (200 ft) above the ground, no safety nets here, and dislodge the nests with 10-m (30-ft) poles with torch lights attached to their ends. The nests contain solidified bird saliva which is highly regarded by the Chinese as a medicinal cure-all. The collectors will sell the nests for $225 to $330 per kilo ($100 to $150 per pound). Make no mistake, this is fatally dangerous work and over a recent three year period over 40 collectors are said to have fallen to their death. The collecting of the nests is supposed to be limited to certain times of the year but in practice it goes on every day. As you walk along the three-kilometer (two-mile) walkway to the cave entrance, as well as giving way to the nest collectors, you are also likely to encounter locals carrying huge bags of guano on their backs. Guano is bat and bird excrement which is sold as a rich fertilizer.

Where to Stay

The National Park has its own accommodation center at the entrance to the park with

bungalows for $22 a night and a room for half that. Cooking facilities are provided so bring your own supplies. If you go during the week during local school term time, there will always be room available. At weekends it is best to make a booking through the Miri office, ((085) 36637), or from Kuching, ((082) 248988.

In Niah town, where the buses stop, there are three unimpressive hotels. The **Yung Hua Hotel**, ((085) 737736, is the best at $13 for an air-conditioned double room. I am not sure why you would stay in town rather than at the park headquarters, because the town has nothing to recommend it unless you are staying at the park and forget to bring provisions with you. There are no shops or restaurants at the park but

there is a supermarket in town where you could buy food and drink.

Getting There

The Niah National Park is located some 120 km (75 miles) southwest of Miri and it is easy to board a bus from Miri that will take you to Niah town. From there it is a M$10 boat ride to the park entrance. The problem is that the last bus back to Miri leaves the park at 1 am and that turns a one-day trip into a mad rush because the journey by road takes at least two hours and from the park entrance it is a good 30-minute walk to the cave entrance. However you have the option of staying a night at the park or hiring a taxi for your return journey. From Miri a taxi will cost $7 straight to the Park entrance but for the return journey you need to ask the park office to phone for a taxi. Alternatively, the boat service will take you back to Niah town where there are plenty of taxis.

Another alternative is to take a tour from one of the Miri tour operators. This makes sense if you only have one day, but if you have time to stay overnight then a tour trip is not necessary. If you are going on your own, do bring a torch with you. The caves are dark and the torch will help you see the tiny figures of the nest collectors perilously perched above you. It is also possible to take a bus from Bintulu to Niah.

ABOVE: Visitors to the Deer cave will be amazed by the multitudes of the bats that fly out of it at dusk.

MULU NATIONAL PARK

The Niah Caves are world famous and yet, archaeology apart, they pale in comparison to the relatively unknown **Mulu Caves**. Indeed, if time is a premium I would suggest jettisoning plans to spend a day or two at Niah and devote the time to Mulu instead.

Physically the caves are stupendous. Sarawak Chamber, though not longest, is capable of holding eight 747 jumbo jets lined nose to tail. Mount Mulu itself, only 2,376 m (7,795 ft), is a naturalist's paradise, although it was first climbed only in 1932 and the National Park opened only in 1985. In the park may be found 170 different orchids, 10 different pitcher plants and 262 species of birds including all eight types of hornbills.

Further on, the Melinau River appears to stop at the face of limestone cliffs. The river, in fact, flows underground into the cave system, the beginning of which is **Clearwater Cave**. Over 60 km (37 miles) in length, only a small part of it is open to visitors as yet, but this is enough to make the day's traveling worthwhile, especially if you have a knowledgeable guide. The other cave open to the public is **Deer Cave**, two kilometers (one-and-a-quarter miles) in length and less than 100 m (328 ft) high. The best time to make this visit is in the late afternoon to catch the wonderful sight of thousands and thousands of bats streaming out at dusk on their hunting expeditions.

Where to Stay

If you are part of an organized trip, the tour company will have arranged accommodation for you, most probably in one of the private resthouses on the other side of the Melinau River to the Park Headquarters. They have their own generators. If you are managing your own way there you must make arrangements at the National Park Office in Miri to stay in one of their resthouses. Bottled gas cookers are available but you need to bring your own food and mineral water. This is best purchased from the supermarket in Miri but if you have the time there are shops in Maraudi. Don't forget to buy a good torch.

Getting There

The bad news is that it takes a day's journey from Miri just to reach the park. First of all you have to reach the small town of Marudi on the Baram River, either by boat for three hours or by plane for 15 minutes. From Maraudi it is a three-hour journey by boat to Long Panai and then another four-hour journey to the park itself. The last 45 minutes take you up the narrow Melinau River to the start of the national park. For the individual traveler, the tricky bit is the last leg of the journey because the cost of the boat depends on the number of passengers, and if no one else was traveling you would be faced with the full $60 charter fee. At the time of writing there is only the one boat from Maraudi that departs for Long Panai, at midday, and if you missed this you would need to stay the night in Maraudi. Accommodation at Maraudi is given in the Maraudi section below.

The good news is that Mulu is open all year round. Information and booking are available from the National Park Office, Section Forest Office, 98000 Miri, ((085) 36637, and this is the same office that handles Niah Park.

An alternative, well worth considering, is a package trip through one of the travel companies in Miri (or through Asian Overland in Kuala Lumpur). They will arrange all travel and accommodation and a typical four-day/three-night tour is $150 per person. after the TRAVELERS' TIPS section.

MARAUDI

Maraudi is not worth visiting in its own right but Malaysian Airlines stops here on the route from Miri to Bareo in the Kelabit Highlands. There is also a regular boat service from Kuala Baram, and this forms part of the route to Mulu Park. You can change money here and there are shops if you forget to buy something in Miri. There is basically just the one main street and it's a 10-minute walk from the airport.

WHERE TO STAY

The best place to stay is the new **Hotel Zola,** Lot 14–15, P.O.Box 271, Maraudi, where decent rooms go for $18 after discount, $4 less if you want to forgo a carpeted floor, ((085) 755311. The **Mulu Air-Cond Inn** is functional and adequate. Rooms are $10, ((085) 755905. Another reasonable place is the **Maryland Hotel**, ((085) 55106; fax: (085) 755333, with rooms from $12 to $15. On the main street there are a couple of eating spots plus an air-conditioned fast-food place that seems wonderful if you have been in the forest for a few days.

BAREO AND THE KELABIT HIGHLANDS

Bareo, sometimes spelled Bario, is home to a Kelabit community set high on a valley floor in the highest inhabited part of Borneo — the 1,127 m (3,700 ft) Kelabit Highlands. While Kelabits are the only inhabitants of Bareo, the surrounding uplands are home to Muruts and Sabahan, and the forest is home to the Penan, now living a semi-nomadic existence in one of the few un-logged parts of Sarawak.

Bareo is different from anywhere else in Sarawak. It is flat and cool and the paddy fields of this agricultural community are spread out in a way that is more reminiscent of Bali than Borneo. The land is especially rich and Bareo has maintained its reputation for producing the best rice in the country. In the morning, before the daily Malaysian Airlines flight arrives, you will see sacks of the rice piled up near the airfield waiting to be taken down to Maraudi. Vegetables and fruit are also grown for the Miri market, and in the past, salt was a valuable produce because of the salt springs in the area. Salt is still collected and an hour's walk to the main salt spring is one way of spending a morning around here. Bareo is very much a self-sufficient community and villagers still organize hunting trips into the forest for fresh meat. In the morning, groups of Penan hunters, tattooed and easily recognizable by their basin haircuts and loincloths, who bring in wild boar meat to sell. If you stay here and have a meal you can be sure of the most organic ingredients because the farmers use no chemical fertilizers or sprays and the meat will be fresh from the jungle.

If you do come to Bareo, and I highly recommend it, do try to plan for it by trying to bring with you a copy of Tom Harrison's *The World Within*. Toward the end of World War II, Tom Harrison and seven other men were dropped in here by the Australian air force, their mission being to organize local resistance to the Japanese. Harrison was intensely interested in the culture of the Kelabits and his book is a unique mixture of military memoirs and anthropology. He was able to observe and study the Kelabits before their whole lifestyle was transformed by the Christian missionaries who felt obliged to disapprove of so many of their traditions, beliefs and practices. Harrison lived in Bareo for some time (the airfield you land on was built by his team) and was deeply respected by the people. I witnessed this myself when visiting a longhouse near the salt spring, for pinned to the wall was an old black-and-white photograph of Harrison, next to a color print of the Blessed Virgin. The Kelabits are now nearly all Christians, although many of them still have stretched earlobes and tattoos.

Another noticeable feature about Bareo is the presence of the Malaysian army here. They have a camp on the other side of the airfield and the odd group of soldiers moving around, with and without their weapons, is a common enough sight. This goes back to the early 1960s when Indonesia was vigorously pursuing its claim to Sarawak, and British and Gurkha troops were stationed in the Highlands. This threat is now a thing of the past and one wonders if the army now is more concerned with the protest movement against the logging of the forests. This is not far from the area where Bruno Manser lived with the Penan people for some time, evading numerous attempts to capture him and very successfully bringing the plight of these people onto the world stage. A fascinating book is available, *The Battle for Sarawak's Forests*, that records in words and pictures the struggle of the native people who depend on the forest for their food and shelter.

WHAT TO SEE

First and foremost Bareo is a place to unwind and relax, taking strolls around the countryside and observing the way of life of the farmer villagers. There are a number of treks available. A three-hour trek takes you to **Pa'Berang**, a Penan settlement where accommodation could be arranged at a longhouse. Walking to the salt spring has already been mentioned and this trek could take in the Batu Narit rock carving at **Pa'Umor**. **Pa Lungan** is another interesting four-hour trip. Nearby hills can be climbed without too much effort and they afford terrific views of the countryside around Bareo.

The longer treks offer fascinating possibilities. Two days would bring you to the Indonesian border with Kalimantan and this can now easily be crossed. A night could be spent in Indonesia before returning to Malaysia, or you could fly out from Ba Kelanan. From Bareo you could also set out to climb **Gunung Murud**, 2,422 m (7,946 ft), first climbed in 1922 by Mjoberg with a team of 70 porters. This would take about a week, as would the return trip to Batu Lawi, 2,043 m (6,703 ft), not a climb for the inexperienced. Full details, again, in the Briggs book. What is within anyone's capabilities, though it might sound audacious, is to organize a four-day trip into **Pa Tik** and spend the time with the semi-nomadic Penan people. All you would need to bring with you is a spirit of adventure and cans of food and dried soup. The Penans were never head-hunters and have lived in the forest for centuries until the chain-saw massacre, 240,000 hectares (590,000 acres) of their jungle being logged annually, began forcing them to "settle" in longhouses.

Reliable guides for any of the treks just mentioned can be arranged through the tour companies in Miri or directly through Peter Matu (Kelabit Highlands, 98050 Baram, Bareo, East Malaysia) in Bareo. Guides cost about $12 a day and accommodation would be in longhouses along the way. Not just an adventure but an education too. The owner of the resthouse in Bareo can also arrange trips and guides.

WHERE TO STAY

In Bareo itself there is only one official resthouse, the **Bareo Airtel Lodge**, just next‘ to the airstrip. A three-bed room is $6 regard-

less of the number of people using it and meals are available at $2. The visitors' book makes for interesting reading and could give you a few ideas on how to spend your time. At the actual airstrip there is a coffee shop serving drinks and simple food. All other accommodation will be at longhouses, either Kelabit or Penan, and you should think of paying $4 or $5 a night for your lodging and breakfast.

GETTING THERE

Getting there is indeed half the fun. Bareo is only accessible by air on the rural service offered by Malaysian Airlines, and a Twin Otter flies in from Miri, and returns the same day, on a daily basis. The plane stops at Maraudi so you could join it there. The flight takes 40 minutes, and for the first half of the journey from Miri all you will see, trickling through the forest canopy below, is a network of pathways created by the logging companies for their lorries as they systematically cut down the trees. The trees you do see are not part of the original rain forest. Around Bareo itself though, the loggers have been kept at bay and the lorry paths are no longer seen.

Until the new airstrip is completed, there can be a problem with the existing short, grass airstrip which prohibits landing if there is low cloud or continuous rain. Flights can be canceled and the 19-seater Twin Otter can easily fill up. So make reservations as far in advance as possible. I was once caught in Bareo this way, and there were two alternatives: trek for two full days to Ba Kelalan where flights to Miri are rarely canceled, or negotiate a place with one of the private air charter companies that fly produce in and out of Bareo. They charged me the same rate as Malaysian Airlines.

Permits are required for any visit to Bareo and the Highlands and these are available from the Resident's Office in Miri.

OPPOSITE TOP: All manner of people, goods and animals pass through Bareo airstrip in a day. OPPOSITE BOTTOM: These express boats hurtle through the water dodging each other as well as the log barges and river debris.

Sabah

LAND BELOW THE WIND

Sabah is Malaysia's largest state. Its center-piece, for the visitor, is Mount Kinabalu and as the peak requires no special skills to climb it, there are a variety of outdoor experiences on offer and in which the visual splendors of southeast Asia's highest mountain can be enjoyed.

Near the town of **Sandakan** there is an amazing orangutan settlement where the animals are nurtured and protected. Also near Sandakan you can visit a group of islands where endangered turtles lay eggs and are guarded by Malaysian soldiers with M-16 machine-guns.

Kota Kinabalu, the capital, is pleasant enough and close to some particularly lovely islands that form Kinabalu National Park. The towns of Tenom and Beaufort also possess a fair amount of charm. The appeal of Sabah, however, is not found in its cities and towns, where there is really very little to do or see, but in its natural environments. Sabah is well worth visiting because of its charming countryside, excellent nature reserves and challenging mountains, but extensive travel can be very costly as Sabah is, by far, the most expensive state in Malaysia. Not all the roads are comfortable to travel on and Malaysian Airlines flights become indispensable. If you want to see more of Sabah, the tour companies mentioned below offer various trips to the interior, in addition to the more regular trips to Mt Kinabalu and Sandakan.

BACKGROUND

Before the Europeans came, Sabah was loosely attached to Brunei. Strangely enough, it was an American by the name of Moses who first obtained trading rights from the Sultan of Brunei and these rights passed through various hands before ending up with an Englishman who established the British North Borneo Company in 1881. When independence was granted in 1963, there were strong objections from both Indonesia and the Philippines, but eventually these were settled. Any instability in Sabah today originates from Malaysia's internal politics. The recent discovery of natural oil off Sabah's coasts has strengthened the calls of some local politicos for more financial and political autonomy.

The largest ethnic group in Sabah is that of the Kadazans, an agrarian people subdivided into the Tuaran Lotud, the Tempasuk Dusuns and the Rungus. The Bajaus, originally from the Philippines, settled in the northern coastal region. The jungle people of Sabah are the Muruts. There has also been a long history of intermarriage between these groups and the Chinese, Filipinos and

Indonesians, and what you see in Sabah today is a mixture of all these races and tribes.

KOTA KINABALU

Planes to Kota Kinabalu, the capital of Sabah, depart from Kuala Lumpur, Kuching, Miri and Singapore. Kota Kinabalu is the starting point from which one may set off for Kinabalu National Park and all inland destinations.

OPPOSITE TOP and BOTTOM: Giant rainforest trees form a dense cover on the slopes of Mount Kinabalu. ABOVE: An orangutan, released from captivity, learns jungle survival techniques from a ranger at Sepilok Orangutan sanctuary.

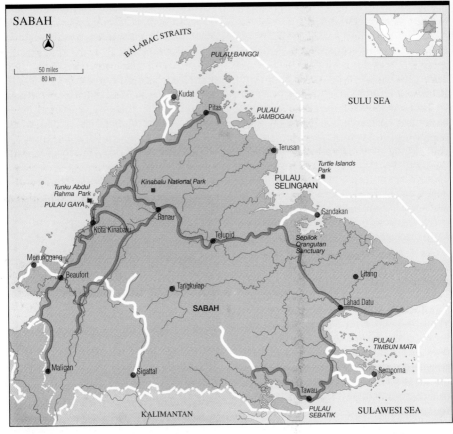

GENERAL INFORMATION

There is a tourist office at the airport but the main State Tourist Information Centre is at N° 51 Jalan Gaya, ℂ (088) 219310. It is a 10-minute walk from the Hyatt Hotel and the staff is helpful and informative. The Tourist Development Corporation of Malaysia also has an office on the ground floor of the Wing On Life Building in Jalan Sagunting, ℂ (088) 211732, . If you are planning to visit Kinabalu National Park, the Parks Office is in the Sinsuran Complex on Jalan Tun Fuad Stephens, ℂ (088) 211585. If you are planning to visit Sandakan, consider going by air, as the journey by road takes eight hours. The Malaysian Airlines number is ℂ (088) 240560.

The minibus station for Kinabalu, Beaufort or Sandakan is at the town *padang*.

A knowledgeable tour company in Kota Kinabalu is Popular Express Travel, ℂ (088) 214692, N° 33 Jalan Tugu Kampung Air. This is out near the Centrepoint shopping complex but it also has a desk at the Tanjung Aru Beach Hotel. Next to the Hyatt can be found Coral Island Cruises, ℂ (088) 223490, if you are interested in an organized trip to the islands or night fishing. Api Tours, Lot 49, Bandaran Berjaya, P.O. Box 12853, ℂ (088) 221230, is a big tour company offering all sorts of tours within Sabah, including white-water rafting on the Padas River, and they have an office at the airport as well.

WHAT TO SEE

There is not a lot to see and do in the town itself apart from making arrangements for onward travel to Kinabalu, Sandakan and maybe Beaufort and Tenom.

However, the **Sabah Museum** is worth visiting. The outside is a stylized longhouse and inside there are interesting displays of local culture. Near the museum is the **State Mosque**, open to visitors, providing that they remove their shoes. Both the museum and the mosque are a short taxi or bus ride from the center of town. The bus runs along Jalan Tunku Abdul Rahman.

The town's newest and biggest shopping center is **Centrepoint**. There is a Yaohan department store here, a few small handicraft shops and a comfortable food center on the bottom level. If you are shopping for souvenirs or presents, there are a few handicraft shops in the area near the Hyatt Hotel, and in the hotel itself there is a fair bookshop if you want something on local history or anthropology. Tunku Abdul Rahman Park, the most interesting place to see near Kota Kinabalu, requires just a 20-minute journey by boat.

Tunku Abdul Rahman Park

The islands off the coast of Kota Kinabalu form the **Tunku Abdul Rahman Park** and they are a stunning sight from the air. The surrounding turquoise water, the coral and the white beaches are ideal for snorkeling or a day out with a picnic, and two of the islands provide accommodation. It is easy to reach the islands from the jetty behind the Hyatt Hotel, and the return fare is less than $5.

If you are staying at the Tanjung Aru Beach Hotel there are various day trips available, including a glass-bottom boat cruise over the shallow reefs. A marina next to the hotel hires snorkeling equipment and arranges scuba diving courses.

Gaya Island is the largest of the islands and has many secluded beaches. From Camp Bay on the south of the island there are 21 km (13 miles) of forest trails. Bring a pair of binoculars if you like bird-watching. **Mamutik Island** and **Manukan Island** both offer basic wooden chalets that sleep four and cost from $50 to $75. Manukan is the larger of the two and has more facilities, including a restaurant. Inquiries and reservations should be made at the National Park Headquarters in Kota Kinabalu, ((088) 211652/211585. This office also handles arrangements for Kinabalu National Park.

The top hotel in town is the **Hyatt** in the center of town at Jalan Datuk Salleh Sulong, ((088) 221234; fax: (088) 225972. A standard double is $100. For beach lovers, there is the **Tanjung Aru Beach Hotel**, 88999 Kota Kinabalu, ((088) 58711; fax: (088) 217155. It is a bit pricier than the Hyatt, but offers a whole range of water sports. Back in town, the **Hotel Shangri-La**, ((088) 212800; fax: (088) 212078, has doubles for

around $75 and is the best hotel after the Hyatt.

The **Nan Xing**, ((088) 239388; fax: (088) 233778, is on the central Jalan Haji Saman. This is a good Chinese hotel offering most of the essential services provided by international hotels but only charges $40 for a doubles. The Cantonese restaurant here is also worth eating at. In the same price range and on the same road is the **Hotel Capitol**, at N° 23 Jalan Haji Saman, ((088) 231999; fax: (088) 237222.

ABOVE: Houses built on stilts teeter precariously over the sea at Pulau Gaya.

145

Ang's Hotel is a well established place at N° 28 Jalan Bakau, ℂ (088) 234999; fax: (088) 217867, and the rooms here are $24.

Another old regular is the **Sabah Inn**, ℂ (088) 53322, at N° 25 Jalan Pantai, but I would much prefer the **Town Inn**, at N° 31–33 Jalan Pantai, ℂ (088) 225823; fax: (088) 217762. It is in the same block as the Sabah Inn but you have to go round the back to find the entrance. It is worth the trouble because it is very clean, attractive and modern, and has rooms at $25. A few rooms for less than $20 can be found in the Segama Complex, located near the Hyatt, and they are all much the same. The **Hotel New Sabah** in Block A, ℂ (088) 235875, is typical.

The above is only a selection based on my personal experience, and Kota Kinabalu is overflowing with hotels and offers a wide choice. The Sabah Hotels Association annually publishes an informative list, available from the tourist office at the airport or in town, with details of all the hotels.

WHERE TO EAT

There is a large variety of food choices in Kota Kinabalu. The two international hotels have their own weste rn and Asian restaurants, and the **Nan Xing Hotel** has a good Cantonese restaurant. At the Hyatt, the **Phoenix Court** serves a typically mixed Sichuan and Cantonese menu, and the **Semporna Grill** is good for seafood. In Wisma Merdeka on the second floor there is the Japanese **Azuma** restaurant, ℂ (088) 212225, and on the fourth floor of the Gaya Centre, **Jaws Seafood** restaurant does delicious Thai-Chinese food, ℂ (088) 236006. There is also a Korean restaurant, **Korea House,** ℂ (088) 58127, that should be reasonable.

The coffee house at the **Capitol** offers breakfast for $3 and reasonable local and western meals for around $5. Next to the Capitol is a fast-food place called **Fat Cat**, acceptable for an inexpensive western breakfast, though the main dishes are tasteless.

The bottom level of the **Centrepoint** complex is devoted mostly to food outlets, and there is a range of informal places offering western fast food, and Malay and Indian dishes at very reasonable prices.

GETTING THERE

Malaysian Airlines flies from Kuala Lumpur and JohoreBahru in peninsular Malaysia and from Kuching, Sibu and Miri in Sarawak, as well as direct from Singapore. If you are traveling from Singapore, money can be saved by going from JohoreBahru instead of Changi, and Malaysian Airlines runs a bus from the Novotel Inn hotel in Singapore, straight to the airport outside Johore Bahru.

Malaysian Airlines and Cathay Pacific also fly from Hong Kong to Kota Kinabalu, as do Malaysian Airlines and Philippine Airlines from Manila. Flights are also available to and from Bandar Seri Begawan (Brunei), Seoul, Taipei and Tokyo. The international airport at Kota Kinabalu is well organized: there is a coupon system for the taxi ride into town as well as a tourist office from which you can book a hotel room and collect information and maps.

ABOVE: Porters carrying the night's food up to the resthouse on Mount Kinabalu.
OPPOSITE: The view from St. John's peak, Mount Kinabalu, best seen at dawn when the sun rises on a landscape of wind whipped rock.

BEAUFORT AND TENOM

The train to Beaufort and Tenom runs through the dense jungle, parallel to the banks of the Padas River. It starts at Kota Kinabalu, goes to Tanjung Aru, then to Tenom in the interior. It follows the coast as far as Beaufort and then turns inland across the Crocker range. The most scenic part of the rail journey is from Beaufort to Tenom. You can make a booking at the Tanjung Aru station, ℂ (088) 52536.

KINABALU NATIONAL PARK

The park covers an area of 754 sq km (291 sq miles). And Mount Kinabalu, the highest peak between the Himalayas and New Guinea, towers above at 4,101 m (13,455 ft). Only a small percentage of visitors to the park climb the mountain, and it is worth giving it a try. The climb is, surprisingly, not terribly difficult. Around the park headquarters there is and incredible variety of exotic plants and flowers. Here you will

At Tenom there is the **Orchid Centre** and if you are interested you should try and ring beforehand, ℂ (087) 735661, to see if a guide can be arranged. Tours are also available from tour companies in Kota Kinabalu. Tour companies often suggest you travel past Tenom to **Keningau** and **Tambunan** but there really isn't much of interest. Most of the forests have been logged.

WHERE TO STAY

There is not much choice. The best in Tenom is the **Hotel Tenom**, P.O. Box 198, ℂ (087) 736378, and in Beaufort the **Hotel Beaufort**, ℂ (088) 211911. Rooms are from $7 to $12.

find the largest flower in the world, the *Rafflesia*, a red flower up to one meter (three feet) in diameter and weighing up to two kilograms (four-and-a-half pounds), as many as 26 different rhododendrons, and 1,200 species of orchid. There are also the **Poring Hot Springs** on the southern park boundary.

WHERE TO STAY

All accommodation must be reserved in advance through the park office in Kota Kinabalu. If you are planning your trip from abroad, you should write, as far in advance as possible, to Sabah Parks, P.O. Box 10626, 88806 Kota Kinabalu, Sabah. ℂ (088) 211585.

Busy times are the school holidays in April, and July through August.

There is a range of rooms and chalets to suit most budgets: a bunk bed in a hostel is $3, a twin-bed cabin is $22, a deluxe cabin $37 and VIP chalets with a kitchen for just under under $100. If you are climbing the mountain, arrangements for accommodation at the overnight huts can be made. Cabins are also available at Poring Hot Springs for $7 per person.

Outside of the park, accommodation is available at **Hotel Perkasa**, about four kilometers (nearly two-and-a-half miles) past the park entrance on the main road to Ranau. The postal address for this hotel is W.D.T. 11, 89309 Ranau, ((088) 80316; fax: (088) 889101. Room rates go from $40 to $80, and a shuttle bus runs between the hotel and the park. New places are being built in the vicinity of the park, so if the park accommodation is full, it would be worth checking with the Tourist Office in Kota Kinabalu.

WHERE TO EAT

There are two restaurants at the park headquarters that serve local and western dishes. The food is adequate, though it might be a good idea to supplement this with some basic provisions from Kota Kinabalu. There is a shop selling some items of food, but if you are going to spend two days climbing the mountain, stock up in Kota Kinabalu with as much as you can carry.

CLIMBING MT KINABALU

If at all possible, you should set out to reach the top. No special equipment or training is necessary, although you should be reasonably fit.

Getting to the top is a terrific feeling but this need not be a do-or-die effort. The trail starts at 1,830 m (6,000 ft) and goes uphill for eight kilometers (five miles) to the summit, but there are a number of resting spots and huts with bunk beds at 3,300 m (11,000 ft), and one hour further up at 3,800 m (12,000 ft). At either of these places you may rest overnight and rise very early the next morning to reach the top before the clouds

set in. At the first resthouse, Laban Rata, there is a restaurant.

On the way up you will pass different types of vegetation and you are bound to see the amazing insect-trapping pitcher plants. The journey upwards goes from rain forest through to slightly different vegetation as you meet the cloud layer, and then passes through an area of dwarfed and stunted trees clinging to tiny pockets of soil in the cracks in the rock face. At around this level, the oxygen gets thinner. The last leg of the journey begins the next morning in the dark. Follow the ropes up the rock face with the aid of a torch and, with hope, a good moon. When dawn comes you will be on bare granite, well above the tree line, and the summit beckons. At the peak the view is breathtaking. Look across at the black depths of Low's Gully, 1,000 m (3,280 ft) down. If you descend quickly, you can be back in the park headquarters by the afternoon. A trip to the **Poring Hot Springs**, 43 km (27 miles) away, will help relieve any muscle aches. Don't forget to collect your official document that certifies you reached the top. This records the name of the guide who went with you. Guides are compulsory but there is talk of changing this rule, though they are often very helpful, especially for the beginning of the last leg of the journey in the dark.

Bring some warm clothing with you. Toward the top the air is thin and a pair of gloves and a scarf are a great help. It is very cold early in the morning and a sudden downpour of rain may make it essential to carry some rain gear and/or an extra set of clothes. Sleeping bags can be hired from the park if you don't have your own.

GETTING THERE

From Kota Kinabalu the journey takes a couple of hours and it is best to leave early in the morning when there are plenty of minibuses leaving the padang area. You could also hire a taxi direct from Kota Kinabalu, or even from the airport. Expect to pay around $35, depending on your bargaining skills and whether the taxi is taking anyone else part of the way. The big hotels and tour companies offer packages that arrange everything for you.

SANDAKAN

BACKGROUND

This town, 386 km (240 miles) from Kota Kinabalu on Sabah's east coast, was once the capital of North Borneo. Toward the end of World War II it was the starting point for a forced march of thousands of allied prisoners of war. Only a handful of prisoners escaped with their lives after mass executions near Ranau. Today it is a thriving commercial center, despite, or perhaps due to, the total depletion of the area's forests. Most visitors fly in from Kota Kinabalu to visit the orangutan settlement and the turtle islands.

GENERAL INFORMATION

Independent travelers will need to make a visit to the East Coast Parks, P.O. Box 768, Sandakan, ((089) 273453, to make a booking for the Turtle Islands and inquire about a speedboat there and back.

It is also worth checking with S.I. Tours, ((089) 219717 or 214615, to compare their rates. They also handle trips out to the orangutan sanctuary.

WHERE TO STAY

The place to stay in Sandakan will be the **Ramada Renaissance** when it opens in early 1992. The pre-opening sales office is KM1, Jalan Utara, 90007 Sandakan, ((089) 213299; fax: (089) 271271 and Ramada Worldwide has an office in Kuala Lumpur, ((03) 241-4081; fax: (03) 242-1493. You can expect room rates to be in the international price range, i.e. at least $75 for a standard double. The **Hotel City View** is the best hotel at the time of writing and if you are just staying overnight, it has a lot to recommend it. It is situated in the main road, Lot 1, Block 23, 3rd Avenue, P.O Box 624, 90007 Sandakan, ((089) 271-1122; fax: (089) 273115. A double goes for $60 but, as their card states that "a discount rate of 35 percent will be given to our valuable room guests." The rooms are small but provide most of the essential services you are likely to require for a short stay.

If you are staying longer and would benefit from a pool, gymnasium, golf, tennis or a business center, then the Ramada Renaissance is a better bet. If you want to stay below $25 the best place is the **Malaysia Hotel**, at N° 32, 2nd Avenue, P.O. Box 214, ((089) 218322, followed by the **Hung Wing Hotel** at Lot 4, 3rd Avenue, ((089) 218957/218855.

WHERE TO EAT

A pleasant meal can be enjoyed at the **Perwira Restaurant** for about $15 for two.

The restaurant is a little way out of town, too far to walk but worth the short taxi ride. It is next to the Hotel Rama, ((089) 273222, which is not recommended unless you arrive late and nothing else is available. If you are staying in town, the **Hotel City View** is fine for a light meal, and round the back near the market there are some Muslim coffee shops serving food. Both the **Restoran Habeeb** and the **Restoran Buhari** serve good food for two for around $4.

Boy in traditional Malay costume, East Malaysia.

SEPILOK ORANGUTAN SANCTUARY

Now an endangered species because of the destruction of its natural habitat, the result of the systematic logging of the forests, orangutans captured in logging camps or kept illegally as pets are brought to the sanctuary for rehabilitation. Since its foundation in 1964 over 100 apes have been successfully released back into the forest.

A visit to the sanctuary is a memorable experience and quite different from viewing

them in a zoo. Adult males weigh up to 100 kg (220 lb), stand about a meter (just over three feet) tall, and despite their dangling arms they bear an uncanny resemblance to humans. Their faces display personality and there are many stories of their gentle and playful ways. Many female orangutans who have spent some time in rehabilitation at the center return to the sanctuary from the forest when about to give birth.

The sanctuary is 30 minutes by car from Sandakan. In town, the best place for taxis, and the occasional bus that goes there, is around the waterfront near the fruit and vegetable market. Package trips can be organized from Kota Kinabalu or in

Sandakan. You should plan to visit the sanctuary in the morning to catch the feeding sessions.

TURTLE ISLANDS PARK

The park is made up of three islands located some 40 km (25 miles) north of Sandakan and close to the Philippines, whose islands can be seen in the distance.

Every night of the year, Green and Hawksbill turtles come ashore to lay their eggs and you are virtually guaran-

teed a sighting. Park staff live on the islands and each night they are engaged in the task of tagging new arrivals, collecting their eggs and transplanting them to the protected hatcheries where they are safe from human and animal predators.

A visit to the park is a wonderful experience not just for the opportunity of seeing the turtles lumbering ashore and laying their eggs, but also for the equally magical sight of tiny turtles hatching from the protected eggs and later being released into the sea.

You will be told when the turtles have arrived, usually around nine or ten at night, and a warden will escort you to the beach where you can observe the egg-laying at close quarters. Later you can help the wardens collect the newborn turtles that are emerging in the hatchery. Often, some of them will find a way through the wire netting and you'll have to scamper off trying to catch them. When the buckets are full of hundreds of little turtles and you return to the beach, where they are tumbled onto the sand.

Accommodation is available on **Pulau Selingaan** in comfortable chalets for $10 a night, and there is a small restaurant serving

meals. Reaching the island now takes less than an hour in a 100-horsepower speedboat, but the price is high at $90 for the return trip. If you are lucky, a boat will be going anyway, and an extra place can be arranged for around $25. A package trip, arranged in Kota Kinabalu or Sandakan, reflects this level of pricing. The only consolation is that perhaps the price of getting there actually helps to keep the turtles relatively undisturbed. The creatures are very sensitive and the slightest noise can cause them to negotiate a cumbersome u-turn on the sand before returning to the sea. It is no surprise that they are fast disappearing from peninsular Malaysia's east coast.

Sabah

SIPADAN ISLAND

This island lies off the small coastal town of **Semporna** and is an absolute must if you are interested in scuba diving. The diving season is mid-February through mid-December. The reefs on the edge of the 600 m (1,960 ft) drop-off are magical, and sighting 10 turtles on one dive is not at all uncommon. **Borneo Divers** are the undisputed operators and all inquiries should be directed to them at Rooms 401–404, Fourth

floor, Wisma Sabah, Kota Kinabalu, ((088) 222226; fax: (088) 2211550. A complete package, including airfare from Kota Kinabalu and all accommodation and food, would be $550 for three days/two nights. For anyone over the age of twelve who can swim well, there are introductory courses.

In Semporna, the best place to stay is the **Dragon Inn**, P.O. Box 6, 91307, Semporna, ((089) 781088, where rooms average $40.

OPPOSITE LEFT: Giant insectivorous pitcher plants abound on the slopes of Mount Kinabalu. OPPOSITE RIGHT: The turtle's long crawl ashore ends as her eggs are carefully collected. ABOVE LEFT: Snorkelling off the coast of Sandakan, Sabah. ABOVE RIGHT: A young inhabitant of Pulau Gaya.

Singapore

BACKGROUND

Singapura is the Malay word for this island and it comes from a Sanskrit word meaning Lion City. Not that lions are known to inhabit this part of Southeast Asia for when the Englishman Raffles landed here in 1819 the island was inhabited by only a few Malay fisherman. Raffles, however, saw the potential of the deep and well-sheltered harbor, and he pulled a fast one by exploiting a local dispute about ownership of the island. Raffles set up a sultan of Johore who was more than willing to let the East India Company establish a trading post in return for an annual payoff. Immigrants were welcomed and within decades Singapore was a thriving port gaining the kind of reputation that ensured commercial success. Such a reputation has continued up to the present day, as will be immediately noticeable the moment you arrive at the city's airport. The impact is not quite so dramatic if you arrive by train or coach across the causeway from Malaysia, but it won't be long before you notice the difference.

GENERAL INFORMATION

For tourist information, Singapore is one of the most efficient spots in the world. Hotels abound with free leaflets and magazines which carry useful information about the city. *Citymag* is the best tourist magazine and, at the time of writing, is still free of charge. *The Secret Food Map of Singapore* is a map that makes you want to go out and hunt down their recommendations, but don't be surprised if a restaurant doesn't seem to be where it is supposed to be, as the map is getting a little outdated. The Singapore Tourist Information Board has two offices, one at N° 01–19 Raffles City Shopping Centre, ((65) 330-0431 or 330-0432, open until 6 pm, and the other at Scotts Shopping Centre, ((65) 738-3778, open till 9:30 pm. The Airport also has many racks of leaflets for you to pick up on your way through, as well as a free hotel booking service. Most of the big hotels have agents handling city tours and short trips to JohoreBahru and the Indonesian island of Batam. Travel agents are ubiquitous in the

Orchard Road plazas but one worth drawing your attention to is the Malaysia and Singapore Travel Centre, ((65) 737-8877. They know their stuff and deserve credit for establishing the Battlefields of World War II tour.

Check the TELEPHONES section in TRAVELERS' TIPS for useful Singapore numbers.

WHAT TO SEE

Most of Singapore looks as if it was built in the last 25 years, however, a few places of

interest have survived the ravages of modernization and more recently places in the last stages of decay have been saved due to a belated conservation effort. Nearly all the districts mentioned below have countless eating possibilities, so check the WHERE TO EAT section if you are going to combine your sightseeing with a meal in the same area.

CHINATOWN

Much reduced in size but holding its own, Chinatown finally came to the attention of

OPPOSITE: Sir Stamford Raffles broods over the city that he founded. ABOVE: A shophouse in Singapore's Chinatown.

the government as a major potential tourist attraction and now what remains is safe from the developers, if not safe from the kitsch merchants. It has undergone a massive cleanup in recent years but the essential nature of the area is intact and men who make lion heads for lion dances still sit out on the street in the cool of the evening, fortune tellers still make a living along South Bridge Road and temple shops keep up with the times by selling paper VCRs and washing machines to be burnt and so sent up to the heavens for one's ancestors.

What follows is a suggested walk taking you through the most authentic and interesting part of Chinatown, although it is by no means and exhaustive tour.

Start from the **Furama Hotel** and walk toward the People's Park Complex. At the junction of Cross Street is the old **Customs Building** built in the thirties which is quite an imposing sight. Opposite is the old Great Southern Hotel. It was the first hotel in Singapore to have a lift and it held cabarets in the tea garden on the roof. Next door is the **Majestic Theatre**, originally built to house Cantonese operas but later converted to the cinema it is today. Continuing along New Bridge Street, take the next left turn, **Mosque Street**, which has not yet been tidied up and marks an abrupt change from the bustle and proportions of New Bridge Street. Here you will see the amazing ability of plants in the region to find a sprouting place absolutely anywhere. One gets the feeling with some of these buildings that if the plants were taken down the structures that support them would crumble away to

nothing. At night the curious or voyeuristic can see wonderful cameos of human life, very different from the Western norm, by peeking up into the second-story windows. This street was populated by the Hakka clan. Originally built as stables, many of the buildings on here seem to be on their last legs. Many of the wooden staircases leading to the upper stories look barely surmountable. At the end of Mosque Street turn right into **South Bridge Street** where you will come across the **Jamae Mosque**, built in the 1830s. If you would like to go in, please remember to remove your shoes first. Further along is **Pagoda Street**, a one-time haunt of opium smokers, many of whom were coolies, near slave laborers, brought into Singapore to work on the river. Further along is the **Sri Mariammam Temple**, open till eight in the evening, where the name of the first Indian immigrant to Singapore in 1819 has been recorded in stone. Continue along South Bridge Road to **Smith Street** on which, it is said, 25 brothels operated in 1901. Cross the road and go up **Ann Siang Road** where you will find a shop making Lion Dance heads and, opposite that, a temple shop selling all the paraphernalia one's newly departed relatives might need in the afterlife, all made out of paper. Walk back down South Bridge Road and back to Smith Street where, when in season, the pervasive aroma of durians will greet you. If you're feeling daring you could even buy one and try it. It is reputed to be a very powerful aphrodisiac. This road will bring you back to **Eu Tong Street** where in the evening you can have your fortune told.

TANJONG PAGAR

The area of Tanjong Pagar includes **Neil Road**, **Tanjong Pagar Road**, and the smaller roads between them. At one time this whole area was a huge nutmeg plantation but later became a major road from the docks at the top of the road to the warehouses along the Singapore River. On the corner of the two roads is the old **Rickshaw Station**, which once had 10,000 rickshaws and their human beasts of burden hanging about round it, now a restaurant. Walk up Tanjong Pagar Road and take in the vista of the renovated shop houses. The graceful houses on one side of the road have been restored to their original grandeur, while those on the other side await renovation. Go back through **Duxton Road** and browse around the many craft and artifact shops here. Genteel pubs and restaurants are easy to find in an area that, as recently as the 1950s, housed opium dens and gangsters. Well worth visiting is the **Tea Chapter** at N° 9A–9B Neil Road, a tea shop serving Chinese tea in the traditional manner in a pleasant atmosphere.

luggage shops along the road cater mostly to visitors from India who buy things here which would be expensive or unavailable in their own country. This area is best seen either early morning when you can enjoy a wonderful South Indian breakfast, or later in the evening when the area becomes crowded and the temples are busy.

You should start your visit to **Serangoon Road**, nicknamed **Little India**, at its junction with Bukit Timah Road. Buses that will take you here are N° 64, N° 65, N° 92, N° 111 or N° 139. The market at the top of the road is

SERANGOON ROAD (LITTLE INDIA)

On a busy night, the chaos of New Dehli or Bombay is almost palpable. Crowds gather around the temples or on street corners while fortune tellers and their parrots linger and garland makers hawk wares used for religious services, weddings and festivals. Shops also have catalogues of photographs from which to choose garlands, and prices for these braids of *margosas* and jasmines run into hundreds of dollars. From the temples along the road a great cacophony of sound emerges. Shops sell everything from gold jewelry to garish sari material to clay oil lamps and huge boxes of spices. The many

mildly interesting and upper-levels stalls sell standard Singaporean clothes or cloth. You may find interesting shops or restaurants on several of the side streets. **Racecourse Road** has a string of tasty and inexpensive restaurants. Back on Serangoon Road is **Sri Srinvasa Perumal Temple**. The site for this temple was acquired in the nineteenth century but most of the outlandish exterior was built after 1960. The temple is dedicated to the Hindu god, Vishnu. Inside,

OPPOSITE: Still handmade in Chinatown, dragons are very much a part of the Chinese New Year celebrations. ABOVE LEFT: Souvenirs at prices to suit all pockets color the streets in Chinatown. ABOVE RIGHT: Celebrating the Chinese New Year in Chinatown.

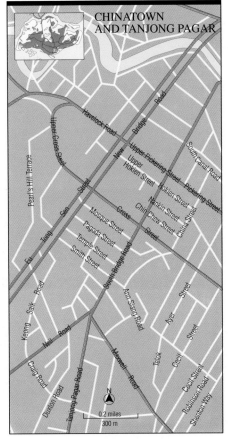

CHINATOWN
AND TANJONG PAGAR

long hair, smokes a surreptitious cigarette while waiting for the next devotee.

Further down Serangoon Road is **Desker Road**, a well established red light area frequented by locals. Sightseers and interested parties should peer down the alley that runs down the back. Further down Serangoon Road still is the **Veeramaknaliamman Temple** dedicated to Shiva, another manifestation of the one god of Hinduism. It is from this temple that the annual *Thaipusam* festival begins, where penitent sinners skewer themselves with steel rods and carry enormously heavy decorated weights which are attached to their body with more skewers.

You should time your trip to Serangoon Road to coincide with a meal time. Great Indian food can be found in Singapore and much of it is in and around Serangoon Road.

SENTOSA

Originally an island military base, Sentosa is now being marketed as a leisure center and is indeed about to burgeon with new multi-million dollar projects including several five-star hotels. A walkway is in the process of being built which will provide a pedestrian link with the mainland, but until that is ready, the island is approached by ferry from the **World Trade Centre** or by cable car from Mount Faber, which is nearby. Sentosa can certainly offer a day off from the traffic and noise of the city. On weekdays in particular, Sentosa is a little haven of peace and good taste and a positive heaven for nature lovers. Corridors of vegetation are being carefully preserved across the island and several areas are kept undeveloped, assuring visitors an enormous range of birdlife visible, with some patience, from any of the paths or exhibitions there. The Nature Walk will reveal to the visitor two species of carnivorous pitcher plants and secondary rain forest plants. There are also small areas of mangrove swamp with the associated wildlife.

worshipers buy offerings of coconuts or bananas which they take to the Brahmin priest at one of the smaller sanctums inside, who then blesses the devotee with ash, and red dye. The fruit represents vasanas, the desires of man and its offering symbolizes an attempt to divest oneself of desire, thus taking an essential step toward self-fulfillment. Vishnu followers are given a V-shaped mark on their forehead rather than the more usual red spot. After having their offerings accepted the worshiper circumambulates within. Indian temples, and this one particularly, are very unlike a place of worship that western tourists might be accustomed to. They are noisy and seemingly irreverent places, with children running around, cars parked in the precincts, lounging brahmins, and an odd mix of erotic and outlandish deities. A digital clock is suspended above an elephant-headed, many armed figure; the brahmin, in a white sarong and with

If nature isn't your cup of tea, there is still much to see there, including a coralarium, the undersea world, an exhibition of boats, a butterfly park, a roller skating rink, a lagoon with water sports, and well presented remains of the military fortifications of World War II. In the evening there are the dancing fountains and a culture show. The island offers a wide range of places to eat, or alternatively there's the World Trade Centre itself or the Food Centre across the road near the bus station. Transport around the island by bus or monorail is included in the price of the entry ticket, or you can hire bicycles from the ferry terminal or the lagoon. In the World Trade Centre there are some interesting things to see, most notably the *Guinness Book of Records* **Exhibition**.

JURONG BIRD PARK

Many birds of the region can be seen here, some completely free, others in cages, and some in a gigantic walk-in aviary. There are two bird shows, one with performing parrots and a magnificent eagle swooping low over the audience, and another displaying the skills of hunting birds.

The MRT goes out to Jurong station and a cab will take you the rest of the way. A sunny day at the bird park can be a hot and debilitating experience, so make full use of the open air buses traveling around the park and plan your visit around the shows. There are plenty of places in the park for snacks and drinks. Near the park is a crocodile farm where terribly unhappy crocodiles languish in concrete pits.

HAW PAR VILLA

Situated on Pasir Panjang Road, a 20-minute car journey from Orchard Road, is **Haw Par Villa**, which has existed in one form or another for almost a hundred years. Once a private residence of the makers of Tiger Balm ointment, it is now a kitschy theme park focusing on Chinese mythology. Its major attraction is the Wrath of the Water Gods Flume, for which you may have to queue patiently for the pleasure of a stomach churning ride. For the squeamish, there is the Tales of China boat ride, a five-minute exploration of the myriad ways in which wrongdoers are punished in hell. If you don't like the sound of either of these, laser and film shows on Chinese mythology, a puppet show, and a very realistic

mechanical old man who tells stories are alternatives. Chinese operas and improvised theater for children are performed throughout the day. It is perhaps good for a half-day's entertainment, especially if you are interested in Chinese imagery and the stone statues which originally made up Tiger Balm Gardens. Entry is S$15 for adults, S$12 for children and all rides, shows, etc., are free. Buses N° 10, N° 30, N° 51 and N° 143 will take you there. The nearest MRT stop is Buona Vista from where you can take the SBS service N° 200 or get a cab.

RIVER TRIP AND HARBOR BOAT TRIP

The Singapore River has undergone many changes since Stamford Raffles sailed up it in 1819. He saw dense mangroves, crocodiles, virgin jungle and envisioned a vital trading post, a link between Europe, India and the East. Only ten years ago, the riverside was a furious chaos of coolies, *tonkkangs* and sampans, godowns and lorries and unlicensed hawker stalls. Now the only vessels on it are the tourist bumboats.

An interesting day out along the river should start at the **North Boat Quay**, where the marble Raffles gazes at his achievements. This is the spot where he first disembarked. Hallpike Street, now no longer signposted, was the first street to be built in Singapore. It runs along the side of the car park next to the departure dock of the bumboat rides. The attorney general's chambers are nearby,

ABOVE: Part of the Irish contribution to the Singapore skyline — the parliament building designed by George Coleman in 1826.

as is **Parliament House**, designed by the Irishman George Coleman in 1826. It was originally a private house, built for John Maxwell and has been added to many times since the original construction was undertaken. Most of it dates back to 1875. **Empress Place** used to be the immigration department where people queued daily and waited, scrambled and sweated in the crumbling, boxed-in cubicles with tired old fans failing to disturb the air and government regulation linoleum crumbling gently beneath their feet. It was boarded up in the mid-

eighties and several years later there emerged the magnificent new Empress Place restored and in pristine condition. It is now used as a mall and exhibition hall which houses international exhibitions, including many brought specially from China and never seen before outside the Republic. The original tiles were discovered underneath the linoleum and replacements were commissioned from Thailand. Many of the original items, like the safes built by the safe makers to the bank of England, are still in place.

After visiting Empress Place, a walk along the other bank of the river, crossing it via **Cavanagh Bridge**, will reveal some still undisturbed shop houses, although they are

a dying breed. Cavanagh Bridge was built in Glasgow in 1869 and shipped out here. It was named after Sir Orfeur Cavanagh, a former governor of the colony. Beside it is a tax office, once the General Post Office and at various other times the Singapore Club and a hostel for female British prisoners of war. Shenton Thomas, once governor, hid here on Friday February 13, 1942, after Government House was bombed. Singapore's Union Jack lay hidden here for three and a half years until it flew again in 1945. The building is on the site of the original Fort Fullerton, built to protect the town from invasion from the river in 1829. During the Japanese occupation the severed heads of those found looting were displayed here as a deterrent to other would-be looters. The steps leading down into the river from the side of the building date back to the construction of the boat quay in 1842.

You might like to take one of the bumboat rides which offer a trip up the river, showing the about-to-be renovated godowns (warehouses) and then back down to the river mouth itself and into Marina Bay with a view of the merlion fountain.

If you're in a nautical mood, a trip out into Marina Bay and beyond is a fascinating experience. There are several organizations which arrange trips out into the bay, the best being **Watertours,** ((65) 533811, which has an authentic-looking Chinese junk and an excellent tour guide. There are several different trips to choose from but the best is the twilight cruise which includes a good buffet meal, an informative talk by the guide, and great sunsets, all at a decent price. It leaves from Clifford Pier at 6 pm and returns at 9 pm.

THE PADANG

Cricket was first played here in the 1820s and close by is the **Singapore Cricket Club**. The Padang itself has witnessed some of the less happy moments of Singapore's history, such as the day in February 1915 when a match was interrupted by the news that an armed uprising was taking place. The Fifth Light Infantry of the British Indian army, the only unit stationed on the island, mutinied after having heard a rumor that they would be battling fellow Muslims in Turkey. Another historic event occured on February 17, 1942, when the defeated British were lined up here, before being marched off to Changi prison. Cricket wasn't played here again until the Japanese prisoners of war cleared the area of shell craters in 1945. Now the green is once again the site of cricket matches and the annual celebration of Singapore's independence. Opposite is **City Hall**, a Victorian building where Lord Louis Mountbatten accepted the surrender of the Japanese forces in 1945.

the city and offers some splendid views. The hill was also the scene of some of the historic moments of World War II. The headquarters of the British military command were here in underground rooms which are still intact but not yet open to the public. It was here on February 15, 1942, that the decision was made to surrender to the Japanese.

THE BOTANIC GARDENS

Situated just beyond the Orchard Road area at the junction of Holland and Cluny Roads

FORT CANNING PARK

Archaeological evidence has been found on this site proving the existence of a civilization four hundred years before this area Government Hill. There is an old Christian cemetery here whose gates still remain, although the tombstones have all been moved to the sides. This ground has been a holy place for many cultures and turning left out of the cemetery gates you will come to the **Iskandar Shah Shrine**, a Muslim place of worship where the body of the last ruler of ancient Singapura is said to be interred. The park itself makes a pleasant evening walk above the bustle of

are the Botanic Gardens which offer the interested visitor a great introduction to the flora of the tropical regions. It was in these gardens that the first rubber trees were planted in the Far East by the Irishman "Mad" Ridley. It was from these plants that the huge rubber plantations of Malaysia began. A plaque marks the spot where the first tree was planted. The park also contains an area of primary rain forest complete with macaques, Singapore's only surviving wild monkey, and snakes such as the spitting

ABOVE: The Botanic Gardens — a haven from the rush of Orchard Road. OPPOSITE: The Victoria Theatre, a showpiece of colonial architecture.

cobra, said to have a deadly aim at six meters (20 ft). The park has many other attractions including a very informative orchid garden where you can buy cuttings. The trees are all labeled with their common name and place of origin. Opposite the main gates of the park is one of my favorite hawker centers, where you can get such delicacies as *roti john* or *tahu goreng*, possibly the best in Singapore.

BUKIT TIMAH NATURE RESERVE

While Singapore appears to many people to be entirely urbanized, there are a few

areas which have not yet spawned the inevitable blocks of flats. One of these is **Bukit Timah Hill**, an area of secondary rain forest, which means that it has been felled at some time but the remaining plants have regenerated. At the lower parts of the hill you can still see trees remaining from the time when this area was planted with nutmeg and rubber trees. A road goes all the way to the top of the hill and there are still other pathways to explore. The macaque monkeys are abundant, particularly at the top of the hill. The best times to visit are very early morning, or early evening, when birds are around, due to the large numbers of insects. One particularly spectacular bird is the racket-tailed drongo with enormous streamers trailing out behind it. At the

---

ABOVE: Alkaff Mansion with the city skyline behind.

bottom of the hill is a small information hut which sells a fascinating booklet about the nature reserve.

SINGAPORE ZOOLOGICAL GARDENS

Having had some of life's most depressing experiences in zoos — neurotic and sickly tigers at Jaipur, enfeebled penguins hunched together in communal misery at Warsaw, or frost-bitten parrots keeping up a brave face in the depths of a Regents Park winter — I can cheerfully recommend Singapore Zoo as an idyllic setting to both voluntary visitors and to residents of the zoo. Set in one of Singapore's pockets of countryside it offers its visitors user-friendly information about the animals and

natural barriers such as lakes or pits rather than cages. There are daily animal shows featuring trained elephants, apes and seals as well as a children's petting zoo. While you are at the zoo there are the nearby **Mandai Orchid Gardens** which sell cut orchids from all around the world. Bus N° 171 from Queen Street takes you straight there.

EMERALD HILL

At the bottom of the road where it joins Orchard Road is **Peranakan Place,** a collection of restaurants and bars with a vaguely Peranakan theme. There is also a small **museum** which is well worth a visit.

The term Peranakan refers to the descendants of the early Chinese immigrants to the Straits settlements of Melaka, Penang and Singapore. who intermarried with local women. This unique cultural blend survives to the present day. The museum, ((65) 732-6966, is situated in an original Peranakan house. A museum guide will start your tour on the doorstep of the house and you can spot the place easily enough by walking up the right side of Emerald Hill Road, past the street tables, until you see a house flanked by two large white lanterns which are embellished with red Chinese characters that spell out the family name.

Peranakans were descendants of predominantly wealthy Chinese traders, so the prosperous interior of the house is typical. What made the Peranakans special was their multicultural assimilation which led to the development of a distinctive culture that had its own style of architecture, furniture, food, dress and even language — a patois of Malay and Chinese with English, Indian and even Portuguese.

The terraced houses on this road are good examples of Peranakan architecture, sometimes referred to as Chinese Baroque, reflecting the unique blend of Chinese and neoclassical forms from Europe. The European influence had its origins in Melaka (the west coast Malaysian town that was once a Portuguese colony) and was introduced into Singapore by way of the Straits-born Chinese.

The style of the roofs are Chinese, with green or red bamboo-shaped tiles, but the

timber fretwork is Malay in origin. Printed scrolls above the windows and doors are Chinese but the Doric and Corinthian columns and louvered timber shutters are very much European.

The cowboy saloon bar-looking doors on the front of these houses are called *pintu pagar*, made to provide ventilation while at the same time offering privacy to the family.

Take a walk past the Peranakan Place buildings all the way up Emerald Hill Road. Begin your tour at Nº 12 where you can observe the peep hole in the ceiling that allowed a *nonya* to see who was at the front door without revealing herself. Nº 14 has a ghost-busting hexagonal mirror above the door, known as a *pakwa. Pa* is Chinese for the lucky number eight and kwa stands for the elements like fire and water. Keeping on the left side, you come to a crossing, and facing the junction on the right side of Emerald Hill Road is a house with the most unfortunate *feng shui* (the art of geomancy as it relates to the positioning of buildings and sometimes even furniture so as to ward off evil spirits and attract good ones). Because it faces an open road the spirits had a clear runway for a speedy entrance and pity the poor householder who didn't take sensible precautions. If you peep in at the door you'll see how the owners have placed a temple directly in the line of any advancing nasties. A temple in your front room might not be convenient but it certainly beats having an uninvited ghost. Coming back down the road look for the lozenge-shaped small side windows. They are in the shape of a bat, the Chinese word for which, *fu*, has the same sound as another word meaning good luck and prosperity.

ARAB STREET

The area around the Golden Landmark Hotel still reflects the large Arab influence in Singapore which reached its peak at the turn of the century. Still standing is the **Sultan Mosque,** built in the 1920s, representing a bizarre architectural blend of influences

from Persia, Turkey and North Africa. Remove your shoes before enter the mosque. All around the building and along North Bridge Street are many interesting shops selling perfumes, batik, cane items and the like. Also very close by is the resurrected **Bugis Street** hawker center. Many of those who remember the original Bugis Street sigh with sadness at its parting because of its unique atmosphere and impromptu shows by the transvestites. But now, shifted slightly to the left, Bugis Street is with us again, transvestites and all. It is

open 24 hours and offers beer gardens, hawker food, a *pasar malam*, shows and much more.

WHERE TO STAY

TOP CLASS

Most of the mega-hotel chains are represented in Singapore, offering their paying guests every luxury imaginable.

The legendary **Raffles**, ((65) 339-8377; fax: (65) 339-1713, was closed for three years for major renovation but reopened in 1991. If you don't stay here then at least call in for a drink and a bit of nostalgia. First built in 1886 by the Sarkie brothers, Armenians in origin, it was originally a tiffin room and boarding house. By the mid-twentieth century it had collected its string of famous names: Coward, Chaplin, Fairbanks and Maugham and had become a rallying place for colonialists where they could be sure of not running into any riffraff. In more recent

---

OPPOSITE: Some of the happiest captive animals in the world entertain hundreds of people daily at the Singapore zoo. ABOVE: One of the many exotic creatures at the Jurong Bird Park.

times Raffles opened its doors to one and all but now, sadly, its renovation has again rendered it beyond the pockets of the average tourist. The least expensive doubles are $373.

Another hotel steeped in history is the **Goodwood Park**, at N° 22 Scotts Road, Singapore 0922, ((65) 737-7411; fax: (65) 732-8558. Originally the Teutonic Club, it opened in 1900 to entertain the German community in Singapore. Taken as a spoil of war during the First World War it became a club for the British colonialists in the

pore 0923, ((65) 737-2233; fax: (65) 732-2917, was the first high-rise building erected in Orchard Road. It underwent major renovations in the eighties and offers all the luxuries including the highest pool in Singapore. Compared to the other big chains it is a restrained and quiet hotel with good restaurants and an excellent lounge bar in the lobby. The lobby leads into a mall of designer shops. A double room here costs $170.

Still in the Orchard Road area and in the same price range is the **Royal Holiday Inn** at N° 25 Scotts Road, Singapore 0922, ((65)

1920s. It assumed its present identity in 1929 and rivaled Raffles as a haunt for Europeans, including British royalty. During and after the Japanese invasion the hotel became a residence of army officers and witnessed war crimes trials after Singapore's liberation. The hotel boomed in the fifties and sixties and attracted the glitterati of those years — Cliff Richards, Acker Bilk, Shirley Bassey, Matt Monroe and many others. A double room here costs $230.

Most of the other hotels in Singapore saw their birth in the seventies and eighties. The **Hilton** at N° 581 Orchard Road, Singa-

737-7966; fax: (65) 737-6646. Once owned by the Sultan of Brunei, the hotel has a special entrance for the Sultan to use when he is in town which leads directly to his gold plated suite. The interior of the hotel has been brought up to the standards befitting a place patronized by the richest man in the world.

Nearby is the **Dynasty** at N° 320 Orchard Road, Singapore 0923, ((65) 734-9900; fax: (65) 733-5251, owned by a local family. It has a magnificent set of carved panels in the lobby depicting Chinese folk stories. A standard double is $150.

Further down Orchard Road, and with an incredible array of restaurants, bars and discos, is the twin-towered **Mandarin Hotel**

ABOVE: One of the world's greatest hotels, the legendray raffles, now restored to its original luxurious splendor.

at N° 333 Orchard Road, Singapore 0923, ((65) 737-4411; fax: (65) 732-2361. Big and impersonal, but centrally located, its restaurants and facilities are top class. A standard double is $184.

In the Marina Square area, the best is the **Oriental** N° 3335, Raffles Avenue, Singapore 0103, ((65) 338-0066; fax: (65) 339-9537. A business hotel with real style it has great views from the rooms and the atrium bar is a treat. Doubles here are $189.

There are also excellent hotels outside the main Orchard Road area. In Chinatown, The **Furama** is at N° 60 Eu Tong Sen Street, Singapore 0105, ((65) 533-3888; fax: (65) 534-1489. It has an excellent Cantonese restaurant which serves delicacies such as bear's paws, snake, deep fried duck tongue and more on request. A double room costs $115. In the Arab Street area is the **Golden Landmark** at N° 390 Victoria Street, Singapore 0719, ((65) 297-2828; fax: (65) 298-2038, with a slightly frenetic lobby but good restaurants and close proximity to the new Bugis Street development. A double here costs $109. Close to the river and its burgeoning new tourist attractions is the **New Otani**, at N° 177A River Valley Road, Singapore 0617, ((65) 338-3333; fax: (65) 339-2854. A Japanese hotel with great range of food and beverage outlets including the wonderful **Sebazuru** restaurant (see WHERE TO EAT), and great views of the river. Doubles go for $172.

MODERATE

Most of these hotels are out of the main Orchard Road area; the closer they get to the center the higher the room rate. At the top end of this range are places like the **Cockpit Hotel** at N° 6–7 Oxley Rise, Singapore 0923, ((65) 737-9111; fax: (65) 737-3105, which has a slightly worn appearance and where rooms go for $83. At the other end of Orchard Road is the **Ladyhill**, at N° 1 Ladyhill Road, Singapore 1025, ((65) 737-2111; fax: (65) 737-4606. This low rise hotel occupies quite a large area, has a nice pool, a good coffee shop and Singapore's best Swiss restaurant. Doubles are $92.

Well away from the center of town is the **Apollo Hotel**, at N° 405 Havelock Road,

Singapore 0316, ((65) 733-2081; fax: (65) 733-1588. Room rates here are $83. This hotel is nicely situated next to a huge department store, has an excellent and inexpensive Indonesian restaurant, a bar which hass old time dancing and the biggest Chinese nightclub in Singapore.

Quite close to Orchard Road is the **RELC Hotel** at N° 30 Orange Grove Road, ((65) 737-9044; fax: (65) 733-9976, where a double with breakfast is $69. It has a convenient location close to the center, but with limited restaurant facilities and no pool, though the rooms are still very good.

The **YMCA** is probably the best deal in Singapore at this price range. Close to the center at N° 1 Orchard Road, ((65) 337-3444; fax: (65) 337-3140, rooms cost $44. You can even get room service from the McDonald's downstairs.

The **Strand Hotel**, N° 25 Bencoolen Street, ((65) 338-1866; fax: (65) 336-3149, has decent rooms at $49. Also in this area is the **Bencoolen Hotel** at N° 47 Bencoolen Street, ((65) 336-0822; fax: (65) 336-4384, at the same rate.

One last good place is **Jack's Travelodge** at N° 336 River Valley Road, fax/((65) 732-9222. No pool but a public one nearby and a large shopping plaza; also good restaurants are close by. Rooms are $48.

INEXPENSIVE

Places that can be called inexpensive are growing rarer in Singapore as the older buildings get razed or renovated. The **Air View Hotel** at N° 10 Peck Seah Street, ((65) 225-7788, has air-conditioned rooms with bathroom for $27 while the **Tiong Hoa** at N° 4 Prinsep Street, ((65) 338-4522, is quite central, and has air-conditioned rooms at $23. The **New Mayfair,** at N° 40–44 Armenian Street, ((65) 337-5405, has rooms at $28 while the **New Seventh Storey**, at N° 229 Rochor Road, ((65) 337-0251, has similar rooms for $37.

WHERE TO EAT

If choosing one from the many top-class hotels in Singapore is difficult, deciding which of the thousands of eating places to go to is impossible. All the cuisines of the Far East in their myriad forms are amply represented here, as are those of the West and even the Middle East. What follows is based on novelty value, quality, and just plain prejudice. It is categorized according to the amount of damage to the wallet.

TOP CLASS

For sheer class and elegance the **Restaurant de France**, ((65) 733-8855, is a must. Deco-

suggested. **Greece, My Love** would be my second choice. Its advantage over Marina Village is its open air amphitheater with excellent live music. Ring (225-3055 to make reservations for any of these restaurants

Back in town at the Hyatt Regency is my personal favorite, **Nutmegs**, (733118, which serves Californian *nouvelle cuisine*. Decorated in a striking black and white art nouveau style, this restaurant is small, intimate and very popular. Deep fried potato skins dipped in sour cream are typical of its innovative style of cooking. Like many other

rated in regency style and divided into three areas, one of which is an indoor patio garden, the service here is unobtrusive but complete. Just watching the preparation of the dessert is a wonder, that is if you can find the will to choose from the dessert trolley. A meal here for two will set you back about $100, including wine.

Another place that prides itself on its expensive food is **Marina Village**, a collection of high-class restaurants offering Moroccan, Italian, Greek, Swiss, Chinese, Spanish and Malay cuisine. Not all of them are worth the trip or the cost, but my favorite, **Marrakech** the Moroccan restaurant, has both a beautiful decor and delicious food. It is also one of the most popular so reservations

restaurants in Singapore this one does some excellent lunch time offers. Reservations are essential.

Singapore also has its share of excellent Japanese restaurants, of which my favorite has to be **The Sebazuru Restaurant**, (339-2854, in The New Otani Hotel. You can choose between teppanyaki, sushi, sashimi or mix-and-match. The most fun has to be the teppanyaki where you sit around a grill watching the antics of the chef. The restaurant is on the sixth floor and has nice views out over the river and skyscrapers.

Al fresco or indoors, Singapore seafood is an amazing experience.

It is difficult to know how to economically categorize Chinese restaurants. Dishes such as shark's fin or bird's nest soup will hike up the price of your meal enormously. The following Chinese restaurants can be very expensive or only moderately so, depending on what you choose to eat and how many of you are dining.

In Orchard Road the **Long Jiang Sichuan** restaurant, (734-9056, in the Crown Prince Hotel is a good value. Specializing in Sichuan cooking, the restaurant serves an enormous range of Chinese dishes, including many Cantonese dishes popular in the West. It has a very down-to-earth atmosphere; not the ideal location for a romantic dinner for two, but the food is excellent and you can choose your price and quantity of food. Another very nice spot is the **Pine Court,** (737-4411, at the Mandarin Hotel, with an atmosphere redolent of imperial China and excellent Peking food.

Another exceptionally popular restaurant is the **Wah Lok Cantonese Restaurant**, (330-3588, at the Carlton Hotel. Reservations are always necessary. Not all the good Chinese restaurants are in hotels, however, and if you are adventurous, the **East Ocean Seafood Restaurant**, (533-5088, in People's Park Complex in Chinatown, is a fascinating place. It serves creative Cantonese food, and like the other restaurants can be as expensive as you want to make it.

Have you ever eaten Chinese food sitting on top of a grain silo? Well here's your chance. The **Prima Tower Revolving Restaurant,** (272-8822, is built on top of a fully operational grain silo in the middle of an industrial estate near the World Trade Centre. Built on the waterfront, the restaurant has one of the best views in Singapore. The cuisine is vaguely Cantonese, the decor is 1970s shabby and full of huge family groups who go there for the Peking duck or chili crabs or red fish on a hot plate.

Teochew food is becoming increasingly popular in Singapore recently, and more and more small restaurants are opening up. One of the best of these is **Teochew City**, (532-3622, a branch of which is on Battery Road in the city. Teochew food is quite homely in style and subdued by Singaporean standards, but would suit lovers of Cantonese food who find the Singaporean tendency to put chili in everything disturbing.

It is possible to write an entire guide book just about Chinese food in Singapore, so perhaps I should stop there and mention a few other cuisines in this price bracket. Thai food has to be one of the most tasty cuisines in the world and Singapore has some truly magnificent examples. Best in my opinion, are the **Her Sea,** restaurants, owned by the Watties chain. One is in Forum Galleria, N° 01–16 Orchard Road, (732-5688, and the other, less crowded, is at B1 N° 55 United Square, N° 101 Thomson Road, (252-5830. A fairly dull decor belies the amazing complexity of tastes: hot, sour, spicy, and aromatic. Olive rice and grilled sea bass have to be the best thing to eat in Singapore. Reservations are necessary at the Orchard Road branch but less so at United Square, which incidentally is also the home of a classy little pub serving imported beers. Another good Thai place is the **Thanying** at the Amara Hotel in Tanjong Pagar Road, (222-4688.

MODERATE

The restaurants listed above are appropriate for special occasions and match the best that Europe can offer. Slightly more homely but still excellent food can be had at a price range of about $30 to $60 for two people, including wine.

In terms of entertainment value the best place in this price range has to be **Alkaff Mansion**. Built in the late nineteenth century this is one of the four houses lived in by the Alkaff family, wealthy merchants who began their life in Singapore as traders in coffee, spices and sugar. Abandoned in the twenties, the house was spotted just as it was about to disappear into the lianas and at some cost was brought back to its original grandeur. An evening visit here is an event, particularly if you decide to try the *rijstaffel* served by a long train of gorgeous ladies. The food, Singaporeans would say, is *okay lah* (meaning nothing special) but the place makes up for that. It is a little out of town, (278-6979, and it is best to get a taxi.

If you like western food, Singapore has many small restaurants serving all types of

European cuisines. **Casablanca,** at Emerald Hill, (235-9328, is interesting both for its western cuisine and its interior. The menu is quite small and bistroic with daily specials chalked up on a board. The building is still in its original condition right down to the uneven stone flags on the floor and the nineteenth-century tiles on the walls. The architecture is typical of houses of that era, very long with a narrow frontage and an air-well to bring fresh air into the windowless interior. Another pleasant aspect to this restaurant is its outdoor area.

Another style of cooking you might like to try is Vietnamese food, or at least its Singaporean variant. None of the Vietnamese restaurants in Singapore are authentically Vietnamese; all are strongly influenced by the Chili Syndrome but the style is distinctively different. **The Sai-gon** restaurant in Cairnhill Place at the top of Emerald Hill is probably the best of the bunch. It is pleasantly unpretentious with a kitchenstyle look about the place, cane chairs and pink tablecloths. No one actually speaks any Vietnamese and the clientele is 50 per-

Another European cuisine represented in Singapore is Russian. The **Shashlik Restaurant** in Far East Shopping Centre, 306-19, N° 545 Orchard Road, (732-6401, is a slightly eccentric place run by some very elderly people who have made and served Russian food all their working lives. Good food and good fun.

In the same street as Casablanca is **Aziza's**, (235-1130, one of the few Malay restaurants in Singapore. The restaurant is full every night so reservations are a must. Food is spicy and based around the typical herbs and spices of the Malay *kampong*, coconut, chili, and lemon grass. Wine is also served at this restaurant.

cent Singaporean and 25 percent Japanese. The food is good and quite inexpensive. Most unusual are the starters, for example *chao tom*, minced prawns cooked on a piece of sugar cane which you can bite into, or *cha goi ton thit*, spring roll wrapped in lettuce with fresh raw herbs. Reservations are not necessary.

If you want to try authentic Japanese food without paying Japanese prices, then there's a great place tucked away in the Cuppage Plaza. It is tempting to be diverted by the open-air eating spots outside but a trip up to the second floor is well worth it,

ABOVE LEFT: A songbird fancier's café.
ABOVE RIGHT: Satay stall at the Satay Club.

for here you'll find **Izakaya Nijumaru**. Izakaya means pub and this establishment is more of a pub serving food than a restaurant serving beer. The walls are pasted with notices of the food specials (nothing is in English) and the busy atmosphere is proof its popularity. It closes at 10:30 pm, and between 8 pm and 10 pm it is packed, with no reservations allowed. Go before 8 pm, (235-6693, and just order one of the set meals if you're new to Japanese food. A favorite is the Tempura Set and at $6 this would make an excellent introduction.

Most Indian restaurants of note appear in this moderate price range and downwards. Only two hotels have Indian restaurants, the Holiday Inn Parkview and the Imperial. Both are pricey by Indian restaurant standards, serving Moghul food, rich in nuts and *lassi*. The **Omar Khayaam**, (336-1505, near the American embassy in Hill Street is prettily decorated, has a small but selective range of Moghul and North Indian-style food, does good *naan* and makes very rich aphrodisiacal coffee made and served at your table. Reservations are not always necessary.

Just round the corner is **Annalakshmi**, (339-9990, an ultra-vegetarian restaurant run by an interesting group of people dedicated to the propagation of Indian culture. All the staff are volunteers. No alcohol is served here and prices are high by Indian restaurant standards. On Saturdays there is a buffet which will astound you with the variety of vegetable tastes. The menu alters, depending on who is volunteering that night. On some weekend nights there is also a cultural show, and reservations will be necessary.

South Indian food tends to be vegetarian and an excellent example of good South Indian food in a pleasant air-conditioned environment is at **Bombay Woodlands**, (235-2712, at Forum Galleria near the Hilton, where you can try a *thali*, the set meal, or pick your own items. *Bhatura* is an enormous deep-fried bread, the size and appearance of a rugby ball, which collapses as soon as you touch it and it is served with a variety of sauces and vegetables. *Masala dhosa*, a rice flour pancake wrapped around vegetable curry with other dips, is also good. Best of

all here is the pistachio or almond shake. Calorie filled but heavenly. Eating here really is very inexpensive compared to many other places mentioned in this section.

If you like tongue-lashing spiciness, then there are several good Korean restaurants in Singapore; the best one is at Tanjong Pagar Road and is called **Hae Bok's**, (223-9003. Outside the restaurant you can look at plastic replicas of what you are about to eat while inside you will be regaled with all manner of starters while you make up your mind what you want. These starters are all complimentary and the staff choose which ones to give you. If you happen to see something else that they haven't given you, just ask for it. Many of the dishes are cooked at your table-side or you are left with just the fixings and a little spirit stove. Singapore has a special cuisine all its own consisting of seafood dishes with lots of chili. The following restaurants are typical of this style of cooking and are a bit out of the way, so you will be able to see some parts of Singapore that are not on the usual tourist routes. The **Long Beach Seafood Restaurant** at N° 610 Bedok Road Singapore 1646, (445-8833, is a good distance from town, about S$7 by cab. Quite old by Singaporean standards, this place was once a seafront hotel but reclamation has it stranded well inland now. It serves vast numbers of people every night and has a whole army of waiters. A typical Singaporean dish to try here, if you aren't an animal liberationist, is drunken prawns, which are drowned in brandy before being boiled. Other dishes to try are chili crab and barbecued fish. The fish is all caught locally. A similar menu but more frenetic atmosphere can be had at **Palm Beach Seafood Restaurant** at National Stadium Drive (next to gate 1 entrance), (344-1474. Here you can try not only excellent Singaporean cuisine but you can watch Singaporeans' uninhibited eating habits. Reservations are always necessary and when you arrive you will see people queuing up the road to get in. Inside is bedlam. Don't choose this place to propose marriage. There is no menu, or none that I have ever seen. Just ask what is good. Prawns in black bean sauce is amazing and pepper crab is also delicious. For crab-eating etiquette just look around you,

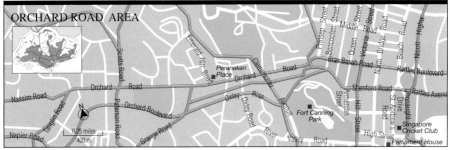

and duck occasionally as bits of shell fly about.

One last seafood place you might like to try if neither of the other two appeal is the **Ng Tiong Choon Sembawang Fishing Pond,** at N° 59 Lorong Chuntum, Singapore 2775, (758-9909, which is absolutely miles away from town but organizes minibuses from the Grand Central Hotel. Ring the restaurant for details. A cab will cost about S$13. If you don't have time to visit much of Malaysia, this place will give you a feel of what small-town Malaysia is like. It is surrounded by fields and rubber trees and built over a pond where during the day you can fish. It is very pretty at night, and unlike the other seafood places which can get noisy. It has a large menu, but notice that some items do not have prices. Be sure to ask before you order. A meal for two here would cost about $35. Few tourists come here but many Singaporeans do.

INEXPENSIVE

This is the most subjective list of all, based entirely on personal preference. No two Singaporeans will agree on the best hawker food even though they spend much time discussing the topic.

My favorite hawker stalls are by the main entrance to the Botanic Gardens. Chiefly selling Malay food, this place does the best *tahu goreng* (fried tofu in peanut sauce) in town and wonderful *roti john*. There is also a *roti prata* stall.

A great place to eat if the heat outside gets you down is the food court at the **Funan Centre**. On the top floor it has many stalls including a wonderful place called **Naan 'n Curry** which serves quite mild curries with beautiful Indian breads.

Marina South is not only a great hawker center but great fun. You can get there by cab, about S$4 from town, or by the N° 400 bus. Nearby Marina Village organizes buses from Shenton Way and Orchard Road. The hawker center is very clean and new. Stalls include a Japanese steamboat stall, a Thai stall (but check portion sizes), as well as the more regular places. Nearby is a bowling alley that caters to children, and up the road is Marina Village which has live music most nights. If you don't sit down the music is free. If you do sit down you get to pay high prices for drinks. There are many shops selling tourist goodies and particularly kites which you can fly on the beach. Most tourist literature promotes the **Newton Circus** hawker center but this place is not recommended. Coach loads of tourists arrive by the hour and prices have inflated accordingly. The food is no better than the places just mentioned.

Serangoon Road is a wonderful place for inexpensive Indian food. **Racecourse Road**, which runs parallel with it, has half a dozen air-conditioned places. Just walk along and choose one that takes your fancy. Two excellent vegetarian places are **Madras New Woodlands Restaurant** on Upper Dickson Road, a turn-off on your right on Serangoon Road, and Komala Vilas on Serangoon Road itself.

SHOPPING

This section basically covers Orchard Road though you'll find shops just about everywhere in Singapore. Most of what you want will be found in Orchard Road, with one or two exceptions. If you are interested in computers and software the place

to go is the **Funan Centre** near the Peninsula Hotel, and if you are shopping for artifacts I would recommend Holland Village (see below). The **People's Park Complex** in Chinatown has a few interesting stores for general souvenir stuff, but for high-quality gifts visit **Marina Square** and **Raffles City**. These are the most modern shopping complexes and they are connected to the Westin, Pan Pacific, Marina Mandarin and Oriental cluster of hotels.

Starting at the bottom end of Orchard Road, **Tanglin Shopping Centre** is on Tanglin Road next to the Ming Court Hotel. Tailors and antique shops are here, as well as regular souvenir shops.

Across the road, at the beginning of Orchard Road, is **Orchard Towers**. At night this is the disco center of town. Someone may whisper surreptitiously in your ear — copy watch? — and if you look interested they will suggest you follow them. You may follow safely but remember the sale is illegal and heavy fines are meted out to persistent hawkers — and don't come back with your broken watch in three months expecting to get a refund. Be prepared for some serious bargaining. Copy watches are easily made, so how much are they actually worth?

For real designer items visit the **Delfi Orchard** (Etienne Aigner, Givenchy and Waterford Wedgewood) and the **Hilton Hotel**'s shopping gallery (Louis Vuitton, Bulgari, Loewe, Montana, Ferre, Armani, Maud Frizon, Gucci, Jaeger *et alia*).

The blue-glassed **Forum Galleria,** next to the Hilton, has Toys 'R' Us and Electric City. Just past the Hilton is the **Far East Shopping Centre,** more interesting for the sculpture of Mother and Child that stands outside it than for anything you'll find inside.

Tangs department store is not bad for a little bit of everything at fixed prices. It is the only major shop to be closed on Sunday. The highly popular **Lucky Plaza**, next to the Dynasty Hotel, has a good mix of shops selling electronic stuff like cameras plus lots of jewelry stores. Many of the shops here will not have fixed prices and bargaining is necessary. If possible, try to establish the fixed price in a department store or, for electronic items, in a place like Cost Plus in Scotts Road.

The dazzling blue building is **Wisma Atria** and there is a mix of designer stores here plus four floors of the Isetan department store. Before reaching Centrepoint there is a whole bunch of smaller complexes on both sides of the road.

At **Centrepoint** you will find a Marks and Spencer with prices that will make many sigh nostalgically for their own branch back in England. Robinsons is the biggest outlet here and it's pricey but the

clothes are good. Hidden away are some good boutiques and cut price factory outlet stores which might appeal, although generally Singaporean clothes tend to be a little bit too frilly for Western tastes. Robinsons is probably the oldest department store in Singapore. If you are interested in art — Chinese calligraphy, paintings, artifacts — visit **The Orchard Point** at N° 160 Orchard Road (just past Centrepoint and on the same side), near the Park View Holiday Inn and diagonally opposite Somerset MRT station. There are over eighty galleries here. Toward the end of Orchard Road is the flat roofed **Plaza Singapura**. Japanese based Yoahan has a large department store here offering a good mix of everything at affordable prices, and the Plaza also has some good shops selling Chinese rosewood furniture.

OPPOSITE TOP and BOTTOM: Shopping in the extensive malls and arcades is a favorite pastime in Singapore. ABOVE: A young spectator enjoying one of Singapore's many street fairs.

NIGHTLIFE

Most of Singapore's better discos are all gathered under the one roof of Orchard Towers, at the bottom of Orchard Road. The most impressive and liveliest is **Top Ten**, (732-3077, on the fourth floor. One floor down is **Caesar's**, (737-7665, and as you might expect there's a Roman theme here with scantily clad hostesses in togas. Lots of the big hotels have discos and **The Kasbah** at the Mandarin Hotel is worth mentioning

if only because it is one of only two clubs in the whole of Singapore with a license for topless acts. The chic place to be seen in is **Chinoiserie** at the Hyatt Hotel because it attracts trendy and rich young professionals, but there is nothing special about the music or the atmosphere. If you want good live music, but no dancing, one of the best places in town is **Anywhere**, (734-8223, at the Tanglin Shopping Centre. It's small, windowless, dark, a bit scruffy and very crowded, but it is a great relief from the squeaky-clean discos and bars which characterize too much of the tourist's Singapore. The resident band partly owns the premises and there's terrific rapport with the audience. A good spot for jazz, calypso or whatever happens to be playing is the **Saxophone** bar and restaurant, (235-8385, in Cuppage Terrace. There's a good Indian restaurant next door if you don't fancy the continental food at Saxophone. The music goes on till

ABOVE and OPPOSITE: Compelling character make-up of Chinese opera singers.

midnight. Jazz music is always available at the **Somerset** bar in the Westin Hotel. The atmosphere is a little sanitized for jazz but good bands are brought in from around the world.

Old-time dancing can be enjoyed at the **Grill Room**, (337-0611, in the Allson Hotel, while just dancing is available at **Club 5** at the Plaza Hotel along Beach Road.

The pub scene is improving a lot in Singapore and there are now a few places worth patronizing. **Brannigans**, at the Hyatt Hotel in Scotts Road, has long been the favorite haunt of young and not-so-young, and **The Bar** at the Holiday Inn across the road is famous for its Burton Bass beer imported from England. Though out at United Square **Brauhaus**, (250-3116, has the best range of imported beers anywhere on the island. There are also excellent Thai restaurants in the United Square plaza. Back in town there's the **Hard Rock Cafe**, (235-5232, in Cuscaden Road within strolling distance of the discos in Orchard Towers. A new pub with live music that became instantly popular with tourists and locals alike is **H2O**, (732-5979, in the International Building along Orchard Road.

Cultural nightlife is experiencing a little renaissance of its own in Singapore and the best way to find out what is on is by checking the daily newspaper which contains a current listings of film, theatre and music.

SHOPPING AND DINING OUT OF TOWN

HOLLAND ROAD

If you only have a couple of days in Singapore and you want to buy lots of electrical items, silks, artifacts or other tourist goodies, then **Holland Village** is where you should go. A taxi or the N° 106 bus from Somerset, Grange Road or Orchard Boulevard, will bring you to a little haven of good taste, good prices and some nice food.

Starting in the shopping center, at N° 02-01 to 03, is the wonderful **Lim's**, which sells many arts and crafts at good fixed prices. It has an enormous range of Korean furniture

and medicine chests and some pieces from Thailand such as faked old tables and chairs and carved wooden flowers. Ask for some discount if not paying by card. Lim's is on the same floor as several other treasure houses with whom you can bargain a little.

Jessica Arts and Crafts, (468-2336, is a little more expensive than Lim's but has some lovely pieces of Korean furniture. These shops deal regularly with people sending goods abroad so they will reliably handle any necessary shipping.

This center also has several dress shops which have batik and other dresses from the region. There are embroidered blouses from China, beaded jumpers and blouses, as well as quilted Chinese and Thai silk jackets. Again, a polite request for a discount should have a beneficial effect but hard bargaining is not expected. There are several shops here which will make dresses or suits from a pattern or from a garment you already own. On the third floor, at N° 03–32, is Pegs which is very popular among expatriates and sells a limited and conservative selection of clothes.

On the third floor are a couple more shops selling antiques, particularly some benevolent-looking Bhuddhas and a shop specializing in brightly painted wood carvings from Bali. There are also some fabric shops which sell mostly European style home furnishing fabric but also have embroidered and woven clothes from India. Newly arrived on the third floor is **J & A**, a carpet shop specializing in carpets from Pakistan, Afghanistan, Iran, Turkey, Kashmir and China. It is part of a bigger organization with a shop in Far East Plaza, so expect to bargain.

Incidentally, if you run out of cash, there's a money changer inside the stamp shop at N° 03–40.

At the end of Holland Avenue is **Cost Plus**, which always has some good offers in electrical goods and other gadgets. But before you buy anything, go round the corner to **Paris Silk Store** in Lorong Liput, (466-6002, and ask for their prices. Good things to buy here are multi-system televisions which will work in the U.S.A and Europe as well as Australia and New Zealand and dual-voltage items which can be used in any

country. Very few of their customers are tourists; they get most of their business from expatriates who like to keep shopping time to a painless minimum. Don't expect a lot of sales chat at Paris Silk. They expect you to know what you want and don't have a lot of time for explanations or comparisons.

In Lorong Mambong there are several cane and pottery shops selling lots of pottery as well as domestic items and furniture. They will pack, ship and insure your purchases.

Having shopped till you've dropped in true Singaporean tradition there are plenty of places to rest and eat and enjoy the rest of the day. Delifrance has an outlet here which is the only one in Singapore to have evening meals. It is called **Le Bistro** and is relaxed, informal and fairly cheap.

A good cheap place to eat is **Shariff** restaurant, an Indian Muslim food place, at N° 29, Lorong Liput, which has the usual assortment of Muslim food. Best is probably the *murtabak*. It's not as crunchily wonderful as the ones at Arab Street but it's edible, filling, tasty and inexpensive. There is a popular steak house on the other side of the road.

If you feel like eating a little further upmarket there are three places here which are recommended. **El Filipe's Cantina**, at N° 34 Lorong Mambong, serves Texmex type Mexican food.

Across the road at N° 23 is **Pasta Ristorante** which serves Italian food. The atmosphere in here is a little more sophisticated although the prices compare well with Casablanca at Emerald Hill. The place is pleasantly furnished and has an Italian countryside atmosphere.

Another good western food outlet is across the road from the shopping center. **Fondue Cafe 81** in Chip Bee Gardens, (475-9069, serves great fondues at good prices.

Alternatively you can climb to the roof of the shopping center and eat *al fresco* at **Chao Phaya Thai Seafood Restaurant**. Foam deities adorn the walls of the air-conditioned section or you can choose your fish outside from a refrigerated market stall. At very reasonable prices you can enjoy typical Thai seafood. After eating, the place to be seen at is **Java Jive** at N° 17D Lorong Liput,

(468-4155. It is a *karaoke* joint where the songs are sung by everybody.

JOO CHIAT ROAD

Architecturally, Joo Chiat Road is a fascinating place with some interesting shops to browse in. Most of the shop buildings date from the 1920s and a distinctive feature of many houses are patterned wall tiles that are remarkably well preserved. The facades of many buildings are built around mock Doric columns with Corinthian tops, though in some cases the columns are an integral part of the building's structure. Later into the night, this is a red-light area with an abundance of drinking lounges.

At N° 86, on the right-hand side as you walk down Joo Chiat Road from Geylang Road, is an interesting Chinese shop (**Teng Chip Bee** (344-2859). It sells religious paraphernalia and it is well worth looking around in. There are some neat little anti-evil spirits mirrors and excellent Chinese lanterns made of wood and glass.

The music lounges close by are interesting. They look innocuous enough from the outside but when you step inside, be prepared for a black abyss of nothingness. Absolute pitch blackness in fact, with an occasional crooning coming from nowhere in particular. This is not the kind of entertainment you are probably accustomed to. One of these lounges, appropriately enough, calls itself The Alien.

Further down, beginning at the junction with Ceylon Lane, is a block of houses well worth admiring from the other side of the road. The style is unique and if you want to see more of this it is well worth continuing down to the junction with Koon Seng and Dunman Road. Cross back to the right side of Joo Chiat and pause at the corner directly opposite the brightly lit restaurant. Across from you diagonally are two rows of terraced buildings facing each other.

On your way to this junction there are a number of eating places which seem to have imbued the eclectic nature of the surrounding architecture. There is, for instance, the **1st Muslim Thai Seafood Restaurant**, and the older **Malaysia Restaurant** at N° 290, which serves Chinese Muslim food.

Turning left into Joo Chiat Lane will bring you to a dark junction with Tembeling Road. Don't let the quietness of the place put you off. This is as safe as anywhere else in Singapore and it is well worth a visit, especially if you have an eye for photography. Sited on this corner is an ancient Taoist Temple. If you are standing on the other side of Tembeling Road at this corner, look for the two-story Peranakan house, with a Romeo and Juliet balcony.

Continuing down Tembeling Road toward the East Coast will provide opportunities to see the interiors of Singaporean homes. The street is wonderfully quiet, broken only by the occasional noise of neurotic dogs from nearby middle class homes. The houses in Tembeling Road are old and include older-style Peranakan houses (N° 218 on your right as you get near the East Coast Road) is a good example).

Katong Antique House at N° 208 East Coast Road is a very special shop, specializing in Peranakan culture. You may well find that a item that catches your eye is not for sale because the owner likes it himself! Such non-commercialism in Singapore is a rarity indeed. If you do buy something you can be sure that the full history and background of the piece will be explained in loving detail.

Next door is the **Peranakan Inn and Lounge**. Further along is a new addition to the Katong eating scene, the **Sundanese** Restaurant at N° 218 East Coast Road, serving food from West Java cooked by a chef from Jakarta and claiming to be the only Sundanese eating place in Singapore.

For a dessert, move next door to the **Hua Tuo Health Living Club**, the red sign for which is in Chinese. It is a mixture of medicine shop and dessert bar, as each of its desserts is purported to have a medicinal effect.

The **5 Star Hainaese Chicken Rice House** is highly recommended by Singaporean gourmets. It may sounds rather plain, the highlight is not boring old chicken but the rice itself which is cooked in the chicken broth.

At the end of this strip there is a satay and Muslim stall and on the opposite side of the road the Chinese Carlton restaurant. Further back, opposite the Sundanese place, is the **Mun Hiang** Hokkien restaurant.

Another place on East Coast Road which is full of a sense of the old Singapore is **The Red House Bakery.** This is at the other end of the East Coast Road and is difficult to miss because of its deep red exterior. This was once a well-known meeting place where would-be-parents-in-law met to discuss and finalize matrimonial arrangements. The coffee shop is a perfect antidote to the plastic and chrome polish syndrome that dominates the Orchard Road area. The original red and white tiles set off the old marble table tops

The **Meridian Hotel** has an interesting exhibition of drawings created by an inmate incarcerated in Changi prison when the island was occupied by the Japanese (1942–45).

It has a good 24-hour coffee shop and a rather uninhabited disco called Expressway, with no cover charge and drinks at bar prices. It is only open on weekends, (542-7700, from 8:30 pm to 2 am, but not much happens before 11 pm.

The **Europa** bar is rarely visited by tourists but this is the place to visit if you want to

and the faded wooden dividers. One of the ceiling fans looks like the genuine prewar variety, as does the weighing machine near the entrance that still claims to operate for one cent. A good place to relax and chat, where one could begin to feel a sense of what Singapore might have been, many years ago.

CHANGI VILLAGE

A whole day could be spent at Changi, visiting Changi Prison and the RAF museum in the afternoon, spending some time on the beach (although it gets crowded at weekends), then moving on to the village in the evening for a meal and entertainment.

enjoy some commercial rock music. The bands (two that alternate throughout the evening) play inside where tables and standing space are at a premium. To secure a table you would have to be lucky or just turn up early in the evening. Meals are served inside until 9 pm meals, and the music starts at 7 pm.

The Europa has a venerable history. Starting out as a pub for the British army, it is now run by the third generation of the original owners. Locals from the army base rub shoulders with expatriates and Singaporeans from all parts of town.

The hawker center is a reasonable one with a good mix of Chinese, Malay and Indian stalls. A popular spot, especially with local professionals, is **Charlie's Corner** (N° 01–08 Block 2: (542-0867), serving a range of around 70 types of imported beers, however it closes at 11 pm and is never open on weekends.

GETTING THERE

See the GETTING THERE section under TRAVELERS' TIPS for information about getting to Singapore by air, train and bus from outside the region and from Thailand. Travel

newspaper has a travel advertisement page daily and there you will find numbers of reputable travel agents who handle bus tickets. The local bus for JohoreBahru, the N° 170, leaves from the Queen Street station, and buses to Melaka and some other parts of Malaysia depart from the station at the junction of Lavender Street and Kallang Bahru, (293-5915.

For taxis from Malaysia into Singapore it is easier to arrange and more economical to travel as far as Johore Bahru and then get the shuttle train or one of the JohoreBa-

between Malaysia and Singapore is possible by a variety of means. There are many flights each day between Kuala Lumpur and Singapore, including a shuttle service where you just turn up and wait for an available seat. There is also an afternoon and night train service between the two cities and which takes about eight hours. If you travel down to JohoreBahru there is also a local shuttle train service running a few times each day, costing only a few dollars. Check the times with the Singapore railway station, (222-5165.

Long-distance buses run from Kuala Lumpur, Penang, Melaka and other major destinations in Malaysia to and from Singapore and Johore Bahru. The *Straits Times*

hru taxis that travel regularly across to Singapore. The same applies for travel in the opposite direction, although there is a taxi company in Singapore that will pick you up and drive to any destination in Malaysia. The Kuala Lumpur Taxi Service is located at N° 191 New Bridge Road, (223-1889.

There is also a boat service to and from Tioman that departs daily and costs $70 return, (733-5488.

ABOVE: Holiday makers at Changi beach having fun as another planeload arrives.
OPPOSITE: Singapore's major industry: shipping.

Travelers' Tips

GETTING THERE

BY AIR

Both Malaysian Airlines (MAS) and Singapore International Airlines (SIA) have established routes to and from Europe, the USA and Australia. Singapore's Changi airport is regularly acclaimed as one of the world's most popular airports. Both Singapore Airlines and Malaysian Airlines offer extremely good service, and most other international airlines serve Malaysia and Singapore as well. The least expensive flights usually involve several stopovers and roundabout routes. You get what you pay for, so if you are contemplating a cheaper flight check out the details carefully and try to establish a comfortable balance between convenience and finance.

At Malaysia's Subang Airport there is a system for purchasing taxi coupons for the trip into town. The prices are fixed according to the distance, so be wary of entrepeneurs establishing their own prices. At Changi airport, however, you will be amazed at the efficiency with which you and your luggage are comfortably settled in your cab for a smooth ride into town.

BY TRAIN

From Thailand, an inexpensive and comfortable way to reach Malaysia or Singapore is by train. Departure from Bangkok is in the afternoon, arriving at Butterworth the following midday. Two hours later, an express leaves for the capital and reaches Kuala Lumpur at 8:20 pm that night. Changing platforms and waiting till 10 pm allows a connection with the night mail to Singapore which pulls in at 7 am the following morning. Berths are available.

From Singapore there are various trains to Kuala Lumpur, including an early morning express and a night train that leaves at 10 pm and arrives at Kuala Lumpur at 7 am. A first class air-conditioned berth is well worth the extra money if you fancy a wee bit

of luxury. There is also a shuttle train service between JohoreBahru and Singapore.

BY BUS

The only reason for contemplating a bus journey into Malaysia from Thailand would be the unavailability of trains on a specific day. While bus and coach travel is fine within Malaysia and Singapore, there are few advantages to traveling by bus instead of train.

USEFUL ADDRESSES

MALAYSIAN TOURIST BOARDS OVERSEAS

U.S.A.
Malaysian Tourist Information Centre, N° 18 West 7th Street, Suite 804, Los Angeles, CA 90017. ((213) 689-9702; fax: (213) 689-1530.

Britain
Tourist Development Corporation of Malaysia; N° 57 Trafalgar Square, London WC2N. ((01) 930-7932; fax: (071) 930-9015.

Germany
Tourist Development Corporation of Malaysia; Rossmarkt 11, 6000 Frankfurt am-Main. ((069) 283782; fax: (069) 282215.

France
Tourist Development Corporation of Malaysia; N° 29 Rue Des Pyramides, 75001 Paris. ((331) 426-03999.

Australia
Tourist Development Corporation of Malaysia; Ground floor, N° 65 York Street, Sydney, NSW 2000. ((02) 294-41: fax: (02) 262-2026.

Singapore
Tourist Development Corporation of Malaysia; N° 10 Collyer Quay, 01–03 Ocean Building, Singapore 0104. ((65) 532-6351.

SINGAPORE TOURIST BOARDS OVERSEAS

U.S.A.
Singapore Tourist Promotion Board; 8484 Wilshire Boulevard, Suite 510, Beverley Hills,

---

Kapitan Kling Mosque, Georgetown, Penang.

CA 90211. ✆ (213) 852-1901. There is also an office at 590 Fifth Avenue, NBR 12th floor, New York, NY 10036. ✆ (212) 302-4861. Its Chicago office is at 333 North Michigan Avenue, Suite 818, Chicago, IL 60601. ✆ (312) 704-4200.

Britain
Singapore Tourist Promotion Board; First floor, Carrington House, N° 126–130 Regent Street, London W1R 5FE. ✆ (071) 437-0033.

France
L'Office National du Tourisme de Singapour;

Centre d'Affaires Le Louvre, 2 Place du Palais-Royal, 75004 Paris Cedex 01. ✆ 429-71616.

Germany
Fremdenverkehrsburo von Singapur; Poststrasse 2–4, D-6000 Frankfurt. ✆ (069) 231-4565.

Australia
Singapore Tourist Promotion Board; c/o Forum Organization, 55 St. George's Terrace, Perth WA 6001. ✆ (09) 325-8033.

ABOVE: A dancer in traditional dress, Portuguese settlement, Melaka.

Travelers' Tips

TOUR OPERATORS

Regarding specialist tours of Malaysia it is well worth writing directly to **Asian Overland Services**; N° 33-M Jalan Dewan Sultan Sulaiman Sulu, 50300 Kuala Lumpur, Malaysia. ✆ (03) 292-5622. Fax: (02) 292-5209. They have the best contacts throughout Malaysia and are recommended for reliability. In England a well-established travel company that handles small group exploratory holidays is **Explore**, N° 1 Frederick Street, Aldershot Hampshire GU11 1LQ, ✆ (0252) 333031; fax: (0252) 343170. **Trailfinders** is another well-known company that specializes in Southeast Asia and prides itself on offering the lowest fares as well as giving expert advice and discounts on hotels, car rental and local tours. They can be found at N° 42-50 Earls Court Road, Kensington London W8 6EJ, ✆ (071) 938-3366; fax: (071) 937-9294. For details of other operators you should contact any of the above offices of the Malaysian Tourist Board. They will provide details of recommended tour operators and charter flights.

See the GENERAL INFORMATION sections in the text for details of tourist information centers within Malaysia and Singapore.

TRAVEL DOCUMENTS

MALAYSIA

American, British and Commonwealth and most European citizens do not require a visa. A valid passport will ensure a month's stay but this does not automatically cover Sabah and Sarawak. These states have their own immigration procedures and another stamp will be made in your passport.

SINGAPORE

As with Malaysia, American, British and most other European citizens do not require a visa. A fourteen-day stay will be automatically granted. Any extension should go through the Immigration Office, ✆ 5322877, but it is just as easy to pop into Malaysia by visiting Johore Bahru for a day. On your return another fourteen-day visa will be granted.

CUSTOMS

Duty-free goods allowed in are one liter of spirits, one liter of wine, 200 cigarettes or 50 cigars. This applies to travelers arriving in Malaysia or Singapore but note that it does not apply to travel between the two countries. Clearing customs is quite straightforward for most travelers but both countries are extremely alert to the problem of drug trafficking in this part of the world. If you arrive in Singapore by train you will notice the caged police dogs strategically placed to monitor every passenger that passes by. Be warned: the penalties for attempting to bring in drugs are, literally, fatal. Malaysia's anti-narcotics laws mandate the death penalty for anyone found guilty of drug trafficking, which is defined as possession of 14 g (half an ounce) or more of heroin or morphine, 900 g (31 oz) of opium or 180 g (six ounces) of marijuana. The execution of two Australians in 1987 proves that this policy is rigorously enforced. Singapore's policy is basically the same.

WHEN TO GO

Whatever the time of the year, Malaysia and Singapore will be hot and humid. Temperatures hover around 30°C (86°F) during the day and even at night are seldom lower than 20°C (68°F).

The wet season only makes itself felt along the east coast of peninsular Malaysia and Sabah and Sarawak, as these areas receive substantial amounts of rain between October and February. Even then, the rain does not make travel impossible, although Taman Negara, the wonderful national park in peninsular Malaysia, is closed around this time.

WHAT TO TAKE

It is difficult to think of actual items that would be either unobtainable or extrava-

gantly priced in the cities of Malaysia or Singapore, so it is hardly appropriate to draw up a survivor's kit. Even if you are planning to spend most of the time in the jungle interior, a quick visit to one of the big shopping plazas would provide most of what you need. The cost of film and development, for example, is inexpensive compared to Europe or the U.S.A. You certainly do not need a full wardrobe of clothes, as the climate tends to dictate a simple style of dress. A pair of shorts is a good idea and stick to light cotton clothes generally. Because of the heat, a can of powder for the relief or prevention of prickly heat can prove to be an essential item, but again this is easily purchased anywhere upon your arrival.

GETTING AROUND

BY AIR

If you are planning to travel to Sabah and Sarawak, or just hoping to see a lot of Malaysia and Singapore in a short amount of time, then air travel is essential. Malaysian Airlines has an extensive and well-established network of routes which are particularly recommended. If you are planning to travel from Singapore to Sabah or Sarawak, it is well worth considering a Malaysian Airlines flight from JohoreBahru instead of one from Singapore itself. Malaysian Airlines organizes its own buses that depart from the Novotel Orchid Hotel in Singapore straight through to the airport at JohoreBahru. It will take a little longer but you will save a few dollars. Malaysian Airlines also operates special advance booking fares if you can commit yourself to a fixed schedule and give fourteen days' notice.

Two other smaller airlines are well worth knowing about. **Tradewinds**, ((65) 229-7096, is Singapore's second airline and they run a twice daily service to Tioman island and semi-weekly flights to Kuantan. **Pelangi Air** is based in Malaysia, ((03) 770-2020, and they run a thrice weekly flight from Singapore to Melaka, Sitiawan (for Pangkor island) and Kuala Lumpur. They also handle the flight into Taman Negara as well as some other internal routes.

By Train

There are a number of advantages to traveling by rail in Malaysia: the trains are modern, reliable and comfortable and the fares are very reasonably priced. The only drawback is that you can't go everywhere by train, and in fact there are only two main lines other than a small one in Sabah. One runs from Singapore through to Thailand via Kuala Lumpur and Butterworth. This is the most traveled line, partly because of its

international connections and also because it passes through the main population centers. The other main line is a branch-off from the first one at the town of Gemas, and from there, a line runs through to the state of Kelantan in the northeastern corner of Malaysia and onto Thailand.

Reservations are a very good idea, especially for the Singapore-Bangkok route, and they can be easily arranged at the main line stations. At certain times of the year, Chinese New Year and the Christmas period particularly, reservations are essential. The difference between third class fares and first or second class makes it well worth paying the extra. Third-class is more crowded, more uncomfortable and less airy. Second class and first class are indistinguishable for day-time travel, but the night sleepers in first class have air conditioning and private twin bed compartments, though the second-class sleepers are, by no means, uncomfortable. The food on the trains is barely okay, so for a long journey it is better to bring along a picnic.

There is also a rail pass valid for foreign tourists that allows unlimited travel by any train on Malayan Railway (KTM), including Singapore. The current cost is $40 for 10 days and $85 for 30 days and half price for children between four and twelve years old. The rail pass can be purchased at Singapore, JohoreBahru, Kuala Lumpur, Penang or Butterworth. Further details can be obtained from the Director of Passenger Services, KTM, Jalan Sultan Hishamuddin, 50621 Kuala Lumpur, ((03) 274-9422; fax: (03) 274-9424

If you are in Singapore or JohoreBahru, there is a shuttle train service between the two countries. See the JohoreBahru section for details. Finally, within Singapore, the Mass Rapid Transit (MRT) system is a fast way to get around.

By Bus

Malaysia has an excellent network of bus lines connecting all the towns and cities. For certain routes, like traveling down the east coast, they are indispensable because there is no train alternative and flying is non-stop and relatively expensive. On some routes, getting from Kota Kinabalu to Mt Kinabalu for instance, taking a bus is the only way to travel.

In Singapore the government-owned local buses will take you everywhere and there is a bus running to and from JohoreBahru in Malaysia. Driver conductors do not dispense change, so keep some coins handy. There is also an **Explorer's Ticket**, available from hotels and tour agents, that allows unlimited travel for one or three days and comes complete with a map detailing the major attractions. Better still is the **TransitLink Farecard** which is a common stored-value card for buses and the MRT system.

By Car

In Malaysia, the roads are in good condition and are well signposted. Petrol stations are never a problem to locate, though on long car journeys it makes sense to fill the tank when reaching a town. While the roads are safe to drive on, other drivers are best treated with a wary respect. Taxi drivers in particular seem to possess distinct suicidal tendencies when it comes to overtaking on a bend, and though it is tempting to try and emulate them when stuck behind some interminably slow lorry, the fact that horrific crashes are not uncommon should give you pause for patience.

In the towns and cities there is little concept of lane discipline and giving way to other vehicles is not really understood. Westerners may also find the constant use of the horn a little irritating but this should not be taken personally.

There is little free parking anywhere in Singapore and you will need to purchase booklets of parking coupons that are used in most public car parks. The coupons are available from 7-Eleven stores and newsagents and other small stores. Driving around the city center, you will notice the metal girders that straddle certain roads with signs reading *Restricted Area*. If the sign is lit up (morning and evening rush hours) you can't drive beyond the sign without a special sticker on your windscreen showing that you have purchased a license for that day or month. The signs border all approaches to the designated central business area and the license system is designed to moderate the quantity of traffic at those busy times of the day. Each day has a different color coupon so it's easy to spot lawbreakers. Licenses can be bought at strategically placed booths on roads leading into the city.

BY TAXI

In Singapore taxis are plentiful and well regulated. If you want to go into the business areas during the rush hours, you will have to pay the S$3 extra for the coupon, unless it has already been paid for by a previous customer and is already pasted on the windscreen.

In Kuala Lumpur taxis are not as plentiful but they are cheaper, and as long as you ensure the meter is turned on, the fare is regulated. In other towns in Malaysia it is best to agree on the fare before setting off, and often it is a good idea to just check with someone in your hotel about the current rate for a particular journey. In places like

Penang the rates are well established and usually adhered to, and even if they add on a ringgit or two you will most likely find the rate reasonable.

For travel within Malaysia, long-distance taxis are a real bonus and should always be considered. It is simply a matter of turning up at the *teksi* area, announcing your destination and waiting until a taxi has its quota of four passengers, which does take very long. The drawback is not the waiting but rather the kamikaze driving that the drivers sometimes engage in.

BY THUMB

The Visit Malaysia Year in 1990 did a great deal for encouraging a positive attitude toward visitors and this, combined with the natural friendliness of Malaysians, makes for good hitchhiking prospects. If you are contemplating a long journey it is often a good idea to wait around a petrol station on the outskirts of town and approach a friendly face. Looking like an obvious tourist makes all the difference because hitchhiking by anyone else would be unheard of. Tourist or not, women should exercise discretion when hitching alone. If you are wondering about the hitch-hiking possibilities in Singapore, forget it. The island is just too small and too fast and too busy to accommodate the very notion of thumbing a ride.

OPPOSITE: Buses are still the principle means of transport for Singaporeans despite the new MRT system. ABOVE: Young people at the central market display their colorful sense of fashion.

EMBASSIES AND CONSULATES

MALAYSIA

American Embassy N° 376 Jalan Tun Razak, 50400, Kuala Lumpur. ((03) 248-9011.

Australian High Commission N° 6 Jalan Kwan Seng, 50450 Kuala Lumpur. ((03) 242-3122.

British High Commission N° 185 Jalan Ampang, 50450, Kuala Lumpur. ((03) 248-2122.

German Embassy N° 29 Jalan Ampang Hilir, Off Jalan Wickham, P.O. Box 12511, 50780, Kuala Lumpur. ((03) 456-2894.

SINGAPORE

American Embassy N° 30 Hill Street, Singapore. ((65) 732-9211.

Australian High Commission 25 Napier Road, Singapore. ((65) 737-9311.

British High Commission Tanglin Road, Singapore. ((65) 473-9333.

German Embassy 545, Orchard Road, N° 14-01 Far East Shopping Centre. ((65) 737-1355.

ABOVE: Orchard Road, the shopper's paradise. OPPOSITE: The beautifully ornate façade of one of Melaka's town houses.

HEALTH

Compared to most other Asian countries, Malaysia and Singapore present the least problem to visitors concerned about matters of health. No special vaccination certificates are required unless coming in from certain African or South American countries. Consult your doctor if in doubt because sometimes a few jabs make you feel better. Travel insurance is a far better idea and is highly recommended. For any emergency you should go to the local hospital. AIDS is not as big a problem in Malaysia or Singapore as it is in neighboring countries, and there is no need to bring your own disposable syringes. If you are spending some time in the interior in Sarawak, malaria tablets might be a good idea. Again, consult your doctor if in doubt.

MONEY

Dollar prices in this book are in United States dollars unless shown otherwise as Malaysian ringgit or M$, or Singapore dollars, S$. At the time of going to press, exchange rates to the US dollar were M$2.66 to US$1 and S$1.75 to US$1.

In both countries the most common coins are 10c, 20c and 50c and $1, while notes come in $1, $5, $10, $20, $50, $100, $500 and $1,000. Singapore has recently also introduced a $2 note which can be confused with the similarly red-colored $10 note. The Brunei dollar is on a par with the Singapore dollar and occasionally you will be given a Brunei one-dollar note in your change. This is quite acceptable and can be used anywhere.

Exchanging money is rarely a problem in Singapore or Malaysia unless you are spending some time in rural areas, like the national parks, when you need to bring sufficient cash with you. Generally, hotels and the large department stores should only be used as a last resort because their rates will be slightly less than those obtainable in banks or from money changers. In the states of Kedah, Perlis, Kelantan and Terengganu, banks will be closed on Fridays and open from 10 am to 3 pm on Saturdays through to Wednesdays and from 9:30 am to 11:30 on

Thursdays. Elsewhere in Malaysia banks are open from 10 am to 3 pm and from 9:30 am to 11:30 am on Saturday, closed on Sundays. In Singapore banking hours are from 10 am to 3 pm on weekdays and from 9:30 am to 11:30 am on Saturdays.

ACCOMMODATION

Both Malaysia and Singapore are well geared to meet the accommodation needs of most visitors and Malaysia is better than Singa-

EATING OUT

Eating is one of the joys of Malaysia and Singapore. There is a terrific variety and standards are very high. Fancy restaurants can be found in Kuala Lumpur and Singapore and while a certain standard of dress is expected, it is rarely insisted on. The general rule is one of informality and there is a complete absence of the snobbery that is sometimes found in restaurants in Europe and America. A real bonus is the price, for

pore in providing for all budgets. The general standard is very good, and unpleasant events like thefts or sudden electricity cuts are a rarity. Nearly all the hotels referred to in the WHERE TO STAY sections provide air-conditioning, hot and cold water and a private bathroom. Exceptions are some of the beach areas on the east coast and islands like Langkawi and Tioman.

As a general rule it is worth looking at a hotel room before committing yourself, and asking for a discount never hurts. The rates quoted in this book all refer to a standard double and, in the case of the international hotels, these published room rates can often be reduced if you go through a travel agent in Kuala Lumpur or Singapore.

whether you are dining in a five-star hotel or a street cafe it is usually difficult to imagine a meal of a comparable standards available for the same price back home.

Finding food is never going to be a problem in Malaysia or Singapore except during the month of Ramadan when Muslims are forbidden to eat between sunrise and sunset. In traditional Malay areas like Kelantan or Kedah this may cause occasional snags during the day but nothing serious.

SHOPPING

Malaysia produces some beautiful batik and basket ware, found mostly on the east coast and in the northeast. Brightly-colored paper kites make suitable small gifts and they come ready packed. Filigree silver and pewter ware are other good buys, found mostly in craft shops in Kuala Lumpur. In Sarawak, baskets and mats made from rattan, bamboo and pandanus are a good value and the craft shops in Kuching have the biggest variety. There is also attractive, locally produced pottery characterized by geometric black and white designs, sold along the main road from Kuching to the airport. In the state of Johor, locally pro-

duced pottery, as well as a tremendous amount of imports from China, is on sale in the town of Ayer Hitam. Any road journey into Malaysia from Singapore or JohoreBahru will pass through this town. Back in East Malaysia there are wood carvings and other locally made artifacts and the craft shops in Sarawak's capital are far superior to those available in Kota Kinabalu, the capital of Sabah. The museum shop in Kuching is as good a place as any in this respect.

Singapore offers just about everything that every other Asian country produces, at tourist prices. So if you are traveling around Thailand or Bali and you don't want to carry around that gigantic wooden green frog holding a hibiscus that you've taken a liking to, rest assured there are lots of them in Singapore. What Singapore can also offer are good deals in electrical goods and com-

puters. Many tourist shops in Singapore will be able to arrange packing and delivery overseas. Using a charge card is often a good idea for this kind of purchase because it offers some redress if the goods fail to appear, though generally speaking this is not likely to happen.

Shops where bargaining is out of the question are few and far between. I once received a pleasant surprise when considering some antique Chinese furniture on sale in a large department store in Chinatown in Singapore. I half-heartedly inquired if there was any discount for paying by cash (always a good opening move) and was promptly told that 20 percent could be knocked off the marked price.

ETIQUETTE

Politeness is appreciated everywhere in Malaysia and Singapore and you shouldn't allow the occasional encounter with a rude person to blunt your sensibilities. Really losing your temper and blasting away at someone is unlikely to produce an instant solution although it will always produce an instant crowd of curious onlookers. Generally speaking visitors are treated with respect and forbearance and it is good manners to try and do the same when dealing with Malaysians and Singaporeans. When you are concerned about trying to make a point, a show of controlled anger will be far more effective than actually exploding into a rage.

If you are invited into someone's home do remember to remove your footwear at the door. A special point of etiquette applies only to Malay women, who are forbidden to have any physical contact with males over the age of puberty who are not members of the family. This extends to the shaking of hands, and even in sophisticated Singapore many Malay women would prefer a smile and a nod.

A final word about dressing in the more traditional parts of Malaysia. As Malaysia is a predominantly Muslim country, women should dress modestly as is the custom here. One should try to respect the cultural values of the country in which one is a visitor.

ABOVE: A young girl in the traditional dress of Sarawak. OPPOSITE: At the festival of the Hungry Ghosts, in Penang, there is always a colorful display.

PUBLIC HOLIDAYS AND FESTIVALS

The multiculturalism of Malaysia and Singapore leads to a bewildering array of holidays and festivals. Some of these are common to both countries, while others are only celebrated in either Malaysia, Singapore or only in a particular state. Another complicating factor is that many of the holidays are calculated from a lunar calendar and, thus, change every year This is true of Ramadan, the major event in the Muslim year.

lunar cycle. In many respects like Christmas in the West, it is a time for family reunions and general good cheer. Shops abound with special offerings decked out in red and gold, and food delicacies feature heavily in the festivities. Traditionally a time for letting off fireworks, this is now strictly banned in Singapore, although Malaysia grants a dispensation for a set number of days and the skies are lit up at night with rockets. Another common sight is the red packets, *hong bao*, that are distributed to children especially and contain gifts of money. In Singapore a

big parade is held and Orchard Road is closed to traffic. In both countries teams of lion dancers are seen performing and traveling in open-backed lorries.

JANUARY TO FEBRUARY

New Year's Day (January 1)
Thaipusam A Hindu festival in honor of Lord Subramaniam. At Batu Caves outside of Kuala Lumpur and at dawn in the Perumal Temple in Serangoon Road, Singapore, penitents in a trance-like state pierce their bodies with skewers that enable them to carry heavy metal frames called *Kavadis*. At Batu Caves they climb up to a clifftop shrine, while in Singapore they form a procession that leads to the Chettiar Temple in Tank Road. Not to be missed if you have the opportunity.
Chinese New Year Sometimes celebrated in January, the exact date depends on the

MARCH TO APRIL

Ramadan The fasting month of Muslims all over the world, when no food or drink can be consumed between sunrise and sunset. **Hari Raya Puasa** marks the end of the fast and is a national holiday in Malaysia and Singapore (some years this can be in May). In Malaysia it is common for many businesses to close down for three or more days and accommodation in any of the popular resort areas is hard to come by.

Easter In Singapore **Good Friday** is a holiday and in Melaka a candlelit procession is held at St Peter's Church.

Birthday of the Monkey God In Singapore at the Monkey God temple in Seng Poh Road, mediums, said to be possessed by the naughty Monkey God, slash themselves with blades.

APRIL TO MAY

Chithirai Vishu The start of the Hindu New Year, celebrated with prayers and ceremonies at Hindu temples.

Labor Day (May 1) A holiday in both countries.

Vesak Day A public holiday that commemorates Nirvana, the birth, enlightenment and entry into the perfect state of existence of Buddha. All Buddhist temples will have candlelit processions at night after the freeing of caged birds during the day which symbolizes the liberation of captive souls.

Kadazan Harvest Day A harvest festival by the Kadazan farmers in Sabah.

Turtle Season Probably not a holiday for them, but from May to September the giant turtles come ashore along the beach at Rantau Abang on peninsula Malaysia's east coast.

JUNE

Gawai Dayak (June 1 and 2) A harvest festival by the indigenous people of Sarawak.

Birthday of the Yang di Pertuang Agong (June 5) A holiday celebrating the birthday of Malaysia's head of state.

Feast of San Pedro (Melaka) An important event for the Portuguese-Eurasians of Melaka in honor of St Peter, the patron saint of fishermen. Visitors are welcome.

Festival of Arts (Singapore) A month-long event featuring music, cinema, opera, mime, drama, dance and experimental art.

JULY TO AUGUST

National Day Singapore (August 9) A public holiday that includes firework displays, processions and other festivities.

National Day Malaysia (August 31) A public holiday in Malaysia with celebrations particularly in the capital.

Festival of the Hungry Ghosts The gates of hell are symbolically opened and spirits are

ABOVE and OPPOSITE: A kaleidoscope of ethnic dress.

free to roam the earth. Friendly ghosts make house calls to relatives but destitute spirits need appeasing with offerings in the form of burning gifts, including "hell money" (fake currency notes) and mock passports for wandering souls.

SEPTEMBER

Moon Cake Festival Lanterns are lit on the night of the full moon. Moon cakes, said to once carry secret messages during a revolt, are eaten in abundance.

OCTOBER

Thimithi Festival A fire-walking ceremony when Hindus walk across a pit of burning embers in honor of Draupadi. In Malaysia this takes place at the Gajah Berang Temple in Melaka and in Singapore at the Sri Mariamman temple in South Bridge Road.

Navarathri Festival "Nava" means nine and "rathri" night. A celebration in honor of three Indian gods at Hindu temples.

NOVEMBER

Deepavali Hindu celebration of the victory of light over dark. A public holiday.

DECEMBER

Penang Festival Festivities and special events of all sorts.

Christmas Day (December 25) A public holiday in both countries.

MAIL

Poste Restante is available in Singapore and Kuala Lumpur at the main post offices. Chinese, Malay and Indians place their family names first, so be sure to check under your first name as well.

TELEPHONES

Making local or international calls is usually no problem. Small hotels that offer international calls are usually quite willing to let you use their service although it is wise to confirm the rate before making the call. In Sarawak and Sabah the rates are more subject to the whim of the proprietor than in Singapore or mainland Malaysia. In Kuala Lumpur and especially Singapore an increasing number of public phones operate on a card system and the phone cards can be purchased at a post office.

HELPFUL NUMBERS

Malaysia
Police/Emergency Services (999
Directory Assistance, local: (103; other states in Malaysia: (101
International Directory Assistance (108
Kuala Lumpur Airport (Subang) (746-1014/1235
Malaysia Airlines have their headquarters on Jalan Sultan Ismail in Kuala Lumpur: (261-0555; reservations: (746-3000.

Singapore
Police, Ambulance, Fire (999
Directory Assistance, local: (103; international: (104; Malaysia: (109
Taxi Service (24 hours) (452-5555/250-0700
Changi Airport (542-4422 (programmed information on arrivals and departures only)

Malaysia Airlines (336-6777
Singapore Airlines is located in the SIA Building at N° 77, Robinson Road, (229-7270.

BASICS

TIME

Malaysia and Singapore share the same time. Both are eight hours ahead of GMT (London), 13 and 16 hours ahead of American Eastern and Western Standard Time respectively, and two hours behind Australian Eastern Standard Time.

ELECTRICITY

Malaysian and Singaporean current is 220-240 volts, 50 cycles, and most of the electrical goods for sale will also run on 220 volts.

WATER

Water is safe to drink throughout peninsular Malaysia, Singapore and the main towns in Sarawak and Sabah. If traveling in the interior in Borneo, mineral water is recommended.

WEIGHTS AND MEASURES

The metric system is used throughout Malaysia and Singapore.

NEWSPAPERS AND MAGAZINES

Daily English language newspapers are published in Malaysia and Singapore, the *Straits Times* and *New Straits Times* respectively. They are both government controlled.

The *Star* newspaper in Malaysia used to be more critical and open-minded but practices self-censorship in order to avoid being closed down. The *New Paper* in Singapore appears on the streets in the afternoon and is very simply written.

Foreign newspapers are easy to buy in Kuala Lumpur or Singapore but they cost three or four times their usual price. Weekly magazines like *Newsweek* and *Time* are

easily available and reasonably priced. The *Asian Wall Street Journal* and the *Far East Economic Review* both fell foul of the Singapore authorities and are virtually unobtainable.

WOMEN ALONE

Women can feel safer traveling alone in Malaysia and Singapore than most other countries in Europe or Asia. Stories of women being subjected to assault or rape

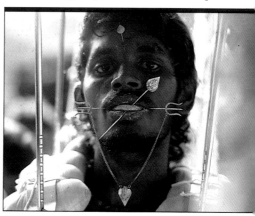

are extremely rare and the only problem area is in the more traditional parts of peninsula Malaysia. Here Muslim men sometimes mistakenly equate some forms of western female dress with a degree of amorality.

TIPPING

In both countries, generally speaking, tipping is not expected, and certainly not in restaurants when the menu specifies the addition of ten percent to the bill. In Singapore tipping is officially discouraged and taxi drivers, for instance, would not expect anything above the stated fare. As a general rule don't tip unless you feel you want to.

ABOVE: A penitent at the Thaipusam festival seeks an indulgence. OPPOSITE: A woman in Muslim dress, Malay village, Singapore.

LANGUAGE BASICS

English is the language of education and commerce in Singapore and it is difficult to imagine situations when you would feel the need for a English-Chinese/Malay/Tamil dictionary. Malaysia is not quite the same, despite its common historical and cultural links with Britain, because of its decision to promote Malay as the official language. The result is that young Malaysians are becoming increasingly unfamiliar with English and a few language basics can be useful.

Unlike Chinese, the Malay language is not a tonal one and is not nearly so difficult to master. There are no articles or complicated tenses. The plural is usually formed by just doubling the noun. **A** is pronounced as in *far*; **c** as in *chip*; **sy** as in *shut*; **g** as in *girl*.

DAYS OF THE WEEK

Monday   *hari senen*
Tuesday   *hari selasa*
Wednesday   *hari rabu*
Thursday   *hari kamis*
Friday   *hari jumat*
Saturday   *hari sabtu*
Sunday   *hari minggu*

GREETINGS

how do you do?   *apa khabar?*
good morning   *selamat pagi*
good afternoon   *selamat petang*
good night   *selamat malam*
good bye   *selamat tinggal*
bon voyage   *selamat jalan*

FOOD AND DRINK

bread   *roti*
tea   *teh*
coffee   *kopi*
fried rice   *nasi goreng*
fried noodles   *mee goreng*
fish   *ikan*
chicken   *ayam*
prawns   *udang*
vegetables   *sayur*
egg   *telur*
sugar   *gula*

meat   *daging*
to eat   *makan*
to drink   *minum*
water   *air*
ice   *air batu*

NUMBERS

1   *satu*
2   *dua*
3   *tiga*
4   *empat*
5   *lima*
6   *enam*
7   *tujah*
8   *lapan*
9   *sembilan*
10   *sepuluh*
11   *sebelas*
12   *dua belas*
13   *tiga belas*
20   *dua puluh*
21   *dua puluh satu*
30   *tiga puluh*
55   *lima puluh lima*
100   *seratus*
1000   *seribu*

USEFUL WORDS AND EXPRESSIONS

East   *timor*
west   *barat*
south   *selatan*
north   *utara*
market   *pasar*
river   *sungei*
toilet   *tandas*
post office   *pejabat pos*
How much does this cost?   *berapa harga?*
today   *hari ini*
tomorrow   *esok*
I   *saya*
a little   *sedikit*
a lot   *banyak*
beach   *pantai*
do not have   *tiada*
excuse me   *maafkan saya*
I am sorry   *saya minta maaf*
how far?   *berapa jauh?*
when   *bila*
where   *di mana*
why   *mengapa*
thank you   *terima kasih*

Recommended Reading

History and General Background Reading

ANDAYA, BARBARA WATSON AND LEONARD. *A History of Malaysia*. St Martin's Press, New York, 1982. An authoritative if somewhat dry history.

FOLLOWS, ROY WITH POPHAM, HUGH. *The Jungle Beat*. Cassell, London, 1990. A young Englishman joins the Malayan Police in 1952 seeking adventure and action. He tells his naive but honest account of the war against the Communist guerrillas in the jungle.

GEORGE, T.J.S. *Lee Kuan Yew's Singapore*. Andre Deutsch, London, 1977. Alex Josey's biography of Singapore's political leader is the standard work but it is far too uncritical; this is the best work on the subject. For a while it was banned in Singapore.

INSAN. *Where the Monsoons Meet: A People's History of Malaya*. Institute of Socal Analysis. 11 Lorong 11/4E. 46200 Petaling Jaya, Malaysia, 1987. (An appealing alternative to the academic histories; a convincing radical view told in comic book/documentary style.

HARRISSON, TOM. *World Within. A Borneo Story*. Oxford University Press, 1984. First published in 1959, this book tells the story of Harrisson's parachute descent, toward the end of the Second World War, into an unknown part of Borneo. His official mission was to organize resistance; his unstated one a desire to boldly go where no (white) person had gone before. If you visit the highlands of Bareo in Sarawak, this book is indispensable.

HALL, TIMOTHY. *The Fall of Singapore*. Octopus Publishing, Mandarin Australia, 1990. A journalistic and unsentimental account of the ignominious fall of Singapore to the Japanese in the Second World War.

LAT. *With a Little Bit of Lat*. Berita Publishing, Kuala Lumpur, 1990. This is the title of just one collection of Lat's cartoons, first published in 1980 and reprinted regularly. The longer you stay in the country the more they grow on you; Malaysia seen and commented on from the inside. The Coliseum in Kuala Lumpur has an original on the wall.

MAHATHIR, BIN MOHAMMED. *The Malay Dilemma*. Federal Publications, Kuala Lumpur, 1982. First published in 1970 this book, by the Prime Minister of Malaysia, is still an astonishing read. Set in stark racial terms Mahathir sets out to explain the case for positive discrimination to favor the Malays. The sort of book you could never imagine your own prime minister ever writing.

PAYNE, ROBERT. *The White Rajahs of Sarawak*. Oxford, 1986. The history of the Brooke family, from James to Vyner, and their tropical kingdom.

TURNBULL, MARY. *History of Malaysia, Singapore and Brunei*. Allen & Unwin, 1989. A readable and reliable historical account.

The Battle for Sarawak's Forests. World Rainforest Movement, 87, Cantonment Road, 10250 Penang, Malaysia, 1989. Essential reading if you are traveling into Sarawak's interior, a collection of documents and articles about the plight of the natives in Sarawak and their struggle against the logging.

Guide Books

BRIGGS, JOHN. *Parks of Malaysia*. Longman Malaysia, Kuala Lumpur, 1991. (If you are intending to selectively visit both East and West Malaysia primarily for its wildlife and jungles then this book is invaluable. Practical and informative, written by an "amateur" enthusiast. Recommended.)

BRIGGS, JOHN. *Mountains of Malaysia*. Longman Malaysia, Kuala Lumpur, 1988. Another specialist guide book, worth every penny if mountaineering is your motive in visiting Malaysia.

CROWTHER, GEOFF AND WHEELER, TONY. *Malaysia, Singapore and Brunei*. Lonely Planets, Australia, 1988. A wealth of detail and general good advice, so essential to the budget traveler, can be found in the Lonely Planet's guidebook. A caveat is that in the 1988 update much seems to have been reprinted from the somewhat outdated 1982 edition.

VENOM AND TOXIN RESEARCH GROUP. *A Colour Guide to Dangerous Animals*. Singapore University Press, 1990. A comprehensive guide to snakes, scorpions, spiders, bees, fishes and other dangerous creatures in the Asia-Pacific region, with suggested first aid and preventive measures.

WEE YEOW CHIN and Z P. GOPALAKRISHNAKONE. *A Colour Guide to Dangerous Plants*. Singapore University Press, 1990. A specialized account of poisonous plants which are common in Malaysia and Singapore.

Travel Books

BARCLAY, JAMES. *A Stroll Through Borneo*. Hodder & Stoughton, London, 1980, and January Books, Wellington, 1988. The title is an amusing understatement typical of the delightful style that characterizes this unpretentious and funny account of travel deep into the interior.

O'HANLON, REDMOND: *Into the Heart of Borneo*. London, 1986. An account of a journey made to the mountains of Batu Tiban with James Fenton. Funny and serious and a great book to take with you to read while traveling in Sarawak.

Stier, Wayne: *Time Travel in the Malay Crescent*. Meru Publishing, Hawaii, 1985. At first the style may disconcert because the whole book is written in the second person singular but the anecdotal manner can grow on you as some of the stories prove interesting.

WALLS, DENIS and MARTIN, STELLA. *In Malaysia*. Brandt Publications, 1986. Two English teachers tell their tale of living in peninsular Malaysia. A perceptive, well-written and reliable account of what everyday life in Malaysia is all about.

WELLS, CARVETH. *Six Years in the Malay Jungle*. Oxford University Press, 1988. Tale told by a civil engineer who came to Malaya in 1913. Pleasantly unscholarly yet full of interesting observations.

Fiction

BURGESS, ANTHONY *The Malayan Trilogy*. Penguin Books, 1972. Written after Burgess was an Education Officer in Malaya in the 1950s, prior to Independence. Typical Burgess.

FAUCONNIER, HENRI. *The Soul of Malaya*. Oxford, 1985. First published in 1931, this autobiographical novel by a French rubber planter is one of the better literary excursions into colonial Malaya.

MAUGHAM, W. SOMERSET. *Collected Short Stories*. Pan, 1986 and *The Casurina Tree*. Oxford, 1985. Authentic tales of the decadent colonials who once ruled Malaysia and Singapore.

THEROUX, PAUL. *Saint Jack* and *The Consul's File*. Penguin Books, 1973 and 1977. Paul Theroux taught at the university in Singapore so this novel and collection of short stories, respectively, have their basis in a firsthand experience of postcolonial Malaya. He also wrote a brilliantly scathing essay on Singapore which is reprinted in his collection of autobiographical pieces, *Sunrise and Seamonsters* (1985).

Quick Reference A–Z Guide
to Places and Topics of Interest with Listed Accommodation, Restaurants and Useful Telephone Numbers

Illustrated Blueprints to Travel Enjoyment

INSIDER'S GUIDES

The Guides That Lead